2/2000

Mario Lanza

Mario Lanza, 1921–1959

Mario Lanza

TENOR IN EXILE

Roland L. Bessette

AMADEUS PRESS
Portland, Oregon

Grateful acknowledgment is hereby made to

Houghton Mifflin Company, excerpts from *My Road to Opera* by
Boris Goldovsky, as told to Curtis Cate. Copyright 1979 by Curtis Cate.
Reprinted by permission. All rights reserved.

Newsweek, excerpts from the 4 May 1951, 13 October 1952, and
24 August 1959 issues, copyright 1951, 1952, and 1959.
Reprinted by permission. All rights reserved.

The New Yorker Magazine, Inc., excerpts from The Current Cinema
(19 May 1951, 26 June 1954, and 31 March 1956) by John McCarten,
copyright 1951, 1954, and 1956. Reprinted by permission.
All rights reserved.

Time, excerpts from the 19 March 1951, 6 August 1951, 13 October 1952,
9 April 1956, and 31 August 1959 issues, copyright 1951, 1952, 1956,
and 1959. Reprinted by permission. All rights reserved.

Published in 1999 by
Amadeus Press (an imprint of Timber Press, Inc.)
The Haseltine Building
133 S.W. Second Avenue, Suite 450
Portland, Oregon 97204, U.S.A.

Printed in Hong Kong

Library of Congress Cataloging-in-Publication Data

Bessette, Roland L.
Mario Lanza : tenor in exile / Roland L. Bessette.
p.   cm.
Discography:
Filmography:
Includes bibliographic references (p.   ) and index.
ISBN 1-57467-044-1
1. Lanza, Mario, 1921–1959. 2. Singers—United States—Biography.
I. Title.
ML420.L24B53   1999
782.1'092—dc21
[B]   98-24135
CIP
MN

Contents

Photographs follow page 96

For my wife,
Phyllis Torres Bessette, M.D.,
and my mother,
Adrienne Gelinas-Bessette (1915–1984)

Preface

My father—a gifted amateur singer with the common limitations of a decent baritone and mid-tenor range but an uncertain high B-flat and unreliable high C—occasionally listened to Lanza and attempted to emulate what he heard. Whether or not he succeeded is unimportant. What mattered was that, even as a child, I regarded Lanza's voice as beautiful, powerful, and different. As I grew older, I discerned that it could be raw, sensual, and uniquely interpretive. I went on to discover and enjoy the likes of Björling, Martinelli, Corelli, Gedda, Bergonzi, and the current triumvirate of Carreras, Domingo, and Pavarotti, recognizing the difference between Lanza's natural production and that of a classically trained voice. Still I regarded Lanza's sound, diction, timbre, interpretive abilities, and power as a combination he, and he alone, possessed.

I found, in talking to many operagoers or lovers of great voice, that Lanza was alternately beloved and scorned. Fortunately, those who admired him comprised the vast majority. A common praise was how the voice reached them, how his artistry touched their lives. If we accept that music is therapeutic and that the prescription varies with the listener, my own antidote—during trying times that included the loss of a brother, the death of a son, the rigors of law school, or the evening after a difficult hearing—was a voice that could reach me like no other: that of Mario Lanza.

Eventually I concluded that his lasting influence on opera and tenors was much undervalued. Many critics are still loath to consider him among the greats despite his enduring popularity; the worst of them are invariably ignorant of his rich, pre-Hollywood concert experience and the fact that nearly every great singer or conductor who heard him sing live concluded that he was second to none.

Who was this man the world knew as Mario Lanza? That was a question I increasingly pondered in view of his immense legacy and how little anyone seemed to know about him. Biographies, memoirs, and record liners were filled with plenty of the usual anecdotes and statistics, but nothing adequately explained the lightning rise to fame, the myriad disappointments of his career, or the intelligence behind his artistry. What of his death and the insulting rumors of Mafia involvement? I was convinced there had to be an explanation—or a series of explanations—for it all.

So I began this book. I could explain more about where it was written and researched, the wonderful people I met and interviewed, or my enhanced appreciation of Mario Lanza's artistry. I think I succeeded in answering the questions that propelled me toward this project. I could tell you a great deal more, but this is a preface, and that is why I will end by saying, "It's all in the book."

Acknowledgments

No writer is always a good spouse, partner, or friend while the research, lengthy pondering, initial writing, refinement, and all that goes into the creative process is ongoing. Those things become magnified if you meet the requirements of your full-time work as a lawyer during the day and work on a book during the evenings and weekends. I thank my partner, Phyllis Torres Bessette, M.D., for standing by and enduring while I worked on this book. Her professional expertise and input were invaluable with regard to the matters of Lanza's health and death.

I thank Clyde Smith for his generosity in granting me access to his collection of articles and clippings as well as rare recordings by Mario Lanza. Frankly, the project would have taken years longer to complete if Clyde had not come forward with so much material during the first year of my involvement. I also thank Terry Smith for her patience and hospitality whenever I visited in search of more material or to discuss some aspect of Lanza's life and career.

Al Teitelbaum, Lanza's manager, was patient and thorough in answering my many questions. He also provided hundreds of photos and documents that were unavailable elsewhere. He and his gracious wife, Beverly, provided wonderful and warm hospitality at their home in Ashland, Oregon, while I spent two days asking questions and probing for a greater understanding of the business side of Lanza's career.

I thank Alan Burns for his thoughtful and lengthy discussions about Lanza's musical development and his early years in New York. I also acknowledge Buddy Mantia, whose support included photos from the legendary collection of the late Vito Torelli.

My sister-in-law, Mary Pearlman, M.D., whose specialty is psychi-

11

atry, provided valuable support by listening to my theories and rumi-
nations about Lanza's behavior and career and pointing me in the right
direction. Truly, she devoted hours to assisting me. I also thank Dale
Kuyper, D.O., for his thoughts during our brief conversations about
the lows and highs of Lanza's career.

I thank Frances Yeend and her husband, James Benner, for their
time in responding to my questions during an interview and responses
to my letters about Lanza's experiences with the Bel Canto Trio. The
same is true for Harold Diner and Gerald Vinci, who played in the
Coca-Cola Radio Show orchestra for the tenor. Those early years were
also enlightened by Albert F. Robinson's thoughtful reminiscences
about his experiences with Lanza in Canada.

I thank Katherine Field for enthusiastically providing her recollections of the tenor's first concert at Royal Albert Hall; Charles Handelman for his outspoken and constructive criticism of Lanza; and Maestro
Julius Rudel for his generosity in appraising the tenor's talent and
impact.

No one who undertakes a biography of an entertainer can go the
distance as swiftly or well without the incredible resources and professional assistance available at the Library for the Academy of Motion
Picture Arts and Sciences in Beverly Hills, California. Similarly, no
biography of Mario Lanza is complete without painstaking research in
the dreary archives of the Los Angeles Superior Court. My search for
the estate files would have been far less effective without the assistance
provided by Alan Achen in introducing me to Chuck Hughes, who
knew where to park and how to navigate the crowds during the height
of the O. J. Simpson circus.

All biographies build on some portion of what has already been
researched, and mine is no exception. The work left by Constantine
Callinicos, both in the form of taped interviews and in his tenderly written memoir, *The Mario Lanza Story*, was indispensable in my approach
to this book. I also extend my thanks to Derek Mannering, who mag-
nanimously shared his thoughts and encouraged me to replace him as
the last person to write a biography of Lanza.

Publication entails many factors, not the least of which is a publisher.
I thank Amadeus Press for its interest and enthusiasm; Eve Goodman for
her encouragement; and Franni Farrell, who came to understand why I
had undertaken this project, for her deft and sensitive editing.

Thanks for various forms of support are also due the late Colleen Lanza, Damon Lanza, Bob Dolfi, Maynard Bertolet, Bob Trumpler, Vince de Fini, my cousin Linda Riley, Tom Paunovich, Elaine Marten, Deena Rosser, Roxanne McQueen, Ann Schaeffer, Linda Rein, Wayne Hales, Jerry Weigold, Rita Barrett, Eddie Durso, Steve Vertlieb, John Durso, Mary Galanti-Popola of the Mario Lanza Institute in Philadelphia, the late Vito Torelli, and my mother-in-law, Estelle Wachtel-Torres, M.D.

I also acknowledge the patience and constructive input from those who read the book in various drafts, including Reba Mae Sarnacki, Arthur E. LaFave, Clyde Smith, Alan Burns, Charles A. McQueen, and Dona Aleta Tracey.

Last, and never least, I thank my daughters, Jennifer Bessette and Angela McKee, for listening to Lanza's recordings without excessive complaints. Their love and support were given without qualification or demands in return.

CHAPTER 1

The Beginning

I never think about my voice. . . . It's just been there since I was
born.

Mario Lanza, 1957[1]

Nothing distinguished 31 January 1921 from any other day in South
Philadelphia, the section of the city known as Little Italy. Men, many of
them recent immigrants, scurried from their modest dwellings to the
streetcar lines and on to their places of employment in the chilly, early
morning darkness. Not much later, the women began their daily mar-
keting, spiritedly exchanging greetings and haggling over price and
quality in stores like Salvatore Lanza's Italian-American import shop at
636 Christian Street, amidst the salami, mortadella, capicolla, tins of
olive oil, and European-style breads. In a small bedroom above this
earthy din, with the rich, ethnic sounds and aroma as much a part of the
house as the red-brick exterior, Alfred Arnold Cocozza was born.[2]

The child's father, Antonio Cocozza, was born in 1893 in Filignano,
a rustic farming village in the Abruzzi region of Italy. Life in the
Abruzzi, a thinly populated area, was limited by the paucity of arable
land and a harsh climate; hardscrabble farming and grazing resisted
even the most concentrated efforts. At the age of twelve, Antonio emigrated to the United States, pursuing no formal education after he arrived. Although he would later work a lathe, fashioning small locomo-
tive parts for a company that did not do as well, his first job found him
varnishing cabinets for the Victor Talking Machine Company, the
employer his son knew as RCA Victor.

By all accounts, Tony Cocozza was a man of ordinary intellect,
energy, and potential who never forgot the land of his childhood;
throughout his life in America, he quoted Italian folklore and axioms and
then explained them in English as if they were edicts from the court of

15

Solomon. Bicycle racing was a particular but short-lived interest; he once participated in a competitive event at Madison Square Garden. He also played the French horn, to the dismay of those forced to listen. Another passion was opera, though he mostly listened to recordings or radio broadcasts and seldom attended a live performance. Tenor voices, especially those of the lachrymose, Italianate variety, were a special fascination for him. For hours on end, he listened to recordings of Enrico Caruso, whose great emotive voice reached the inner recesses of his heart and soul. His son would share this instinctive appreciation of the tenor voice. Unfortunately it was not the only thing passed from father to son.

In 1918 Tony was drafted into the 37th Division, 145th Infantry, and endured the devastation of combat in the Battle of the Meuse Argonne, an experience from which he never completely recovered. For his brief participation Tony received a Purple Heart and citations for gallantry and bravery. Besides capturing a German soldier, he was sprayed with mustard gas, stabbed in the lower spine with a bayonet, and hit by Boche dumdum bullets, which shattered and crippled his right arm. Although he claimed that the Veterans Administration had declared him totally disabled, Government records show only a 60 percent disability pension for the injury to his right arm.[3] MGM, his son's eventual employer, hailed him in press releases as one of the most highly decorated veterans of World War I, which hyperbole only cheapens a legitimate record of sacrifice and service.

The infant's mother, Maria, was also born in the Abruzzi. When she was barely six months old, her mother, Ellisa, and she emigrated to the United States, where her father, Salvatore Lanza, was already peddling vegetables and fruit from a horsedrawn cart in South Philadelphia. Maria, or Mary, as she was soon called, was the first of their eight children

Salvatore Lanza was earnest, tireless, and stubborn. Through sheer force of will and frugality, he advanced from peddling to the establishment of a store at 636 Christian Street. He prospered and eventually owned the property at 636 Christian and a summer cottage in Wildwood, New Jersey, outright. Truly it was the American dream of the time. Like so many others who began with passage on an ordinary liner and cleared immigration at Ellis Island, the Lanzas achieved a far better standard of living than the Abruzzi would have afforded them.

Ellisa Lanza, a solid, hard-working woman who tended to the home and rearing of their children, was overwhelmed by her domineering husband. She and her family somehow maintained their sanity in cramped quarters above the store, where the children rotated shifts behind the counters. The work ethic paid off, for most of them. Hilda became a laboratory chemist; Arnold was successful as a manufacturer and distributor of cleaning and industrial supplies; Robert, tall, elegant, and handsome, was a sought-after dress designer in New York City; others became principals and educators. But their eldest, Mary, her protestations to the contrary, never had a chance at a career or true independence.

Mary maintained that she had always wanted a career in opera but that her father forbade such pursuits. It is more likely that Salvatore, a competent and moral businessman, did not assess his daughter's talent as overwhelming. True, she could operate the pianola that saw much service in the small formal parlor at 636 Christian, but home and studio recordings have captured her heavy-handed keyboard technique and pleasant but thin vocalizations. When interviewed in 1962, Mary maintained that her son Mario had had the career she had been denied.

In 1920 Tony Cocozza, wearing his military uniform, entered the store at 636 Christian Street, intending to buy salami. He did not. Instead he talked to the lively, bright-eyed fifteen-year-old who was tending the counter. Salvatore viewed Tony as a good prospect for his eldest daughter: he was older and received a disability pension; with an income from honest labor, he would be a good provider. Tony courted Mary in his own way, and they eventually married. Their only child soon followed.

The three Cocozzas joined the maelstrom of 636 Christian Street, living with the nine Lanzas and frequent visitors from Italy. Alfred, who quickly became Freddy, was doted on by his parents, aunts, and uncles; one advantage of the extended family situation was that it temporarily camouflaged the troubled state of the child's immediate family. Neighbors remembered the little boy as rambunctious, insecure, and always nattily attired by his mother, a talented seamstress. Mary continued to work in the store and took in sewing projects. She later worked as a waitress in an ice cream parlor; for five years she hooked sample rugs, and for seven years she served with the U.S. Army Quartermaster as a corsetiere. When she bobbed her lustrous long hair, following the fashion of the 1920s, her father refused to speak to her for six months.

Tony, who was physically capable of performing many jobs, showed no inclination to do more than collect his disability pension and listen to his records morning, noon, and night. Given the clutter, population, and noise in the apartment, Salvatore regarded his son-in-law's constant presence and worn records as annoying. Eventually, he rented space and established Tony in a small candy store. The son-in-law dabbled at the enterprise, running a less-than-timely and unprofitable operation. In two years he was back underfoot at the crowded apartment. Tony Cocozza never functioned as the head of the household or—beyond his disability pension—made a significant contribution as the man of the house. He was too nervous to drive, fly, or work. Mary euphemistically attributed the problems to his exposure to mustard gas during the war.

Freddy was drawn, almost from birth, to the rich musical repertoire that was the constant background in the crowded apartment. He learned the opera storylines and was encouraged, by Mary, to argue with his elders about plot and quality of performance. He sang along with Enrico Caruso and Titta Ruffo. When he was seven, Freddy listened to Caruso's recording of "Vesti la giubba" from *Pagliacci* twenty-seven times in a row. The exercise seemed to imprint a method he later found difficult to abandon: that of learning a piece by listening to a recording or having it played on a piano as opposed to reading the music.

In 1930 nine-year-old Freddy and his parents moved to a two-story home at 2040 Mercy Street. Once again, Salvatore assisted. The home was modest—a replica of the brick row houses that lined both sides of the street—but the six rooms, bath, and small backyard seemed private and palatial compared with Christian Street. The positives were obvious, the negatives probably never pondered. The seeming advantages of a more isolated setting only highlighted his mother's growing anger and marital dissatisfaction. Tony, though affable, was less than Mary felt she deserved.

Freddy attended St. Mary Magdalene di Pazzi School at Seventh and Montrose, Nare Junior High School, and South Philadelphia High School for Boys (Southern High, in local parlance). He enjoyed baseball and boxing. He was very fond of dogs and loved horses with a passion he retained as an adult, stuffing every picture, drawing, or story he could find about them into a collection of bulging boxes under his bed. The boy was bright but could be truculent, defiant, and trouble-some, finding it painfully difficult to acknowledge that anything should be done as expected by those who set the rules.

He grew into a sturdy teen with a naturally powerful physique, which he enhanced through spurts of intense, if not unconventional, weightlifting. Freddy's parents allowed him to exercise in a second-floor room, and he saw nothing wrong with simply dropping the weights when he tired. He was never admonished to do otherwise or show respect toward his home. Both Mary and Tony claim he was not spoiled, but every landlord who transacted business with Mario Lanza would have cause to regret his poor rearing.

Freddy was soon notorious in the neighborhood for his appetite. Overeating and indulgence inevitably merged, although they began on separate tracks. Tony was proud that he never said no to his boy. On weekends, he prepared breakfasts that included two pounds of steak smothered with six eggs and an entire loaf of bread, which feasts he served to his son in bed. Mary too held her son's loyalty through over-protection, indulgence, misplaced praise, and, among other things, food. Mario was never cared for as an individual who had to cope with failure or succeed on the basis of merit, which cost him the chance to develop personal independence and self-esteem. He developed a demanding attitude that was rejected outside of his home. Within that same home, his demands were met—too often—by food, his parents' best expression of love and satisfaction.

Mary countered all criticism of her son with nothing but praise, but she could be harshly judgmental when she believed he had failed her. She raised Freddy to be her friend and discouraged his trusting anyone she viewed as competition for his loyalty. She urged him to be fearless, and Freddy quickly added his powerful fists and a willingness to engage in hijinks to his neighborhood notoriety. When Freddy initiated fist-fights, his mother insisted that the other boy started the affair and thus deserved a beating. When he was caught shoplifting candy from a neighborhood store, it was a mistake; his friends, most of them bad influences, were the culprits. When he was accused of taking improper liberties with girls, it was because they were tramps bent on an amorous adventure with her irresistible son.

Freddy bore a startling resemblance to his mother, and Tony never contradicted his wife's claim to being the solitary contributor to the

genetic assemblage that was their son. Mary was excessively proud that less than seventeen years separated her and her boy—and she took excessive credit for all that her son did well. It was Freddy and Mary who took long walks and went shopping together. Tony remained at home, listening to his records. His walks along the narrow, lively, densely populated streets of South Philadelphia were solitary.

When alone, Freddy tried to imitate what he heard on his father's records. Occasionally he attended operatic performances at the Philadelphia Academy of Music, which was within walking distance of his home, intently observing and evaluating every vocal nuance. Among his friends, he achieved another reputation, for crooning, and was soon known as South Philadelphia's answer to Russ Columbo.[4] Young Cocozza frequently announced, clutching his throat for emphasis, that he had "a million dollars right here."[5]

Mary later recounted several versions of stories that placed her as the only musical influence in her son's life, such as buying the violin he heaved in disgust from the second floor at 2040 Mercy Street, but it was the voices at the Academy that called to and seduced him. When he was fifteen years old, he auditioned for Antonio Scarduzzo, a baritone of local reputation in Philadelphia. Scarduzzo advised him to wait, study languages, piano, and *solfeggio* (sight reading of music). It was pointless. Though he was able to sight read when prodded, he always fell back on his original method of learning new music by listening to records. Thankfully, his musical instincts were excellent, and he remained convinced that he would become a great singer, confidently predicting that he would be "the greatest, sensational dramatic tenor that ever lived."[6]

Freddy spent much of every summer at his grandfather's cottage in Wildwood. One summer, Salvatore, ever hopeful of getting Tony or Freddy to drop a bead of sweat while engaged in honest labor, found his grandson a job driving a streetcar. The situation was short-lived. Freddy found it impossible to charge every customer an appropriate fare (young girls and friends rode free) or to keep to the established route. Arguments between the grandfather and grandson were loud and frequent, but they had no affect on Freddy's behavior or penchant for staying out until sunrise.

Freddy regarded high school as a distraction to his singing and neighborhood marauding, and his lackadaisical study habits translated to poor grades. Extremely dependent, he sought to fill his endless need for approval by acting the rebel. He was late for classes, slammed doors, sneaked up behind his unsuspecting fellows to blast a high note into their ears, or simply used his volume to let loose with an obscenity. He was on the verge of expulsion on several occasions and was not afraid to threaten teachers. A teacher from Southern High School described him as one of the biggest bums ever to come through the public school system.[7]

During his senior year at Southern, Freddy angered a teacher and they exchanged words. Freddy—a menacing 200 pounds plus—slugged the faculty member, who had used an ethnic slur, and the administration at Southern High School decided that they would be better off without Freddy Cocozza wandering the halls. Given his past record, no amount of pleading from his mother could alter their decision to expel him for misconduct. Tony was once again philosophical: Freddy possessed a rare and lovely voice; he could not be expected to behave like other boys, nor could he be treated like an ordinary young man.

Mary enrolled Freddy at Lincoln Preparatory Academy, a private school in Philadelphia, so that he could earn his high school diploma; she still harbored a dream of Freddy becoming a lawyer. He had no interest in attending classes, and it is unlikely that he would have survived the more demanding expectations at the preparatory school. He spared himself the experience—and his parents the expense—by refusing to attend.

Alfred Arnold Cocozza, a Philadelphia lawyer? He possessed outstanding verbal skills and enjoyed argument for argument's sake. But he seldom viewed a problem in its whole form or saw an issue as it related to a cause or solution. Fortunately for the judges, clients, and adversaries who would have been confronted by this specter—let alone law school professors and fellow students—Freddy chose to make a positive contribution in another way. He began his serious training as a singer.

CHAPTER 2

Early Training

The tenor sound that issued from that . . . throat was gorgeous,
unforgettable, out of this world. I could hardly believe my ears.
                                                    Boris Goldovsky, 1942[1]

The Cocozzas were never as poor as Mary later claimed. Tony, though
just barely the nominal head of the household, continued to receive a
disability pension that provided the basics for his family. While it is true
that Mary worked until her son was a Hollywood success, her later
claim of laboring for the U.S. Army Quartermaster in order to pay for
his training was unfair to her husband and more a matter of how she
allocated household resources than a reflection of who paid for what.
The real question was, who would teach their prodigal prodigy?

Freddy Cocozza—who was now experimenting with the stage
name of Mario Lanza, a masculinized version of his mother's name—
tried and discarded several coaches before settling on fifty-two-year-old
soprano Irene Williams for two years of soaring vocal development.
Williams was no lightweight. She had sung with the Mormon Taberna-
cle Choir and been a soloist with the New York, Chicago, Los Angeles,
and San Francisco symphonies; she later performed duets with Nelson Eddy. She had an adequate technical basis and the vocal experience
necessary to train Freddy, but her personality was not up to subordi-
nating such a headstrong student.

The new Mario was a terrible pupil, whose best days were marked
by his total inattention to study. He abhorred trilling up and down the
scales, arguing that he should at once advance to singing the arias he
had already mastered by listening to recordings. He was fond of simply
vaulting, from silence, to a ringing and sustained high C. One day
Williams placed her hands on her hips and asked, in utter disbelief,
"How do you do that?"[2] She, like many, was numbed by listening to the

glorious, endless tones of his upper register and equally impressed by the solid confidence of his lower range. And like many who would follow, she was exasperated by her inability to provide direction to such a talent.

Irene Williams emphasized diction, corrected his Italian, and kept Lanza within the form of the music, yet she receives little credit for her contributions as a coach or teacher. It was her introductions that were key, providing impetus and opportunity for the teenaged tenor— though some would argue that he would have attracted notice even if he had confined himself to singing on the corner of Sixth and Christian. He was gifted, to be certain, but success usually comes through a combination of hard work, contacts, timing, and luck.

The young tenor's first recording, made in 1940 when he was nineteen years old, in honor of his parents' twentieth wedding anniversary, was "Vesti la giubba." Throughout his career he would think of it as his "lucky aria." The upper range was lyrical, as might be expected from one so young, but it was also rich, soaring, and driven by the passion that became his trademark. The lower register was surprisingly complete. Other recordings from the same year ("Ch'ella mi creda," "Torna a Surriento," "E lucevan le stelle," and "De' miei bollenti spiriti") caught the same effortless production of truly unforgettable sound. It was not yet the standard Lanzaesque interpretation, with dazzling overtones, instinctive colorations, and an enormous timbre in every register, but it was compelling, riveting, and unbelievable from a person of his years.

Irene Williams presented Mario Lanza in recitals attended by supporters of the arts in Philadelphia, which city was not a minor player in the worlds of classical music and great voice. In this new "classroom" the young man was taught approach, performance, demeanor, and acceptance of audience reaction. His own reaction was mixed: he told Williams that she had shown him the other side of the tracks, and that he liked what he was seeing; he confided to others that Philadelphia society was more taken with him than he was by it. Mario was capable of a high order of intelligence, but he tended to operate on instinct. Likely he sensed that more than money separated him from upper society people. Rather than identify the source of the difference and determine a corrective course of action, he concluded that they thought themselves superior—and that money was the solution. Throughout his life he would be dogged by his alternating rationalization that "we," the lower classes, were superior and a seething resentment over what "they" thought of him.

The consistent quality of Lanza's recitals led to a burgeoning local reputation. Now Lanza required more than exposure; he needed discovery and patronage—and Williams knew her limitations. She approached William K. Huff, director of Philadelphia Forum Concerts, a venue that occasionally hosted the Boston Symphony under Serge Koussevitzky. Huff came to Williams' studio to hear Mario. He was impressed, but pronounced the voice untrained. He counseled that, with hard work, the young tenor would eventually sing at the Philadelphia Academy of Music. Huff also advised the young man to concentrate on nothing but singing and not to permit himself to be distracted by anything. It was advice that Mario received with enthusiasm and intended, almost to his last breath, to some day follow.

Salvatore Lanza, who reckoned that a man's worth was directly proportionate to the honest labor he performed, erupted during this period, disgusted that his brawny nineteen-year-old grandson had yet to earn as much as a single cent in wages. Salvatore feared that he had another Tony Cocozza on his hands, storming that, like the son-in-law, the grandson listened to records for hours when he should be working. He demanded that his grandson find work. But Mary and Tony were more appalled than Mario about the prospect of his laboring for a dollar, even though his vocal studies hardly kept him so busy that a job was out of the question. Mary refused even to let her darling son assist with household chores. Tony stopped listening to his records long enough to advise his son to satisfy Salvatore Lanza by at least looking for work. Mario, somewhat embarrassed by his grandfather's charge that he was the talk of the neighborhood, was reflective about the whole business. He mused that it might be a new experience he would enjoy, but he never quite mustered the ambition to actually seek a job.

Finally Huff interceded. It was a Wednesday evening during the 1940 holiday season and the stores were open late. Wanamaker's, hoping to lure more than its share of the trade, offered a concert featuring what was billed as the world's largest organ. At the Philadelphia Academy of Music on Locust Street, Serge Koussevitzky was conducting the Boston Symphony. Huff, Irene Williams, and Lanza were in attendance.

After the performance, Huff took the young tenor backstage to meet the noted conductor. Koussevitzky, fatigued from the rigors of conducting a symphony orchestra, had removed his formal attire and was enjoying a ritualistic massage. Accustomed to being asked to assess not-so-great talent represented as once-in-a-lifetime, he told Huff to take his charge across the hall, where the accompanist would play anything the singer requested. Lanza chose "Vesti la giubba." Huff nodded and instructed the nervous young man to sing. Mario was uncertain at the outset, but his tones swiftly grew bolder and more confident. Koussevitzky ordered the masseur to cease. He crossed the hall, nodded toward Huff, and when the aria ended, embraced and kissed Lanza. "You have a truly great voice. You will come and sing for me in the Berkshires."[3]

Mario was elated by Koussevitzky's effusive review. As he later said, "I didn't know what the hell the Berkshires was, but I figured it must be something big and great."[4]

MGM later issued a press release depicting the discovery as a fortuitous accident: Mario was helping to move a piano and was overheard by Koussevitzky. The tale was retold many times; it became part of the semi-plot on the tenor's first film and even appeared in several biographies. The tenor himself eventually adopted and embellished the story.

Now Lanza's career seemed to be on solid ground. He was ecstatic and could talk of nothing else. Mary warned that "they" made and broke promises, that the great conductor would not likely follow through. But Koussevitzky—believing that he had discovered one of the great voices of the century—kept his word, and preparations for Lanza to attend the 1942 Berkshire Music Festival commenced. Mario was enthusiastic. The most glorious part of his life had begun.

If anyone was more enthused than Lanza about his prospects for success, it was Irene Williams. The soprano knew that she had glimpsed greatness. When Lanza left for the Berkshires, she accompanied him to the train station, where she presented him with a contract providing her with 5 percent of any income derived from singing in excess of $5000 and 10 percent of any such income in excess of $7500 per year. Williams claimed the agreement would protect him from unscrupulous agents, apparently never giving a thought to who would protect the young tenor from her. Mario signed the contract, without considering its contents or seeking advice. It was the first of many over which he would be sued and not the last he would disavow, though he was justified in this situation. After his experience in the Berkshires, Lanza needed precisely what Williams was incapable of providing.

The Russian-born Koussevitzky, a dreamer who would have found Utopia too bleak, envisioned the Berkshire Music Festival as a place where exceptional young talent would thrive in an ideal setting while gaining from exposure to the most capable instructors available. Founded in Stockbridge, Massachusetts, in 1934, the festival moved to the Tanglewood estate in 1937. Koussevitzky's vision was a reality almost from the beginning.

In the 1942 season, Koussevitzky's favorites were Lanza and an intense young composer-conductor named Leonard Bernstein. Mario approached training as he always had. If someone walked him through a piece, he produced spectacular results. But if you handed him a score to digest in time for morning rehearsal, the result was a blank stare and an orchestra with little to do. Bernstein attempted to work with him, but both men recognized the futility of trying to mesh their disparate approaches.

Lanza was out of his element that summer. The young tenor knew that he could inspire awe with his voice, but he was cripplingly aware that he was inept in areas where serious students excelled. Partly as a defensive measure, partly indulging his natural tendencies, he drank enough beer that summer to be remembered more for that than his application to musical study. Goldovsky remembered his "pawing the girls and luring them into empty practice rooms."[5] As for singing, he did plenty of it, and those who heard him remembered the voice as beautiful and enormous.

At Tanglewood he was surrounded by more serious musicians than he ever would be again. The Russian-born Boris Goldovsky, a versatile musician whose accomplishments, then and later, included a stint as the director of the New England Conservatory of Music and widely published, highly opinionated opera critiques, recalled Lanza singing part of the duet from the third act of *La Bohème* with a young Mexican soprano named Irma Gonzalez during a workshop production. Koussevitzky, driven to tears, cried out, *"Caruso redivivus!"* ("Caruso reborn!"), and excitedly instructed Goldovsky to teach Lanza the tenor part in Beethoven's Ninth Symphony.[6]

Goldovsky set about the task, resolute about his methods and confident of his abilities. After two sessions, it was apparent that tenor and teacher were growing farther apart. Goldovsky explained his plight to conductor Ifor Jones over lunch. "Koussie wants Lanza to sing the tenor part in the Ninth Symphony, and he asked me to prepare it." Jones responded, "You can't. I know Lanza. It can't be done. You can't teach him anything."[7]

Jones and Goldovsky were correct from their perspectives. If Mario were to learn a piece as complex as the Ninth Symphony in German, a language with which he was unfamiliar, it would have required at least several days of unorthodox feeding and memorization—an impossibly crude process for trained musicians to undertake. If they provided him with a recording and allowed him to prepare in his own fashion, the results would have been spectacular—to the audience, but they would not have been acceptable to Jones or Goldovsky.

First Lanza would have adopted whatever technical errors had been made by whoever sang on the record from which he learned. Then he would have imbued the presentation with his own Italianate, at times thoroughly Neapolitan, style. Lastly the conductor would have found that the orchestral ensemble was following his lead, while Mario was in pursuit of his own adventure. Conductors make prison wardens seem easygoing and eager to accommodate. Granting such independence to a performer would be as difficult for them as it was for Lanza to absorb conventional training.

One might argue that, given the results he could achieve when adequately prepared, such efforts would have been worthwhile. The Berkshire Music Festival has never been a forum for the peculiar talents of hugely gifted but idiosyncratic artists. Rather, it is a place for disciplined and traditional training. Though Lanza possessed excellent musical taste, the Berkshires featured a product for which he was neither a producer nor consumer. Regardless, his talent was too great for a default based on technical deficiencies.

Goldovsky, frustrated by his inability to communicate with Lanza, approached Koussevitzky and explained, "I just don't know how to teach this boy. He's got a beautiful tenor voice . . . but . . . neither Dr. Jones nor I know how to go about teaching him."[8]

After a brief conference, they decided to teach him instead the minor role of Fenton in German composer Otto Nicolai's seldom-performed *The Merry Wives of Windsor*. Goldovksy and Koussevitzky were thrilled by the results. By all accounts, Lanza was outstanding, projecting considerable vocal and personal charisma. Highly respected music critic Noel Straus (*The New York Times*, 8 August 1942) ranked the young singer's voice with or above the best tenors of the day in terms of warmth, quality, and power: "If Lanza's talents are developed in the proper direction, he will own a splendid voice. At present, he needs more fundamental training and style. Yet even now he offers good musicality and diction."

Noel Straus was critiquing voice and potential, not degree of accomplishment on the major operatic stages of the world; still, his praise was considerable in view of a roster that included Beniamino Gigli, Tito Schipa, Giovanni Martinelli, and Jussi Björling. Modern critics too often scoff at the suggestion that Mario Lanza was ever considered a legitimate tenor, but the views expressed by their counterparts during the 1940s is irrefutable evidence to the contrary. The 1940s was a time not unlike the present in that fine young talent was considered inferior to singers well beyond their primes; Straus was reviewing a twenty-one-year-old prodigy and not the "celluloid Caruso" reviled by some critics less than a decade later.

Jones and Goldovsky—who viewed the young tenor as magnificently gifted but ultimately flawed by his inability to learn by their methods—would have preened and strutted if a lesser talent who shared their concept of musicianship had provided a merely good performance as Fenton. But even a respected critic like Straus saw quality and musicianship in Lanza's presentation. Criticism that focused on what the tenor could not do, as opposed to what he did, became more pronounced, despite audiences that were simply dazzled by what they heard.

Mario had emerged from the anonymity of his apprenticeship in Philadelphia and affiliation with Irene Williams. Stories about a fresh discovery were coming out of the Berkshires and talk was circulating, in serious music circles, about a great new talent for opera and recital stages. Rosalind Elias, who later had a successful career in opera, remembered that young singers held Mario Lanza in awe and viewed him as a role model.

Others were also in awe. Concert managers swarmed, and Lanza fortuitously signed with Arthur Judson of Columbia Artists, Inc. He also signed with Michael de Pace, who managed Giovanni Martinelli. Judson and de Pace were unaware of the mutuality of their "exclusive" interests. The tenor often signed "exclusive" contracts with several people for the same purpose.

By now, the young man who was still legally known as Alfred Arnold Cocozza was using his stage name, Mario Lanza, full time. The name had a wonderful sound that exploded, when attached to the personality and voice, with Mediterranean passion. Much has been made of the fact that young Alfred experimented with stage names: Al Lanza, Al Cocozza, and Fred Lanza, for example. That he abandoned his father's name, never considering a pleasant hybrid such as Tony Lanza, is significant. It was Mary who suggested and championed the name Mario Lanza, vowing, "You will have my career."[9]

That Mary would equate her thin voice with her son's prodigious talent was indicative of the frustration she harbored over her early and nearly always unfulfilling marriage. To compensate for this resentment, she placed unreasonably high demands on her son. Whether her motive was to dominate and live through her son—or something beyond that —remained to be seen, though she now claimed to be the one who passed on the voice, the musicality, the money for training, *and* the name.

In the months that followed, the elation of Tanglewood vanished and Mario half-heartedly pursued vocal studies in New York, training with the great Metropolitan Opera baritone Robert Weede. A meeting with Maria Margelli, an associate of Metropolitan Opera bass and eventual star of *South Pacific*, Ezio Pinza, led to an impromptu audition and a mutually beneficial affair. The flashy, diminutive, and somewhat older Margelli knew her way around New York society and music circles and introduced Mario wherever she could. She later declared, "His was the greatest voice I have ever heard and I have heard them all."[10]

The benefits of Lanza's brief but intense fling with Maria Margelli were cut short. America was building its air, sea, and ground forces, and Alfred Arnold Cocozza was about to experience what his grandfather had long encouraged and his parents had long denied him: discipline.

CHAPTER 3

Private Alfred Arnold Cocozza

I had no idea such a voice was hidden in the chorus . . . I walked up
to him and asked, "Where did you learn to sing like that?"

Moss Hart, 1943[1]

Late in 1942 Lanza's soaring prospects collided with an induction
notice from the United States Army. Mario was of course aware that
the world was embroiled in conflict and that the United States was gear-
ing up its war machine, but he felt no inclination to participate and
regarded duty as something for someone else to fulfill. After all, he rea-
soned, some men willingly enlisted and seemed drawn to that sort of
thing. His father had been wounded; why did the United States Army
need him? If the army had known what it was inducting, a truce might
have resulted.

The young tenor, like many recipients of draft notices before and
after him, attempted to gain a deferment or at least delay his induction. In a letter dated 16 December 1942, Michael de Pace interceded
with Philadelphia's Local Board no. 75, explaining that his client had a
bright future, that even the distinguished Giovanni Martinelli was interested, and that military service would interrupt the intense training he
required. If anything, the attempt accelerated the interruption of his
days as a carefree civilian.

The disruption of his career struck Mario as a personal attack, the
worst timing imaginable. But many lives and careers were interrupted
by the war, some ruined or ended by injury or death. Lanza's plight
was much less devastating than that of athletes and actors, who lost
years that could not be replaced. His situation, while a personal disappointment, represented nothing more than a delay.

The reluctant draftee reported for induction on 5 January 1943. It
is unlikely that the Lanza *fortissimo* was evident or that his right hand

was held very high during the oath of enlistment. Mario, again Alfred Cocozza, shipped out by rail for basic training with the U.S. Army Air Corps—soon to be known as the United States Air Force—in Miami, Florida. Maria Margelli took an apartment nearby until his training was completed.

Lanza's service dossier showed his considerable experience and training as a singer but little else in the way of qualifications. The air force, in a decision typical of those that have inspired hundreds of movies and barracks ballads, as well as Joseph Heller's *Catch-22*, decided that the erstwhile Mario Lanza—Private Cocozza to them— would excel as a military policeman. In truth, he had been such a low-level performer during basic training that he earned a lousy assignment. He was transferred to Marfa, Texas, a dusty town in the Davis Mountains famous for nothing. A week there compared with an uneventful year most anyplace else. Margelli, sensing that no relationship was worth that, returned to New York.

Once in Marfa, Lanza was assigned the impossible task of patrolling the Mexican-American border. He was not the worst soldier in the air force, though he could have held his own if such a competition had been held. He employed every challenge to authority his amazingly resourceful mind could devise, always falling short of outright defiance. Not surprisingly, the idea of saluting another man was abhorrent to him. He offered excuses about not seeing officers he was supposed to acknowledge, making amends with an agonizingly difficult, miserable half-salute. It was another "them" versus "me" vendetta for him. His unhappiness was total, but no one addressed his apparent depression. Different priorities take hold when a nation is at war.

Whenever he was depressed or unable to handle what most would consider routine pressures, Lanza turned to food. Mario's weight had approached 250 pounds when he was fifteen years old and then again at nineteen; his severe diets thus did nothing more than shrink fat cells created during his teen years. The astonishing weight gains that marked his later life, of fourteen pounds over a weekend or sixty pounds in less than a month, were the result. After several months of poor adjustment to life as an air force private, Lanza weighed 240 pounds enroute to 300 pounds plus. His uniform was unkempt, his belt missing or barely cinched, the shoes frequently minus laces, the knot of his tie several inches below an unbuttoned collar, and the hat frequently where he was not. The young private remained uneasily adrift, passively defying every regulation that interfered with his miserable existence.

Time passed grudgingly in Marfa. Then, amidst the swirl of dust and tumbleweed, came the first in a series of circumstantial convergences of time, opportunity, and luck. Johnny Silver, a noncommissioned officer who had been a comic in burlesque and who would become a Broadway fixture (notably in *Guys and Dolls*) was scanning service records in search of candidates for variety shows that would be presented at military bases throughout the country. After reviewing Lanza's background, he summoned the young private to his office. His first impression of Mario was that he was so far out of uniform, he could have been shot for desertion.[2]

Nonetheless the men got along well, and after Mario sang, Silver launched a campaign to keep him out of combat. The mere mention of Private Cocozza caused well-meaning members of the upper echelon at Marfa to grimace and break into a cold sweat. Banishment to an overseas assignment would accomplish the dual purpose of ridding the post of a malcontent and sending a message to others inclined to ride out the war as protesters in uniform. Johnny Silver's contribution was, in truth, considerable.

More fortunate circumstances followed, and they were not mere luck. Now that the hapless private had made someone aware of his talent, energies were gladly expended on his behalf. His performance as a soldier had been abysmal, but the voice demanded recognition. His voice was all that Mario would ever have in terms of rank and privilege, even in civilian life.

The singing private was reassigned as a chaplain's assistant, long the refuge of those who find it difficult to adjust to military life. (Such an assignment happens so often, it is a true miracle when an earnest chaplain manages to find a competent assistant.) Soon thereafter, Sergeant Peter Lind Hayes visited Marfa to audition talent for *On the Beam*, a musical he had written with Frank Loesser, who would reach greater heights with *Guys and Dolls*. The most common version of what happened next follows.

It seems that Lanza's throat was inflamed by the red dust that made it difficult to maintain even a shoeshine in Marfa, and it was impossible for him to sing at the audition. Johnny Silver supposedly pasted a second label on a 78 rpm disc recording of an aria from *Tosca* by Metropolitan opera star Frederick Jagel, identifying it as Lanza performing with the Boston Symphony Orchestra. The apocryphal tale continues with Hayes, upon finally hearing Mario, proclaiming that he was much better live. Lanza liked the story so much that he later insisted that Silver had pasted the label on a Caruso recording. It is unlikely that Hayes, a seasoned musical talent, would have been duped by a pre-1920 Caruso recording, but doubtless a live Lanza would have sounded better than a recording by the now mostly forgotten Jagel.[3]

Jerry Adler, whose brother Larry was a member of the Harmonicats, remembered that Mario sang magnificently in the base theater.[4] Hayes later recalled the encounter: "I heard this guy belt out a number and I knew anyone with that voice could do more good singing to entertain our troops than by fighting."[5] So Lanza escaped the drudgery of Marfa and joined the cast of *On the Beam*, touring bases to entertain other soldiers. He was an audience favorite in the impromptu, nearly vaudevillian show. Soldiers who had never been near an opera house were dazzled by the power and passion of the first legitimate voice most had ever heard. He was called the Caruso of the Air Force, which pleased him.

Being less than trim would diminish the returns from his next opportunity. Moss Hart, the successful playwright who, in collaboration with George S. Kaufman, wrote *The Man Who Came to Dinner* and earned a Tony in 1957 for his direction of *My Fair Lady*, was conducting auditions for the 342-person cast of *Winged Victory*, his largely forgettable spectacle about the air force—which suited wartime fervor and tastes to a T. Lanza was selected for the fifty-member vocal chorale under the direction of Lieutenant Leonard De Paur. If his appearance had been more soldierly, Mario might have played a leading role. His weight was still over 300 pounds, and at slightly under five feet, nine inches tall, he was hardly the flat-bellied, iron-jawed GI prototype that Americans envisioned.[6]

The cast of *Winged Victory* included impressive names from the stage and motion pictures: Alan Baxter (*Judgment at Nuremberg* and *Paint Your Wagon*); Red Buttons; Marc Daniels; Ray Middleton; 1951 Oscar winner Karl Malden; Gary Merrill, who was married to Bette Davis from 1950 to 1960; stage and screen actor Barry Nelson; 1954 Oscar winner and actor's actor, Edmond O'Brien; the ill-fated suicide of *Gone With the Wind* and *Superman* fame, George Reeves; and Don

Taylor (*The Naked City* and *Stalag 17*). It also included an aspiring actor from Chicago named Bert Hicks, a mean drunk, always on the fringes of production—whose sister Betty became Mrs. Mario Lanza.[7]

After a particularly long day of dealing with last-minute production problems, Moss Hart was resting when Mario began to sing "Celeste Aida." Hart described the voice as glorious and declared the treatment unsurpassed by any he had ever heard. He searched for the singer and was introduced to Private Cocozza. Hart inquired about his background, where and when he had trained; he was charmed by the "childlike innocence" of the amiable young soldier. "He was outgoing, a darling fellow. The seeds of destruction were there, but not on the surface."[8]

Winged Victory opened at the 44th Street Theatre in New York on 20 November 1943 and ran through 20 May 1944. Lewis Nichols of *The New York Times* called the musical wonderful, though its maudlin symbolism and clumsy, patriotic message condemned it to obsolescence with the end of the war. Private Cocozza performed anonymously to the audiences, just one voice among many others. His parents saw the show and occasionally visited.

New York was still to his liking, and Mario spent much of his off-duty time in typical fashion, which included bedding most any woman who came along. He had no inhibitions about swapping partners and no preference, evidently, for the pleasantries of candlelight and crisp sheets; not too particular about location, he often coupled in less than private circumstances. Heavy or thin, from South Philadelphia to the Big Apple, from Marfa to the other tank towns he landed in courtesy of the air force, he cut a wide and almost never discriminating path among the local women.

He was able to enjoy the passing moment, but for the most part he remained unhappy with his life as an air force private, even in New York. The gorging that accompanied bad times continued; Lanza regularly ate and drank quantities that staggered onlookers. He had no choice but to accept his role as the butt of fat jokes and status as a glutton of legend. But never again would he accept the resulting ribbing so good-naturedly.

Lanza met another up-and-coming singer during his stint in New York. Robert Merrill later recalled Lanza with the advantage of hindsight:

He wanted to be an opera singer, and after hearing him sing, I took him to Mr. Margolis. He did an aria from *Turandot*, and we were both impressed. Mario had a wonderful natural voice and not the slightest inclination to polish it. He asked for advice . . . "Should I learn sight reading? Should I get a coach? Should I study with this Margolis character?". . . but he never took anyone's counsel.[9]

Winged Victory chugged along, its ready-made wartime audience earning more than $600,000 for the Army Relief Fund. The round-faced tenor—fresh, sincere, humorous, and uncomplicated—was a favorite with many in the cast. Mothers adored him as he ravenously devoured and praised even their basic meatloaf. Edmond O'Brien's mother thought him special, and he delighted in singing Irish favorites for her. When *Winged Victory* ended its New York run, the cast was shipped to Hollywood, where George Cukor would direct the film version.

Discipline in entertainment units was country-club in comparison with combat organizations, but the man with the name "Cocozza" on his name-tag found it too severe. His psyche was fragile, and given his coddled upbringing, the inspections, citations for minor violations, and hazings of military life made it a brutal experience for the tenor. He was AWOL on several occasions, causing disruption on the set of *Winged Victory*. His indiscretions were always passive; he never engaged in outright defiance, which made it difficult to correct his behavior. There was no kitchen unit, making KP impossible. Instead, errant soldier-entertainers were assigned to load musical equipment on trucks or trains. Mario got whatever exercise he took in that manner.[10]

Private Cocozza, Johnny Silver, and other soldiers from the cast went to an empty Hollywood Bowl one afternoon in 1944. Photos show the tenor, distorted beyond any proportion he would approach again, singing from the stage. Those in attendance remembered that his voice carried impressively. It was an eerie rehearsal in a place where he would enthrall audiences as the headliner just a few years later.

His depression deepened, and his drinking approached problem proportions. He regularly visited the Rhapsody Record Shop on North Highland Avenue in Hollywood or The Masquers, a hangout for actors, singing for nothing more than praise and recognition. At times, it was drunken bellowing—great by most standards—but nonetheless barroom bellowing. The exposure from those forays and the fact that he was with the cast of *Winged Victory* resulted in occasional invitations to Hollywood parties.

One evening Lanza entertained guests at Frank Sinatra's home, singing well into the morning hours. Soon after, Mario signed a contract with Sinatra's manager—giving him four managers to choose from. Sinatra was enthusiastic about the young soldier, six years his junior: "The kid knocked a hole through me. Talk about people swooning when I sing, the tables were turned . . . for once I really swooned."[11] Frank offered to help the young singer and insisted that he stay at his home. It was typical of Sinatra to be kind to a younger talent, or one that had run its course. It was different with direct competitors. Seven years later, when Sinatra's records were a curiosity and Lanza's sales were unequaled, Frankie derisively mocked Mario's weight.

On 5 October 1944 Lanza attended a farewell party for Irene Manning, who was leaving to entertain the troops overseas. Manning, whose pleasant voice suited operetta, broke into films opposite Gene Autry and also appeared in several musicals (*Yankee Doodle Dandy*, *The Desert Song*, *Shine on Harvest Moon*, and others). The young soldier sang for the seventy-five guests, including Walter Pidgeon—who exuberantly predicted that those in attendance were hearing the "tenor of the century."[12] The listeners were in awe. Hedda Hopper was approaching her heyday in the strangely symbiotic relationship that existed between her, Louella Parsons, and Walter Winchell as purveyors of Hollywood gossip. She was there, and she too was dazzled. Mario remained one of her favorites during the early years of his career, and she spoke well of him on her radio show and in her column. Hopper eventually turned away from him, saying he could no more handle success than an infant could handle explosives. But all that was far away on a night that held so much discovery and promise.

The most fortuitous introduction of the session came as the sun rose over Manning's canyon home. Art Rush, who managed Nelson Eddy, had taken in the entire performance without saying a word, making the young soldier uncomfortable. Finally Rush broke his silence, handing the nervous tenor a card and asking if he could come to his office at two that afternoon. The card read "Art Rush—Western Representative for RCA Victor." The logo in the corner—Nipper, the little white dog with the black patch on one eye listening to "His Master's Voice"—was magical. This was Caruso's label. It was something Lanza had dreamed about since he first knew he had a voice. RCA was the only affiliation he ever seriously considered.

Art Rush was a dedicated, successful, and honest Hollywood agent, which was fortunate for Mario, who was once again about to enter into an agreement with no concern for content, ramification, or compensation. On 6 October 1944 Mario signed with the prestigious Red Seal division of RCA. He received a $3000 bonus to defray the costs of his studies, which was the first time RCA provided an artist with such an inducement. The company had no immediate plans to record the young tenor. The voice was spectacular, but his artistic approach was too unsettled to handle a serious repertoire.

One night soon after, at a bowling alley, the young soldier lined the entire bonus, now converted to ten-dollar bills, along a counter for all to see, among them his friend and future workmate, George London, the Canadian-born Metropolitan Opera baritone. In 1944 $3000 was more than most earned during an entire year. Wisely spent, it would have permitted him to train and subsist for fifteen to eighteen months. But Lanza was not the first fool to be parted from his money, though he was more determined than most. The days that followed were a whirl of activity at posh places like Ciro's, the Mocambo, and Romeo's Chianti Restaurant. He overtipped and overspent as if he were compelled to rid himself of any sign of success. When most of it was gone, he was back to the slim standard his air force pay allowed. "It's only money," he nonchalantly explained to London.[13] The incident was a small-scale example of how he would always live. It's only money? With a few noteworthy exceptions, it flowed into and out of his coffers with an ease that cheapened its value.

The days passed and more introductions followed. Maria Margelli, now settled in Hollywood, reentered his life. This time it was strictly business. She approached Jack Warner, of Warner Bros., who agreed to listen to her great discovery. Margelli drove Mario to Warner's mansion, where he rattled the chandelier with "La donna è mobile." Warner found the voice thrilling and was intrigued, but he regarded Lanza as too heavy for a film career.[14]

The filming of *Winged Victory* was completed. The German counteroffensive called the Battle of the Bulge began on 16 December 1944 and was not contained until early the following month—obviously the United States military needed young men, but it bid farewell to the problematic Private Cocozza on 29 January 1945 at the McCaw General Hospital in Walla Walla, Washington. The initial reason for his discharge was a loss of hearing; the records were eventually changed, citing a postnasal drip.[15] In either case, his discharge was a matter of convenience, and source of relief, to all. He was entitled to a 60 percent disability pension (then $69 per month) from the Veterans Administration. The disability was eventually reduced to 30 percent, and the pension discontinued when Lanza failed to report for examinations. After all, it was only money.

Now the young man would attempt to reignite the career that had been interrupted by World War II. He had sung a great deal during his hitch in the air force, but his methods had suffered. His range had matured and increased, and he still lacked training. It was time for a concept that was foreign to him: hard work.

CHAPTER 4

Marriage and Mary

You must tell them you married a girl who loves you and wants
them to love her.

Betty Lanza, 1945[1]

Mario met Betty Hicks several months before he was discharged from
the air force. Bert Hicks, his friend and fellow cast member in *Winged
Victory*, had shown him a packet of family photos. Lanza lingered over
one of them. "Hey! Who's this?"

"My sister Betty. Went out with my wife and kid in Los Angeles.
Landed herself a great job at McDonnell-Douglas. Great gal."

"Married? Engaged?" inquired Mario. Bert said no. Mario asked
for more pictures.

When the cast of *Winged Victory* settled in Los Angeles, Bert took
Mario home to dinner. He and Betty, who was dressed in red slacks
and an off-the-shoulder blouse, were an instant hit. Bert and Betty's
mother, May Hicks, an attractive and engaging woman, was visiting
from Chicago, and Mario, with his affable and engaging manner, was
already one of the family. "Mom," he pleaded not too convincingly,
"make her stop looking at me."

Later, when Bert was about to be shipped overseas, Mario threw
him a party at Romeo's in Hollywood. It was a gala affair, a privilege
granted to an air force private's dazzling voice. On 29 August 1944,
Betty and Mario returned to Romeo's and dined alone. He proposed.
She accepted. They agreed not to tell anyone and planned to marry, in
a church, after the war ended.

After his discharge, Lanza spent several months in Los Angeles.
He had no prospects beyond his VA pension and belonged in New York
where the best coaches and RCA were available to guide his career.
But his beloved was in Los Angeles and secure in her job as an expe-

diter for McDonnell-Douglas. Betty, equally reluctant to bear Mario's absence, said she would quit her job and go to New York with him on one condition: that they travel as husband and wife.

Lanza, never one to give a second thought to anything that seemed right at the moment, agreed. They obtained a license on 11 April, bought a wedding ring for $6.95 the following day, and were married the day after by Judge Griffin at city hall in Beverly Hills. It was Friday the 13th of April, 1945.

Betty was sweet, immature, uncomplicated, and outspoken, an attractive brunette of medium height, with a slim figure and pretty legs. She wore a dress well and, from most angles, had looks that could have carried her through any number of lesser roles in film. If Betty Hicks had returned to Chicago and married the boy next door, she likely would have become a devoted wife, a good but overly protective mother, and an attentive grandmother. Under normal conditions, she could have managed ordinary problems and led an ordinary existence. As it was, she endured fourteen years of a marriage to Mario Lanza, one marked with passionate highs and violent lows.

After the wedding, the newlyweds boarded a train bound for Chicago, where the groom met the rest of the Hicks family. Then, fully anticipating his mother's unfavorable reaction, he proceeded alone to New York to break the news and find an apartment. He did not have much luck on either front.

Mario hooked up with Johnny Silver, himself just discharged from the air force, and spent more time reminiscing and visiting old haunts than he did scouting for suitable accommodations. With the week drawing to a close, he imposed on Silver with a proposal to share his apartment at the Park Central. It turned out to be an eviction for Silver, who eventually moved to the private apartment Mario never had time to find. Nor did he inform his parents about the marriage. His mother had been momentarily taken aback upon meeting Maria Margelli, but she understood the situation and knew that both would take their pleasure from one another and then move along. But marriage? A daughter-in law? The son was terrified.

Mario called his mother and promised to take the short train ride to Philadelphia. Mary would hear none of that. She and Tony came to New York, loaded with foodstuffs in the best Italian tradition. Mario and Silver met them at Grand Central Station and a pleasant reunion followed, but the nervous son was still unable to tell his parents about the most important event in his life. After they left, he called Betty in Chicago and explained his dilemma. His young bride was wiser than he in this situation. She knew that the marriage could not remain a secret and that more time passing would only make matters worse. Mario, showing the cowardice that only his mother could inspire, with her convergent messages of "fear no one but me" and "fear them," suggested that they both tell his parents when Betty came to New York. His wife was firm: "You must tell them you married a girl who loves you and wants them to love her." She arrived one week later.

Tony and Mary responded to their son's invitation to come to New York a second time for what was touted as a big surprise. Betty went to the movies to provide her husband with an opportunity to break the news. He squandered the afternoon, nervously avoiding what he was supposed to tell them. Finally, with conversation stalled and time running out, Mary asked about the big surprise. Mario stammered around the issue, only managing to convey that he was in love with someone. Mary broke in—he had plenty of time for that after his career was established. She advised him to keep company with the young lady but to get on with the business of singing. Realizing that time and circumstance were about to collide, Mario drew a deep breath and explained that he and the girl were already married. The explosive reaction lasted only a few seconds before composure was restored. The Cocozzas were decent people. They knew enough not to show what Tony called a *brutta faccia* (an ugly face).

Betty phoned after the movie. Her husband happily advised her that everything was fine, to come back home. When she reached the apartment, the door was open. Tony, who made no issue of such things, embraced her. Mary kissed her and called her *mia figlia* (my daughter). Betty later remembered, her eyes misting over as she spoke, "Such beautiful people. They took me in, and it was as if I'd belonged to them forever." They all went to nearby St. Patrick's Cathedral to pray.

Betty did not know it then, but the relationship with her mother-in-law would grow no warmer. Mary eventually came to accept Betty. She at times liked, but never loved her. The biggest problem was her refusal to accept that a wife is her husband's partner and that a mother is not always number one in a son's life. Mary loved only Mario and saw no reason for his love for her to be less than exclusive. When she and Betty

were together, it was Mary who claimed to understand what Mario
needed.

Betty never learned to deal with Mary's competition for her son's
attention. But in 1945, and for several years thereafter, she was dream-
ily happy with Mario and her legal name of Elizabeth Janette Cocozza.

CHAPTER 5

A False Start

I can't go through with this torture. It's all wrong.
Mario Lanza, 1945[1]

The newlyweds quickly depleted their savings, which had no effect on their lifestyle. Mario was an easy mark for every friend who was down on his luck, and New York has long been a mecca for that species. Soon they avoided answering a knock at the door for fear that it might be the landlord or any one of a horde of creditors. Things became so strained that they ran an extension from another apartment for electricity. Despite the charm of youth and the romance of struggling artistry, it would prove to be Mario's most mature performance as a tenant.

In June 1945 Mario made test recordings for RCA ("I'm Falling in Love with Someone," "Mattinata," "Vesti la giubba," and "E lucevan le stelle"). The singing was surprisingly uninspired and weighted by the Caruso influence; the incredible lower, middle, and upper registers were impressive but unfortunately not produced to their best advantage. Later in the year, he again recorded "Vesti la giubba" and added "Che gelida manina" from Puccini's *La Bohème* at Melotone Studios. His overall musicality remained tentative, and the recordings, while interesting with regard to Lanza's artistic development, were not commercially viable. Still, few expected that much from a twenty-four-year-old tenor, and he impressed all who heard him. Art Rush's enthusiasm never faltered and, in those early days, he did much to help Mario.

When it appeared that the Lanzas had pushed their landlord to the limit, the tenor decided that a perfect solution would be a move to a larger and more expensive apartment. Then "Lanza's luck" struck again: Robert Weede, at the height of his career at the Met, offered the young couple his place for the summer. The fashionable apartment at 8 West Forty-ninth Street overlooked the skating rink at Rockefeller

Center. Weede genuinely liked Mario, as did most who met him when he was young, fresh, and electric with promise. He occasionally invited Mario and Betty out to his farm in Nyack, New York, where impromptu singing, fresh air, horseback riding, and even lessons in how to milk a cow provided a contrast to life in the city. When the summer ended, Mario and Betty settled into a modest, fourth-floor walk-up, and on 10 October 1945, they exchanged marriage vows for a second time, at the Church of Saint Colombo, with their loved ones in attendance.

That fall, talk was circulating in legitimate circles about a phenomenal talent in need of poise and training. Weede—one of many Metropolitan Opera stars who sang with both Lanza and the greats who regularly performed at the Met—had already concluded that he was second to none.[2] He aggressively championed Mario as a part-time replacement for Jan Peerce on *The Celanese Hour: Great Moments in Music*.

Mario was flattered to be considered as a replacement for Jan Peerce, the erstwhile Pinky Pearl of Catskills' fame. Peerce was an accomplished violinist and musician whose vocalizations were known for their technical precision but as a rule unexciting; the reputation he had earned in his twenty-five years with the Met (1941–1966) dimmed as a consequence of his singing long after his prime.

The Celanese Hour was a moderately successful show that offered classical and popular music and featured spirited and often technically mediocre performances by an assortment of great, good, and marginal singers. It was Mario's first truly professional engagement and a remarkable honor, in view of Peerce's status and Lanza's embryonic reputation. Lanza was scheduled to make ten appearances at the handsome fee of $300 to $400 per week. The money was good for the time, but the young spendthrift continued to prefer lavish dinners, tailored suits, and easy spending.

Lanza appeared on seven shows (24 October, 7 and 14 November, 16 and 20 December 1945 and 2 January and 20 February 1946), singing a broad repertoire that included operatic standards (among them, "Recondita armonia" and "E lucevan le stelle"), operetta (selections from *The Student Prince*, for example), and popular song ("A Pretty Girl Is Like a Melody," "Blue Skies," and others). He was sometimes joined by a rising soprano, such as Frances Yeend, Natalie Bodanya, or Winnifred Smith; more often, he was hampered by soprano Jean Tennyson, who was marginal on her best days. Her greatest vocal asset was her husband, Camille Dreyfus, the founder and chief executive officer of the Celanese Corporation.

Mario's performances were uneven. Some tones were incredibly lovely and his upper register was facile, often thrilling, but his overall production was unsettled. The voice had darkened during his army years, and the uncoached, mostly freewheeling singing he had indulged in left him with little knowledge of how to integrate the breadth of his range. Occasionally he isolated his registers; once he forgot the words to "America the Beautiful." A performance of the Love Duet from Verdi's *Otello*, dismally encumbered by an insipid Tennyson, was at times beautifully interpreted with a soaring range, but overall, he sang it too lyrically and without confidence. By contrast, he was daringly experimental on a haunting rendition of the difficult "Ah, Moon of My Delight," taking his voice from a ringing baritone to a slender thread of falsetto.

The shows were broadcast live, and Mario paced, shivered, and became physically ill before each performance. Every one was a torture. He worried, more than he should have, about being pushed into a situation for which he was not prepared. He very much regretted making his mistakes before the public. It was not a pleasant experience for him; he had been required to sing arias for which he needed years of training. He was particularly critical of his performance of the challenging duet from *Otello* and happy to retreat from public performances to the status of a novice.

The year 1945 had brought decent earnings from *The Celanese Hour* and an appearance on the *Schaeffer Review*, but the struggling young tenor felt that he was betraying his talent. With the new year, his doubts and outlook worsened. Betty, who desperately tried to develop an interest in opera and offer constructive criticism, assured him that something good would happen in 1946.

It did. With his final appearance on *The Celanese Hour* over, it was time for the reason he came to New York: quality coaching and training. His next public engagement would occur seven months later.

CHAPTER 6

Redirection: Weiler and Rosati

Lanza's is the greatest voice of the twentieth century.

Arturo Toscanini[1]

Lanza continued training with Weede and took lessons from Polly Robinson, whose studio was located at Room 802, Carnegie Hall. Robinson was a competent teacher who was plagued by the bane of all vocal coaches: the paying client who simply cannot sing. Samuel E. Weiler, who would become Mario's manager, was such a student.

Weiler was neither saint nor sinner nor benefactor nor greedy manipulator when he first became involved in Lanza's career. Mario had never known meaningful paternal advice. He came to regard Weiler as his "second father," and for a time, his trust in him was absolute. Sam *was* astute and worldly, and he genuinely liked the amiable and gregarious young man his only client could be. But the break that would occur five years later was venomous, and Weiler's eventual conduct was exploitive and disappointing. Both men retold their stories to conform to their respective needs; Mario's version was more accurate than Weiler's.

It started when Polly Robinson told Weiler, who had just completed another session of nasal, approximate high Gs, "Someday I'm going to let you listen to a voice greater than Caruso's." Two days later, Lanza and Weiler met at the studio. "Here," Robinson announced, "is the voice greater than Caruso." Mario sang, and Weiler took it in. He later recalled, "As God is my witness it floored me. I fell on my nose. I had never heard anything so naturally brilliant. I went home and raved all night to my wife about Mario. 'This kid,' I told her, 'has the greatest voice in the world, barring none.'"[2]

Weiler later claimed that Mario pestered him with dozens of phone calls each day, soliciting his patronage, but in truth the two men talked over dozens of cups of coffee in the Park Central Drugstore in December 1945. The young singer rambled about his goals, frustrations, and need for legitimate training. Sam listened. Later they adjourned to the walk-up to talk with Betty. She said that they had bills at the Park Central, various restaurants, and D'Andrea Brothers (where Mario had been fitted for custom clothing), and that they needed $90 per week to meet expenses. Sam told them that he would be on vacation in Florida for a few weeks, where he would ponder the situation.

Weiler, then a realtor, made inquiries about his prospective investment. Arthur Judson, the head of Columbia Artists Management, assessed Mario as untrainable to date and predicted, "He'll either be the greatest tenor in the world or a singing waiter."[3] Conductor Peter Herman Adler, widely known for his eventual success in bringing opera to television, was one of many legitimate musical figures in New York who knew and were trying to work with Lanza. Adler told Weiler that the young tenor possessed the finest instinctive musicality he had ever encountered. He further advised him that Enrico Rosati was the right man to train him.

On 1 February 1946 Lanza and Weiler entered into a contract that provided the tenor with $70 per week; in return Weiler would receive 5 percent of the tenor's gross earnings.[4] Weiler also agreed to pay the young couple's outstanding debts. Weiler later claimed that he paid Mario and Betty $90 per week, took care of debts exceeding $11,000, and spent $90,000 before his investment began to pay off. Frankly, the numbers do not add up—which is what Mario later claimed.

First, the weekly allowance ceased eighteen months later, when Mario signed with MGM; the total for that expenditure could not have exceeded $7000. And it is improbable that Mario and Betty had debts totaling $11,000: they had arrived in New York less than ten months before the contract was signed, Lanza had earned decent fees, and the couple had lived rent-free in Weede's apartment through the summer. A 1946 debt of $11,000 is the equivalent of more than $100,000 today. New York has always been an expensive town, but newlyweds would not have been able to obtain that much credit or spend that sort of money while living in modest, furnished quarters, without car expenses or children to feed.

Next, Enrico Rosati coached Lanza for fifteen months, at $130 per month; Weiler's expenditure therefore could not have exceeded $1950. Lastly, Mario earned concert fees approximating $30,000 during the eighteen months before the Hollywood bonanza hit. The truth was that Weiler's investment paid off from the beginning. Apart from a few months at the very start, the accounts were in the black.

Not surprisingly, Weiler later inflated his wealth in defense of Lanza's claims that his accounts had been looted. Sam claimed that he owned several hotels, that he was a millionaire, and that he did not need the tenor's paltry income. Others advised that he was not independently wealthy and worked as a realtor for his brother, Jack D. Weiler, longtime president of the Federation of Jewish Philanthropies of New York. He also owned a summer camp for boys and the Echo Lake Camp in Pointelle, Pennsylvania—but no hotels. Between selling real estate and the camp, he managed a comfortable, middle-class existence that included winter vacations in Miami and an apartment in a better section of uptown New York City.

Weiler put up with plenty of difficult behavior from Mario, but his claims of a substantial and risky investment were untrue. The tenor paid his own way, and Weiler reaped more than $250,000 in commissions during 1951 alone. Long after Lanza was dead, he continued to draw handsome fees from the estate. He sued the estate, unsuccessfully, for additional fees on more than one occasion and engaged in lowly behaviors such as bootlegging Lanza's recordings.[5] If Samuel E. Weiler became wealthy, his affiliation with Mario Lanza must be credited, at least in part.

Sam followed Adler's advice. He canceled Lanza's concert and radio work for the next few months and took his client to Rosati, the much-respected coach to Gigli, Lauri-Volpi, George London, and other noteworthy singers. Rosati was not out of the mainstream in believing that a singer required drilling and absolute subordination to craft, though he was one of the few able to browbeat even difficult pupils. The first meeting between Mario Lanza and Enrico Rosati was memorable.

Mario had trimmed down since being discharged from the armed forces, with a punishing regime of health foods and meager portions. He abstained from alcohol totally and became a regular at New York's Vim and Vigor restaurant, where he reported for his daily dose of carrot juice. He was impressively built, slim-waisted, with a bulwark of shoulder and chest, an engaging smile, lively black eyes, and a complexion that many remember as beautiful.

The Maestro, seventy-two years old, white-haired and old-world in his musty studio with books and photos strewn about, glared and ranted at Lanza about his attempts to sing before he was ready, berating him for tampering with his gift and risking its destruction. He played the part of a drill sergeant, in a studied attempt to gain the advantage he needed. Rosati demanded that Mario sing. Mario complied. The old man weakened. He bowed his head, his hand still resting on the keys of the piano. Finally he looked up. "For thirty-four years, since Gigli, I have waited for this voice."[6] Regaining his composure, Rosati engaged in the first of many futile attempts to instill discipline in his charge. He told Mario to report at eight the next morning, adding that he should not be as much as sixty seconds early or late. Mario nodded in agreement, probably even believing, for the moment, that he would comply.

The fifteen months that followed were difficult for pupil and teacher. Mario often arrived late and was usually unprepared. He offered excuses that would have embarrassed a seventh grader, claiming that he forgot his notes on the bus or that Betty had left to shop and locked the apartment, making it impossible for him to retrieve his books. Rosati raged at such a lack of discipline and artistic temperament. "*Porco miserio!*" ("Miserable pig!") he would shout, but he could not bring himself to dislike his gifted charge.

Lanza labored at sight reading and endured the exercises he found so pointless and boring. But Rosati never conceded that his pupil was incapable of discipline; instead, he concluded that Mario was afraid. He was partly correct. Lanza's cockiness was a cover for his persistent state of fear before a performance. The prospects of discipline grew dimmer and the fear increased exponentially for the rest of the singer's life.

It ran against Rosati's training and rigid beliefs to tout a talent that was largely natural with poor application to methodology and discipline, but the Maestro yielded to the immensity of the young tenor's gift. Nearly anyone can learn to read music, but few have the natural instinct Mario displayed. "To carve a work of art," Rosati later said, "you must have the tools and the proper piece of wood. In Mario, I had the proper piece of wood."

For weeks Rosati drilled and trained his resistant pupil to prepare for a certain audition: Lanza was to perform Verdi's Requiem for the legendary Arturo Toscanini. On the day of the audition, Mario phoned to say he was ill. Rosati pleaded. "You are not sick, boy. You are afraid. You must get over this. You must sing."

Toscanini shared his podium with no mere musician. He demanded that orchestra members play the piece as it was written and as he interpreted it, not as they felt it. His tirades and autocratic manner set standards yet unsurpassed, much less remotely equaled. When he recorded with a tenor, it had to be a singer who understood that he was but part of a larger ensemble. Jan Peerce was ideal in that regard. Lanza? As he saw it, he was the primary focus; conductor and orchestra were mere background. Lanza and Toscanini could never have worked together. Mario never sang for him. Both men were under contract with RCA's Red Seal division and pursued their separate paths.

The inability to effectively sight read is a great handicap for an operatic singer. Repertoire development is limited; a recording session involving new material is a tedious enterprise; the mastery of an entire operatic role is a project. Rosati continued to drill his reluctant student and brought him to the point where he knew the rudiments of sight reading, but Mario never advanced beyond being able to identify notes. He simply could not integrate what he saw and understand how it related to the score. Even with Rosati's training, he was like a builder who cannot read blueprints.

Nevertheless, Rosati introduced his pupil to Edward Johnson, the fine Canadian tenor who directed the New York Metropolitan Opera from 1935 to 1950. The Met made inquiries, but Mario, still shaken by his experience on *The Celanese Hour*, offered that his reverence for the Metropolitan was too great for him to make his mistakes there. He was a frequent attendee at the Met and watched with an intensity that made it an extension of his training rather than recreation.

Sam Weiler's role was limited to the management of his client's revenue and expenses. He never recruited business or solicited a contract, though he took good care of himself whenever those opportunities were presented by others. It was Mario's Tanglewood connections with Michael de Pace and Columbia Artists Management, Inc., that began to produce engagements.

Weiler's desire for increased revenue coincided with Columbia Artists' formation of the Bel Canto Trio, a mostly operatic ensemble that toured the United States, Canada, and Mexico for two seasons.

Frances Yeend was the headliner, and Columbia was pleased to have Mario aboard. The search for the third member, a bass-baritone, ended when Lanza insisted that his old friend and fellow-trainee with Rosati, George London, complete the trio. It was a loyalty that would survive Mario's tumultuous history of personal relationships.

Yeend was a promising soprano in the 1940s. In addition to more than 250 appearances as a soloist with major orchestras, her career eventually included a long stint with the New York City Opera and engagements with the New York Metropolitan Opera, the Vienna State Opera, the Munich Opera, and Covent Garden. London was a fine bass-baritone whose work ethic and personality took him to great heights and a long association with the Met. When Lanza's dreams of a career in opera were all but foreclosed, he listened to London's recordings for hours, praising his old friend and wondering where he had missed the turn. The trio began its association in September 1946, with Yeend earning $500, Mario roughly $330, and London $275 for each of the eighty-six appearances they made.

Columbia Artists booked Lanza for a solo concert in Ottawa, Canada, on 13 November 1946. W. Kilpatrick, the field manager for Coronet Concerts, was greatly impressed by the virtually unknown tenor. He entreated Columbia Artists to provide more Canadian bookings for the young singer, calling the concert the high point of his career as a promoter. Allard de Ridder, the conductor, lauded Lanza as the finest soloist he had worked with and also praised the young American as easy to work with, which had more to do with his instinctive ear than success after exhaustive rehearsals. The Canadian people seemed aware that, while they had not seen a world-renowned tenor, they had heard a twenty-five-year-old tenor who was on his way.

The young tenor also appeared in Port Chester, New York; Milton, Pennsylvania; and other small venues. Rosati had unwittingly provided him with confidence, and he seemed to have conquered his fears. Although the Maestro did not feel that his work was finished, the association between teacher and student ended in May 1947. Rosati recalled a meeting attended by Weiler, Judson, and others interested in expediting Lanza's career: "I looked at them sitting there and told them I wanted to wring their necks. 'You have the goose that can lay golden eggs and you want to kill him.'" Mario too later claimed that he had been rushed, that he was not ready. But the potential for concert earnings was substantial, and Weiler saw only Mario Lanza's ability to generate cash. He overrode the Maestro's better judgment.

In any case, Lanza emerged, as a consequence of both Rosati's training and his own maturation, with startling breath control, excellent phrasing, and decent knowledge of how to integrate the broad registers of his voice. He went on to thrill and disappoint Rosati, but the Maestro never lost sight of what might have been. At the end of his life, an inscribed photo from Mario occupied a prominent place in his living room, amidst signed pictures from the greats of opera:

To Maestro Enrico Rosati—any success I am having or will have in the future I owe 100% to you, the greatest undisputed voice teacher in the world, past, present and future. I love you and you will always be close to me wherever I am or in whatever I do. Especially on the stage, however, you will always be there with the third register. All of my love for you, Maestro. Mario Lanza

CHAPTER 7

Costa

[Lanza] was about the most prodigally gifted vocal talent ever to emerge in this country.

George London, 1982[1]

On 14 April 1947, in the small town of Shippensburg, Pennsylvania, Mario met Constantine Callinicos, New York–born and Juilliard-trained but ultimately a minor figure in the world of classical music. His most enduring achievement was that he understood Mario Lanza and had the monumental patience necessary to work with him. His association with the tenor proved to be the height of his own career, and he would become a significant part of Lanza's artistic legacy.

Like all those who called themselves "friends" to Mario, Callinicos was never without financial compensation for the time he and Lanza spent together and, at times, gouged him. Still, it was somewhat different with the small, tender-voiced man Mario called "Costa." Until the end, Constantine remained faithful to the tenor's artistic promise. Perhaps more importantly, Callinicos knew better than to coldly criticize or abruptly correct him. Most of Lanza's best work was done with Constantine, and it was not because of what he did with his baton or the orchestra. Mario and Costa fought and frequently refused to speak with one another, but the tenor invested great trust in him.

Their initial contact was odd. Callinicos was freelancing when he received a call from Columbia Artists about an engagement in Shippensburg with a tenor named Mario Lanza. He had not heard of the place or the performer. When the financial arrangements were made known, a minor percentage of the singer's low fee of $250, he almost refused the offer. But it was the only game—in town or out—for Callinicos on that date, and he relented. He called the unknown tenor to ask when they would be able to rehearse together.

"We don't need to rehearse. I've got other things to do," the singer responded. Callinicos considered this "an astonishing approach" in view of the tenor's limited reputation and repertoire. The men met in the small town only two hours before the concert was scheduled to begin. Costa's reaction was favorable:

> His brown eyes sparkl[ed] as he shook my hand. He was just twenty-six with a fresh, simple, ingenuous vigor that I had rarely seen among professional artists. He had the build and barrel chest of a heavyweight fighter and was in excellent shape. In the first few seconds, I had to judge him uncomplicated and unspoiled, a press agent's delight.[2]

So much for Constantine's judgment. He remembered Betty as vivacious and as pure as her Midwest upbringing. He saw no sign of the troubles that would soon plague the young couple.

Mario nonchalantly informed Callinicos that he had forgotten his tuxedo and suggested that they appear in business suits. A tuxedo, preferably tails, was *de rigueur* for concert work during the 1940s; business suits were for men who crooned in smoky lounges. Constantine was an adherent to tradition. He had accompanied such singers as Metropolitan Opera soprano Lily Pons and the magnificent Heldentenor Lauritz Melchior (who, like Lanza, could not sight read). His tuxedo may have been threadbare and in need of pressing, but a concert accompanist did not appear in a suit. Taken aback, but without options, Callinicos went along with the request. He soon learned that Mario abhorred formal clothes; the "lost" trunk or "forgotten" tuxedo was still standard more than a decade later.

Callinicos had never heard Lanza sing before his first phrase from "Pietà, Signore" in Shippensburg that evening. It bears mention that Costa's recollections of Mario were often romanticized and, at times, slightly inaccurate, but his version of what occurred that evening was supported by local reviews and the memories of those who attended the concert. Callinicos recalled it this way:

> As I started the introduction . . . Mario turned his back to the audience, leaning casually over the piano; he winked, then smiled at me. Then he began singing, and I knew that the tux was unimportant and that the offensive back-to-the-audience was just a

neophyte's lack of stage deportment, for as the rich, glorious tones flowed effortlessly from Mario's throat, I knew I was listening to one of the greatest tenor voices since Caruso. Through Mario's vocal cords, and through those bony cavities in his throat, nose, and mouth which are called the resonators, emerged phrases of such opulence, warmth, and velvety quality I sat there feeling some incredible joke had been played on me. The notes were round and lush, satisfying and meaningful, and his breath control, on the long phrases, was truly amazing.

Lanza next appeared at the Waldorf-Astoria in New York and in White River Junction, Vermont, with remarkable poise and style given his relative inexperience. But the meeting in Shippensburg was the beginning of a bond that endured beyond the last day of Mario's life. Callinicos would reappear several times in Lanza's career, usually when the tenor knew he was in trouble and that Costa's patience was required. Great work and nearly unbearable suffering lay ahead for Mario and his new friend. But who knew anything of that on an evening when a bright-eyed young man hypnotized an audience in Shippensburg and assuredly told his accompanist, "You haven't heard anything yet"?

CHAPTER 8

Concert Road to Hollywood

Maybe I had it too easy at the beginning. Maybe success came too
fast. I did not have the usual rags-to-riches struggle.

Mario Lanza, 1957[1]

Mario's goal remained a career in legitimate opera and a debut at the
Met. Hollywood was on the other coast and, in spite of absurd claims
that his dream, from childhood, had been to portray Enrico Caruso in
a biographical film, the young tenor's eyes were riveted on New York.

Appearances by the Bel Canto Trio were sporadic until the summer
of 1947. Their reputation began to crest on 8 July 1947, when an audience of six thousand roared its appreciation of Yeend, Lanza, and London at an open-air concert in Milwaukee. Critic Richard S. Davis (*Milwaukee Journal*, 9 July 1947) wrote:

> The favorite with the audience was the tenor, Lanza, a singer
> unmistakenly destined to enjoy a handsome career. . . . This
> youngster not only has a firm and ringing voice of adequate power,
> but he has set standards for himself and is eager to meet them.
> Clearly, he is on the way up.

One musician remembered that the young tenor was reluctant to
rehearse and surly when finally prodded to prepare for the concert, but
when he began to sing, "his sins were forgiven."[2]

The Bel Canto Trio performed on Indian reservations and in high
school gymnasiums. Their circuit read like a carnival advance man's
itinerary: Ames, Iowa; Minot, North Dakota; Chihuahua, Mexico; La
Porte, Indiana; Albion, Michigan; Middletown, New York; Sylacauga,
Alabama; Wallingford, Connecticut; St. Paul, Minnesota; Chicago; San
Antonio; Madison, Wisconsin; Wheeling, West Virginia; Halifax and
Sydney, Nova Scotia; and St. John's, Newfoundland.

Fast on the heels of the success in Milwaukee, the trio performed at two outdoor concerts in Chicago's Grant Park. The first was held on Saturday, 19 July; good advance reviews and fine weather had attracted a crowd of fifty thousand people. Lanza sang his signature "Celeste Aida" with the verve he could deliver in his early career. The audience loved it; so did distinguished critic Claudia Cassidy (*The Chicago Tribune*, 20 July 1947): "Mr. Lanza sings for the indisputable reason that he was born to sing. He has a superbly natural tenor, which he uses by instinct, and though a multitude of fine points evade him, he possesses the things almost impossible to learn." The next evening, because of Cassidy's fine review and despite a light rain, seventy-five thousand turned out.

The tour continued, with Mario drawing considerable attention. In Ames, Iowa, pedagogue Tolbert McCrae, the head of the music department at a local college, offered that Lanza had provided him with as much excitement as he had yet experienced, and he had been listening to singers for many years.[3] In Wheeling, West Virginia, he received ovations after each of his solos and impressed critic Marjorie Toatgio of the *Wheeling Intelligencer*.

Meanwhile, in that city on the other coast, the directors of the Hollywood Bowl were scrambling to find a tenor to replace Ferruccio Tagliavini, the Italian-born *tenore di grazia* who had made his debut with the Met that season. It was time for more of "Lanza's luck."

The concert was part of the summer subscription at the Bowl and Tagliavini, whose singing was light, elegant, and refined, had been scheduled to perform with Eugene Ormandy and the Hollywood Bowl Orchestra. Art Rush, who had signed Mario with RCA, was once again the right man in the right place at the right time. He approached the most powerful non-executive in Hollywood, Louis B. Mayer's secretary, Ida Koverman, with acetates of Lanza's test recordings for RCA. Acetates offer poor voice reproduction, but Koverman, a patroness of the arts who knew her way around, had heard enough. She played the recordings for Mayer, who was still the most powerful executive in Hollywood. He was impressed. Then Koverman showed him a photo of the handsome young tenor. Mayer was astonished by the unlikely combination of such a voice and decent looks.

Koverman assured Mayer that the real voice would be even better than the acetates. Then, using the strong-arm tactics she exerted with

legendary graciousness, she coerced the directors at the Bowl to book
Lanza as Tagliavini's replacement. Art Rush provided a sheaf of rave
reviews but management at the Bowl remained skeptical about the
drawing power of a relatively unknown and somewhat chubby tenor
from Philadelphia. Rush provided more assistance by organizing media
releases, and some of Lanza's crusaders from his military days—
notably, Walter Pidgeon—did what they could in the short time before
the concert. Contrary to allegations that the event was a sell-out, the
crowd, at just under four thousand, was smaller than the subscription
average for the 1947 season.[4] What the audience lacked in numbers, it
made up for with enthusiasm.

Mario's good fortune necessitated a break from the trio's tour.
Frances Yeend, just out of the hospital, happily agreed to appear with
him. After all, this would be the biggest venue of their association and
she was as ambitious as her lesser-paid cohort. George London came
along to lend moral support, though he was also hopeful of being
included in the program.

Lanza was unusually apprehensive, even by his standards, as the
concert approached. The orchestra opened with Bach's *Passacaglia
und Fuge*, playing for nearly fourteen minutes while Mario stared and
paced. He knew that this was an enormous opportunity and that the
combination of Art Rush's tenacity and Tagliavini's unavailability had
produced a near miracle. He privately vowed that no one would outshine him that evening and seemed annoyed that Yeend had flown out
for the event, worrying that she might upstage him.

Shortly after the orchestra finished, Lanza was introduced to an
audience that included London, Mayer, Koverman, Betty Lanza, and
dozens of celebrities, among them Edmond O'Brien and the young
tenor's future leading lady, Kathryn Grayson. Many in the audience
came out of curiosity. Others were disappointed with not being able to
hear Tagliavini. The Hollywood Bowl has featured the finest artists
from around the world, and 28 August 1947 was hardly the greatest
night in its history. Few who attended that evening left unaware that
they had witnessed a historic debut, however.

Lanza's first selection was "Una furtiva lagrima" from Donizetti's
L'Elisir d'Amore. He had not warmed up, but it was a good beginning,
sung with appropriate restraint and glorious tone. Polite applause followed. His next selection, "Un dì all'azzurro spazio" from *Andrea*

Chénier, was thrilling from start to finish, with Lanza's dramatic colorations and wide range passionately employed. By the time Lanza finished his third offering, "E lucevan le stelle," the audience was his. Two
selections by the orchestra and solos by Yeend followed. Then Lanza
returned for two Puccini duets, "Bimba dagl'occhi" (*Madama Butterfly*) and "O soave fanciulla" (*La Bohème*). As the duets progressed,
Lanza's confidence soared, and he employed every dramatic intona-
tion and passionate coloration from his considerable arsenal. Yeend,
though her singing was adequate, was miles behind him.

When it was over, the audience applauded well into the night. Few
were more enthusiastic than the despot from Metro-Goldwyn-Mayer.
George London insisted that Lanza's singing, that evening, was better
than any of his previous or subsequent performances. The tenor himself was characteristically jubilant: "What a night! I fractured 'em. Louis
B. Mayer was there and had tears in his eyes!"[5] Mario later recalled this
as the greatest event in his life, after Tanglewood. It was a brilliant presentation—and for a time, he would sing as well, or better.

The performance at the Hollywood Bowl—a startling display of
natural talent, great instinct, and a uniquely passionate approach—
would have brought the audience to its feet at any palace of lyric drama.
The critic for the *Los Angeles Daily News* declared that Lanza's was
the voice that many had awaited for too many years. The review in the
Los Angeles Times (29 August 1947) was even more effusive: "[Lanza]
electrified a large audience that cheered for several minutes. . . . He has
a truly rare asset in a naturally beautiful voice, which he uses with intelligence and a native artistry which, rightly developed, should prove to
be one of the exceptional voices of the generation."

The tenor had poured all his emotions into his performance that
evening. When producers arrived backstage with offers, he was not surprised; it was simply bound to happen. Louis B. Mayer—whose record
speaks for his ability to spot talent—made the unsophisticated young
Philadelphian feel as though he was the most important person in the
world.

A studio audition on the MGM lot in Culver City was scheduled for
30 August. Mayer ordered all his producers, executives, and directors
to the cavernous recording stage known as Studio One. The purpose of
the meeting was not disclosed. L. B. waited as the executives gathered.
Then, in a scene typical for a man who alternated between unbridled

meanness, fawning sentimentality, and Victorian prudishness, he announced with dramatic understatement that he wanted them to hear a voice.

The tenor stood behind a curtain and launched into "Che gelida manina" and "Thine Alone" from Victor Herbert's *Eileen*. Producer Joe Pasternak remembered it this way: "A magnificent singer thundered at us from a battery of speakers. I say *thundered*, the word may not be entirely right. The voice was rich, warm, sensuous, virile, capable of incredible highs and able to go down in register as deep as a baritone. My spine tingled."[6]

Mayer, uncharacteristically succinct, said, "Gentlemen, you've heard the voice. Now I want you to meet the singer." Mario emerged from behind the curtain. According to Pasternak, he was "dark and bushy-haired . . . well-boned, heavy-chested . . . not striking looking, perhaps." Nonetheless, the veteran producer saw something he liked.[7]

Mayer turned to his highly paid minions and announced that the studio was going to sign the young man. Pasternak, who had long dreamed of an "operatic picture" reflected. Was Lanza too stocky? Would an operatic voice translate to box-office success? What about his hair? On the positive side, Lanza was manly and capable in appearance. "All my life I'd wanted to find a face with a voice. Could this be it?" Pasternak mused. "A venture into the cinematic unknown such as I envisioned required a lucky meeting in time, space, and spirit. With Lanza, I felt a beginning was possible. He was the foundation stone." Joe Pasternak approached Mayer: "I like him very much." "He's all yours," L. B. replied.[8]

Other offers were coming fast, and Mario was totally confused. Stunned by the rushing developments, he phoned Sam Weiler and asked for advice. Weiler told him to be polite and hear everyone out. He firmly instructed his client not to affix his signature to anything. Then he flew to Hollywood and negotiated with MGM. He abandoned his business affiliations in New York and moved to California to manage his only client's interests, further refuting his later claims of independent wealth and disinterest in Lanza's money.

The contract with MGM (backdated to the date of the singer's audition, 30 August 1947, with work to commence on 1 June 1948) contained several oppressive provisions. One in particular would prove catastrophic: Lanza was free to pursue operatic and concert engagements for six months of each year, but Paragraph Four denied the singer the right to appear in opera and concert venues, record, or perform on radio if MGM suspended him or declared the contract in default.

Nor was the agreement as lucrative as universally represented. The tenor received a $10,000 signing bonus and guarantees of $15,000 for his first film; $25,000 for his second; $30,000 for his third; $40,000 for his fourth; $50,000 for his fifth; $60,000 for his sixth; and $75,000 for his seventh film. The guarantees for the tenor's first three films were dime-store, and if he became a big star, the guarantees for the remaining films would be obscenely inadequate. If Lanza proved to be a bust, MGM was free to terminate the association at will with one week's notice and was guaranteed one month's unpaid work (stills, conferences, interviews, photo sessions, and so forth) for each film.

"You're going to be our singing Clark Gable," Louis B. Mayer had assured him.[9]

"Right away?" Mario asked Pasternak.[10]

The aspiring tenor was enticed. The front gates of MGM were wide open, and as Lanza entered, the doors to the Metropolitan—and every other legitimate opera house—slammed shut behind him.

CHAPTER 9

Early Warnings

Am I the second Caruso? No. I'm the first Lanza.

Mario Lanza[1]

Joe Pasternak wanted to become better acquainted with the talent he would try to develop, so both Mario and Betty spent several days in Hollywood, impressing everyone they met as vibrant, youthful, gracious, and unaffected. To help them feel welcome, Pasternak took them to lunch in the MGM commissary, but the young couple felt ill at ease in the presence of people they had previously seen only on movie screens. Mario's jubilant sincerity touched the veteran producer. MGM still had to develop a concept for his introductory film, work on which was scheduled to begin the following June. Discussions focused on whether to develop the tenor as a new talent—a serious operatic artist —or as a formula replacement for Nelson Eddy, who had parted company with the studio in 1942.

Lanza rejoined Yeend and London in September 1947, and the Bel Canto tour continued in small cities before surprisingly large audiences. Lanza invariably provided the biggest thrills, and Yeend learned, slowly but surely, that her bigger fees were earned, in part, through her ancillary duties as den mother, babysitter, and nursemaid to Lanza and London. The tenor refused to fly, claiming that his service injuries made it impossible, so Frances nearly always arrived at each town first, assuming the burdens of locating the concert halls, making contact with the local association, and settling into a hotel. George and Mario followed, by bus, car, or train. Sometimes they barely made it in time for their introduction. Betty, whom Yeend termed difficult, occasionally accompanied the group. Her presence did not affect Mario's behavior.[2]

"It's-only-money Lanza" continued to live for the moment. He lodged, usually with London, in the most expensive suites, proved to be a bonanza to room service, and tipped as if he were supporting overseas military campaigns. Frances stayed in less sumptuous rooms. Her future was less certain, nor did she share the seeming advantage of an MGM contract and signing bonus.

The young Philadelphian was again drinking heavily. The late 1940s were part of an extended era where the smell of alcohol on a man's breath during the early morning was acceptable, four to five drinks with lunch a jolly sign, navigating the highways after a long evening a manly enterprise, and abusive drinking—practiced by Humphrey Bogart, Erroll Flynn, and Ernest Hemingway—considered the sure mark of a two-fisted adventurer. Yeend tried to control them, but the team of Lanza and London was too much for her. George London eventually curbed his habit, and fortunately Lanza's drinking did not affect the quality of his performances with the Bel Canto Trio. Yeend expressed it with lively earthiness: "I loved singing with Mario. He had a great thrill at the top and he never spared the horses. He just let it loose!"[3]

The tenor also resumed his adolescent practice of shoplifting gourmet items, candy, and liquor, behavior he regarded as boyishly rebellious. He offered absurd rationalizations about his desires versus the wealth of people who owned small stores, always explaining that, if caught, he was prepared to pay—which made everything fine. He also vandalized recordings by performers he did not like by snapping the edges off the breakable 78s of the time. Why the owners or record shops had to pay for his dislikes is something he never explained. More distressing, Yeend discovered, were the increasingly infantile behaviors that Mario called pranks. For instance, while the soprano earnestly sang beloved opera arias before attentive audiences, the tenor thought it riotously funny to urinate in a bucket offstage, within her sightlines but unseen by the audience.

Although allowing that Mario "had a wonderful voice, and in the early days . . . was an exciting performer," Frances Yeend later described his musicianship as deficient: "He was never secure about some of the entrances in the trios." She was even more adamant in her view that Lanza had been impossible on the road:

> [His career] was marred by behavior of a singularly undisciplined
> and malicious sort. . . . His personal life . . . was characterized by a
> lack of regard for others, both socially and professionally, that was

> shocking. . . . He was blessed with an extraordinary talent that he
> should have made much, much more of than he did. He provided
> a great treat for the ear, but there was nothing for the mind.[4]

By contrast, London recalled the months with the Bel Canto Trio as Mario's most disciplined period as an artist. He remembered his friend as a devout student of anything related to singing, passionately discussing the relative merits of the masters at all hours and willing to travel great distances to hear a rare recording. The difference can be attributed to perspective, as Yeend worked with the tenor only in legitimate situations—*The Celanese Hour* and on tour with the Bel Canto Trio—while London had known him during his worst days in the armed forces. Also, London maintained sporadic contact with Mario following the Bel Canto experience while Yeend did not see him after 1948.

On 10 October 1947, the tenor appeared in Quebec City with soprano Agnes Davis. He earned a fine review from critic Gilles Mercier (*Le Carabin*, 15 October 1947) who noted that the tenor, though youthful, had a fine and passionate voice without apparent limitation. Mercier also lauded the young tenor's interpretive abilities, range, and presentation. The enthusiastic audience called him back for several encores.

On 14 February 1948, the tenor turned straight man for Edgar Bergen and Charlie McCarthy on their radio program, which was broadcast from the Fair Park Auditorium in Dallas, Texas. He kidded with McCarthy and begged for a chance to sing, which prompted a challenge about singers and their being too prideful to work; Lanza persisted and was finally given a chance to sing "Vesti la giubba." He returned to Canada for an appearance as a guest soloist in Toronto's Massey Hall, on 5 March, the first hour of which was broadcast live over the radio. Recordings of three arias—"La donna è mobile," the Lamento di Federico, and "Vesti la giubba"—have survived. The "La donna è mobile" was somewhat lyrical and imprecise but thrilling; its held high B emphasizes Lanza's extraordinary breath control. The Lamento di Federico from *L'Arlesiana*, which would become a staple of his concert repertoire, was well interpreted and lyrical in parts. "Vesti la giubba," an aria he took to the front too many times, was well sung. It was an impressive performance.

Later that month the tenor returned to Hollywood for prerecordings and tests. Kathryn Grayson, his prospective leading lady, announced that she was pregnant, moving the starting date for the film to 3 November. He rejoined the tour, vocally petulant about his status as the second-highest-paid member of the trio.

During late March and into April, the tenor received intensive coaching to prepare for an operatic engagement as Pinkerton in *Madama Butterfly*. Sam Weiler engaged Armando Agnini, the artistic director for the New Orleans Opera Association, whose studio was in New York. The sessions began and nearly ended on a familiar note when Agnini's Viennese pianist began to correct the tenor. Lanza refused to work under such conditions, resulting in a hurried replacement. Leila Edwards, who worked with many great singers—including Robert Merrill—listened and finally told Mario: "You learned from the Gigli recording."

"How did you know?" the tenor asked, surprised by her candor and correctness.

"Because you're making the same mistakes Gigli made!" she laughed. She then instructed him, "Hold the score. Let's start from the beginning, and just try to feel the distance between the pitches."

Now it was the tenor's turn to laugh. "I can't learn music that way. Sing me the phrase and I'll sing it back to you."[5] It was an uncommon admission from a singer whose outbursts were usually a cover for his fear of being criticized and advised, for what seemed like the thousandth time, to learn the basics of his craft.

The coaching continued and, in early April, Sam and Selma Weiler joined the Lanzas in New Orleans for what would be the young tenor's first and last performances in live opera. Mario performed as Pinkerton on 8 and 10 April 1948, in a production sponsored by the New Orleans Opera Association and directed by Agnini. Tomiko Kanazawa, the Cio-Cio-San, made a career of singing the role, for which her delicate Oriental beauty was ideal.

The soprano usually garners the acclaim in *Madama Butterfly*, and Kanazawa was expected to outshine the newcomer in New Orleans. She performed well, but Lanza wowed the audience and reviewers. Critic Laurence Oden (*Times-Picayune*, 9 April 1948) joined the comparatively slim but growing ranks of those absolutely sold on Sam Weiler's goldmine:

Mario Lanza performed his duties as Lieut. Pinkerton with considerable verve and dash. Rarely have we seen a more superbly romantic leading tenor. His exceptionally beautiful voice helps immeasurably. The combination of his good looks and vocal ability should prove helpful in any of his more earnest undertakings.

Jess Walters, a fine bass-baritone who enjoyed a long and distinguished career, appeared as the American consul, Sharpless. He remembered Lanza's voice as beautiful and big.[6]

Walter Herbert, the general director of the New Orleans Opera Association from 1943 to 1954, seized the opportunity and presented Sam Weiler with a contract for Lanza to appear in two performances of *La Traviata* during the 1948/49 season.[7] The contract was signed and Mario looked forward to the dual pursuit of his opera and movie careers. But MGM business prevailed the next year, and the tenor was unable to fulfill the commitment.

Lanza never returned from this detour from his operatic goals. The years ahead would bring the distractions of film, recording, and concert work. They also brought a diminution of already scant discipline, which took the tenor further and further from the operatic stage. Critics often seize on Lanza's limited experience in live opera, alleging that his voice was too small and nothing more than the product of technology. But the cause was never an inadequacy of voice, even on the last day of his life.

The weather in New Orleans was seasonal: hot and uncomfortably muggy. Mario and Betty stayed at the fashionable Monteleone and joined the Weilers for dinner at Arnaud's, a fixture in the French Quarter. Betty ordered chicken curry and fled after one bite. Mario, usually hysterical when anything—real or feigned—affected his wife, remained calm and continued to enjoy his meal. Suddenly he slammed his hand on the table, clattering the dishes. "Don't tell me! Rabbit or not, this is it!"[8] Betty was pregnant.

Mario again joined Yeend and London, his prospective fatherhood giving him a new excuse to celebrate. Albert Robinson, who worked for a branch of Columbia Artists, Inc., and who had been "impressed by his vocal powers" ever since hearing Lanza's audition for Columbia, booked the Bel Canto Trio for concerts in Halifax and Sydney, Nova Scotia, and St. John's, Newfoundland. Robinson was "most fortunate in hearing the trio's concert" in Halifax and specifically remembered the reception that followed: "I congratulated each of the artists in turn, and

Mario remarked to me 'Do you know what I did tonight?' I replied that he had sung beautifully, but he retorted, 'No, I sang *five* high Cs! Caruso never sang more than two in one evening!' It was May 1948 and the concert had been held on a Friday evening. The trio was not due in Sydney until Monday, giving them the weekend in Halifax. George London invited Robinson to lunch on Saturday and Frances Yeend joined him for dinner that evening. Robinson remembered both occasions as most enjoyable.[9]

On Sunday, Robinson ran into Mario and Betty in the hotel lobby and asked them to join him and a young lady from the local concert committee for brunch. The foursome met in the lobby at the appointed time. They were ushered to a handsomely set table, where menus already had been distributed. Mario picked his up and scarcely glanced at it before throwing it down in disgust. "There's nothing I can eat here!" Robinson asked him what he would like. Mario replied that he must have fresh fruit and vegetables. A special salad was ordered for him; the others made their selections from the menu.

During brunch, Robinson attempted to engage the tenor in conversation. "I hear you're going to Hollywood to make a movie."

"Yes, but not until September."

"I suppose there's a lot of advance preparation to be made before they can begin shooting," Robinson continued.

"No, the leading lady is pregnant."

"Well, there is just nothing to be done until her baby arrives," Robinson offered, to which Mario responded suggestively, "Ah, but you'd think there would be!"—a comment that Robinson regarded as inappropriate under the circumstances. After more conversation, Mario left without a word of thanks for the meal. Robinson remembers that Lanza appeared at the concert in Sydney but dropped out of the tour and returned to New York, leaving the Bel Canto Trio without a tenor for the three concerts scheduled in Newfoundland.[10]

Frances and George devised a new program and never sang before an audience with Mario again; he was replaced by tenors with more operatic experience. Despite her reservations about Lanza's behavior and artistic discipline, Yeend said that the Bel Canto Trio's performances were never again as thrilling.[11]

Mario and Betty visited Tanglewood that summer as guests of Columbia Artists, Inc. Many of the instructors remembered him and his great success during the 1942 festival and offered warm greetings. Boris Goldovsky, apparently unable to bear that someone he regarded as merely a very talented but technically poor musician was achieving great success, refused to see him.

The Lanzas returned to Hollywood, where Joe Pasternak was agonizing over preparations to ready Louis B. Mayer's "singing Clark Gable" for his first appearance on film:

> His first screen test proved so shocking that for a day or two there was private talk of forgetting making a picture with him. He was dressed badly—he ran to loose-fitting shirts with long-stemmed collars and his hair looked like a horsehair mattress that had burst its seams. I insisted we make another test. I begged him to lay off the carbohydrates for a couple of weeks, got the barber to chop his hair with a will, and put him into suits that emphasized his height rather than width.[12]

Color film was not readily available at MGM at the time, and Lanza's swarthy Italian looks and curly hair *were* a ghastly combination in the stark imagery of black-and-white test film. With his hair straightened and dyed a brownish red and his olive complexion minimized with pale makeup, he presented an oddly wholesome, somewhat elfin appearance, for all his 190 pounds, in a second color test film. Fortunately, the tinted hair and makeup were scrapped after his first film.

On 24 July 1948 the tenor made his second appearance at the Hollywood Bowl, sharing the billing with Kathryn Grayson. Together they sang "O soave fanciulla" from Puccini's *La Bohème* and Victor Herbert's "Thine Alone"; basso Lee Wintner joined them for Lionel Barrymore's "Hallowe'en Suite." Grayson, whose MGM career was in the doldrums, attempted to outdo Lanza with her florid, at times tremulous, coloratura soprano. Their film association renewed Grayson's stock, leading to memorable roles in *Show Boat*, *Kiss Me, Kate*, and *The Vagabond King*.

The tenor's solo performances on the Agnus Dei and "Nessun dorma" from Puccini's *Turandot* were incredible. He began the Agnus Dei with restrained trepidation, uncharacteristically focused on technique, but when he became comfortable with his timing and orchestral cues, his natural instinct took over, and his passion brought some to tears. His approach to "Nessun dorma"—Luciano Pavarotti's signature piece despite commendable versions by other tenors, notably Jussi Björling—was similar. The dramatic finish—"*Vincerò! Vincerò!*" ("I will win! I will win!")—was held and caressed with absolute confidence. It brought down the house.

Mario and Betty took the old standby tour of homes to the Hollywood stars. Drop-jawed, they wondered if they would ever live in such luxury. In the meantime, they rented a small bungalow in the San Fernando Valley. Betty struck up a friendship with Sylvia Teitelbaum, whose husband Al owned a fur salon on Rodeo Drive in Beverly Hills. Invitations to parties followed. One night at the Mocambo, Al Teitelbaum sat Betty next to Ann Sheridan. Mario was between Sheridan and Joan Crawford. The young couple were awestruck and hardly said a word.[13]

Preparation for the film included weight reduction, which is how Mario met a true friend, Terry Robinson, a streetwise Golden Gloves champion, former Mr. New York, chiropractor, and conditioning devotee who left Brooklyn and came to Hollywood to seek his fortune. Louis B. Mayer, who suffered from back pain, was among Robinson's clients. Robinson and Lanza spent a great deal of time together, not all of it glamorous. Robinson acted as Lanza's personal manager when little business was transacted and remained loyal when everyone else deserted the tenor. Betty often treated him badly despite his devotion to her husband.

In late November 1948, Robinson assisted the young couple in locating a suitable duplex at 236 1/2 Spalding Drive, off Wilshire Boulevard in Beverly Hills, a tasteful neighborhood of tree-lined streets and easily accessible to the studios. Sam and Selma Weiler were nearby. Terry—by now factotum and chauffeur as well as trainer and friend—constructed a gym on the roof for the tenor's workouts. Mario and Betty were ecstatic over their rapid ascendancy from the New York walk-up.

Now it was time to make a movie. Mario was eager—and destined to set new standards for initial box-office impact and truculence on the set.

CHAPTER 10

That Midnight Kiss

I'm greater than Caruso!

Mario Lanza, 1948[1]

No one could deny that MGM's newest property worked hard and followed orders during his first few months in Hollywood. He was dependable, cooperative, and genuinely eager to learn. He trained with Terry Robinson, lost weight, and added tone to his physique.

Ida Mae Cummings, Louis B. Mayer's sister, had the run of MGM's roster of stars for the many charitable functions with which she was involved. She tapped Mario to sing at Pickfair, the legendary estate of Mary Pickford and Douglas Fairbanks, as part of a program benefiting the Jewish Home for the Aged. It was a hot day and more than two thousand women chatted as the unknown tenor climbed the hill toward the bandstand. He was gracious, polite, and honored to perform before the group. "Mario Lanza" was announced—with no discernible effect on the din of conversation. The name simply wasn't enough to overcome bragging about children or comments about the weather or the latest fashions. Then he began to sing. The throng fell quiet. Everyone's attention was fixed on the tenor. He sang song after song that afternoon, to thunderous applause and pleas for encores. The requests continued through dusk.

Lanza made the rounds at Hollywood parties, and invariably he was asked to sing. For a while, he complied, but soon he resented that the voice, not the man, had attracted the invitation. He drew the line when Louis B. Mayer invited him to a black-tie affair at his estate. Mario donned a tuxedo and reported to Mayer's mansion—where he was escorted to a second-floor balcony from which he was expected to sing for L. B.'s guests, dining below. Lanza stormed out, deeply resenting the shabby treatment.

His reaction was typical. Lanza saw things only in black and white; he could distinguish no gray areas and eventually refused all requests to sing, resulting in a reputation as uncooperative and conceited. The tenor never realized that, in the revolving banquet known as Hollywood, the only commodity he brought to the table was his voice. Nearly everyone in Hollywood was used and discarded in some fashion, but the young singer demanded recognition as a man, and there was not much interest in what he had to offer. It was not meant to be personal, but the young tenor took it that way. It was just Hollywood, a concept Mario never understood.

Preparations for *That Midnight Kiss* were underway. Joe Pasternak described the plot, which never jelled, as follows: "Our first picture was called *That Midnight Kiss*. We had the title, and, I think, after we started working on the script, some justification for it was found."[2] The film's plot, such as it was, loosely followed MGM's fabrication about the tenor's discovery by Koussevitzky while moving a piano. The lack of a plot did not detract from the film's start-to-finish romp through the world of lavish sets Pasternak favored.

MGM planned to launch its latest discovery in grand style. The director, Norman Taurog, had won an Oscar for *Skippy* (a 1931 Jackie Cooper film) and was nominated for another with *Boys Town* (starring Spencer Tracy and Mickey Rooney). He was considered an adept craftsman who could adapt himself to any concept and turn out a palatable, box-office success. Charles Previn, cousin to the father of prodigy André Previn, was the musical director. He occasionally admonished his young charge to "save some of those high notes," and Mario seemed to take the advice in stride. "I told him," Previn said, "that he was going to be a big success and that he shouldn't let it go to his head." Giacomo Spadoni, who had worked briefly with Enrico Caruso, coached Lanza and gushed, "I had the feeling I was once again coaching Caruso—not only the quality and range of Lanza's voice but also his physical appearance and bubbling energy."[3]

The pairing of Lanza and the twenty-six-year-old Kathryn Grayson worked surprisingly well on film. Their supporting cast was first-rate: Basque classical keyboard wizard José Iturbi (for whom *That Midnight Kiss* would be the last film); Ethel Barrymore, then seventy years old with one Oscar and three nominations to her credit; Keenan Wynn, one of Hollywood's most versatile character actors; the all-purpose

J. Carrol Naish; Jules Munshin of Catskills' fame; Thomas Gomez, who
was nominated for an Oscar in *Ride the Pink Horse* (1947); and Marjorie Reynolds, who starred opposite Bing Crosby in *Holiday Inn* and as
William Bendix's wife in the long-running television series *The Life of
Riley*.

Production began on 3 November 1948. The tenor was cooperative
and reported on time. Later that month, he joined Jack Benny, Dean
Martin, Jerry Lewis, Don Ameche, and Red Skelton on a radio show,
the *Elgin Watch Thanksgiving Special*, singing "Così, cosa," "E lucevan
le stelle," and "All Ye Thankful People Come," a Thanksgiving hymn.
Photos of the performance show a happy, relaxed group.

The learning process for Lanza was tedious, as always, but prerecordings of the musical selections went in single takes, which would
become his tradition. They included light pop ("I Know, I Know, I
Know" and "They Didn't Believe Me"), operatic standards ("Una furtiva lagrima" and "Celeste Aida"), and a Neapolitan standard ("Mamma
mia, che vo' sapè"). He sang the operatic selections in an impassioned
style, moving away from correct technique to the *fortissimo* that Hollywood and the public demanded. He produced his usual glorious tones
and hung some incredible notes. The only superior version of "Mamma
mia, che vo' sapè," a difficult composition, was recorded by Mario himself on 5 May 1949.

Mario found that making a movie was hard work, what with early
morning arrivals in Culver City, long periods waiting around in dusty
studios that looked more like airplane hangars, and retake after retake
of minor scenes. He returned home each day with detailed descrip-
tions of his activities. Mario and Betty were still giddily in love and
happy in their modest, rented quarters on Spalding Drive, waiting for
their twosome to increase by one. They regarded themselves as living a
simple life; they drove a used car and laughed about the idea of ever
becoming affected by Hollywood or stardom.

On 8 December 1948, Betty went into labor. Mario and Robinson
took her to Cedars of Lebanon Hospital. Betty's labor was prolonged,
and the baby was born the next day while Mario was on the set. When
the new mother awakened, Sam Weiler and the beaming father were at
her side. The newborn was named Colleen and baptized at St. Paul's
Catholic Church in Westwood. Sam and Selma Weiler, both Jewish,
were honored as godparents, promising that Colleen Lanza[4] would be

raised a Catholic. The tenor lavished Colleen and the three children who followed with praise and affection. He was, at his best, a good and attentive father.

Although he occasionally reported to the set of *That Midnight Kiss* with the smell of alcohol on his breath, Lanza's drinking did not affect production. Altogether he missed only five days (20 and 21 December; 31 January 1949—his twenty-eighth birthday—and 21 and 22 February). It was his crude, exhibitionist pranks that astonished cast, crew, and executives. He occasionally relieved himself on the set, choosing a potted plant, a bucket, a corner on a stage where Kathryn Grayson was rehearsing. Louis B. Mayer was furious. He summoned the truant he now called "Caruso" to his office and demanded that the vile behavior cease, and further advised Mario's friends not to leave him alone any longer than they would a small child.[5] Time was a dangerous commodity for Lanza. During the long delays on the set, he hoisted his barbells, working up a sweat and ruining his makeup and hair. Taurog insisted that the singer weigh in each day. His weight varied by approximately twenty pounds during the picture—hardly noticeable in comparison with what was to come.

The humility that had touched Joe Pasternak when Lanza was signed by MGM vanished and a world-class ego erupted. Pasternak remembered the production as "a pleasant enough experience . . . but there was a disturbing quality, even then, that you couldn't quite pin down."[6] When Edmond O'Brien dropped by during filming, the rising star was elated to see him. O'Brien was surprised by Mario's disinclination for reminiscing about their wild time together during *Winged Victory*. Rather, as O'Brien later recalled, "[Lanza] was interested only in telling [me] of the dark, sinister things people were trying to do to him." The young tenor was convinced that some people were attempting to undermine his career and ruin his bid for stardom.

"That old bitch Ethel Barrymore," Mario raged, "she's trying to steal my scenes. I'll tell her where to get off!" O'Brien was stunned. The suggestion that Ethel Barrymore would try to upstage the star of the film was ludicrous. He protested, insisting that Ethel was a seasoned and true professional. Mario interrupted with one of his patented curses: "She's no damned good, she's upstaging me all the time! Who the hell does she think she is?"

O'Brien, remembering the uncomplicated soldier with the glorious voice from *Winged Victory*—both in New York and Hollywood—was startled and shaken. He tried again to convince his old friend that he was mistaken, but the tirade continued. "Maybe I should have recognized it at once," O'Brien later said, "but who looks for paranoia in a friend?"[7]

Lanza's acting was decent for a novice. He had a frequently overlooked flair for light comedy and a great amount of charisma. He kept his inclination for overly bright and wide-eyed hamminess to a minimum in *That Midnight Kiss*. Overall, he came across as a promising newcomer with a magnificent voice.

When the picture was finished, Lanza—showing a colossal lack of insight—petulantly demanded top billing over the well-established Kathryn Grayson, who had starred in thirteen films prior to *That Midnight Kiss*. To place an untried newcomer at the top of the bill would have been a case of horrendous judgment and brutish manners. When the credits rolled, MGM wisely placed Kathryn at the top of the bill and Mario Lanza, in letters the same size, at the end, following the words "and introducing." But the picture was regarded as a Lanza vehicle from the first day of its release. *That Midnight Kiss* is available on video, and it is doubtful that many buy it thinking of it as a Grayson film. In the end, Mario had been right, in his black-and-white way.

Now it was time for him to honor old commitments, make his first commercial recordings for RCA, and await the moviegoing public's verdict. He was bursting with anticipation and annoyed that, though he had starred in a movie, he was not yet a movie star.

CHAPTER 11

Stardom

This boy has . . . a greater voice than Caruso. He has the greatest voice I have ever heard.

Licia Albanese[1]

Columbia Artists had booked concert dates for Mario and Constantine Callinicos before *That Midnight Kiss* was even a concept. The program for the 1949 tour included the Lamento di Federico, "Celeste Aida," "Lasciatemi morire," "Già il sole del Gange," "Nina," the Agnus Dei, "La donna è mobile," "The House on the Top of the Hill," "My Lady Walks in Loveliness," "Tell Me, O Blue, Blue Sky," "Softly, As in a Morning Sunrise," and "Thine Alone." The tour was scheduled to begin on 7 March 1949, in Bluefield, West Virginia, and close in Lincoln, Nebraska, on 25 May with stops in Clinton, Zanesville, and Athens, Ohio; Wilmington, Delaware; Troy, New York; Portland, Maine; Fort Wayne, Indiana; Duluth and Minneapolis, Minnesota; Chicago; New Orleans; Tulsa, Oklahoma; Sylacauga, Alabama; and Centralia and Charleston, Illinois. The young tenor, fresh from the MGM studios, deeply resented the commitment to play in small towns for what he now saw as inferior money.

The tour began with an unavoidable cancellation, as Lanza was called to the MGM lot for retakes. His overall record of cancellations—fifteen of twenty-seven concerts—reflected a combination of his sense that he would rocket to success as a screen star and an outright failure to commit himself to the training and discipline that a talent like his required. He had been slothful in his studies with Irene Williams and Enrico Rosati, yet he craved acceptance as a serious artist. Outwardly, he was cocky about his ability to "fracture 'em" with the beauty of his voice; inwardly, he was as insecure as ever before each performance, worrying that he might forget his lines, miss a note, or produce a sour tone. That fear, along with his musical deficiencies, stunted his growth as a repertory artist.[2]

Lanza set his own irresponsible standard during the 1949 tour. He canceled performances at the last minute, citing phantom pains, throat problems, and even pneumonia. One concert that didn't come off was scheduled for 19 May in Centralia, Illinois, where more than one hundred men had died in a mine disaster in 1945. Lanza remembered the tragedy and looked forward to the concert. When Callinicos arrived in Centralia, he was advised that the performance had been canceled because the tenor was hospitalized in Chicago. The phone rang moments later. It was Mario. "What the hell are you doing in that town?" boomed a healthy-sounding Lanza. "Why aren't you here with me?"

"Here with me" was a suite at the Bismarck Hotel in Chicago, where a lively party was in full swing. Costa was confounded by his friend's lack of concern for the people who had planned their evening around seeing Mario Lanza in concert. Fear was behind the cancellation. "Anyway," Mario told Callinicos, "I don't know some of those numbers they put on the program. Those Hugo Wolf songs I don't know from nothing."[3] Rather than learn his craft or, with regard to the immediate problem, compromise and vary the program, he retreated to drink and the company of strangers, to whom he sang, for free, until well beyond midnight.

In Lanza's defense, he had no effective management at a crucial point in his artistic development. Although the odds of Lanza following anyone's charge to appear on schedule were slim, Weiler utterly squandered his chance to lay down the law. Weiler occasionally met with representatives from RCA and MGM, but his orientation was financial rather than artistic.

Nothing was ever entirely lost with the errant young tenor. When he took the stage, the singing was brilliant and the audiences were dazzled. His methods were unconventional for a classical artist, starting with the "lost" tuxedo. He plugged his unreleased film, engaged in casual banter with the audience, and generally sang as if it would be the last time the song would be heard rather than a stuffy artist concerned with decorum and tradition.

On 5 May 1949 Mario and Callinicos took a break from the already-breakridden tour to record four songs for RCA's Red Seal division at the Manhattan Center, a huge, converted Scottish rite temple on West

Thirty-fourth Street in New York. Several times in 1948 RCA had attempted to produce their untested recording artist. Offered his choice of three conductors, the tenor selected Jean Paul Morel of the New York City Opera, but rehearsals degenerated into a battle between Morel's resolute ideas and Lanza's natural instincts. The young artist, who had not sold a single record, stormed out and vowed never to return.

When Mario proposed that Callinicos conduct the first recording session, RCA flatly refused. He had been difficult to date and David Sarnoff, the ruthlessly driven head of RCA, had no intention of risking a $5000 session with an unknown wielding the baton. When RCA proposed that the tenor put his faith in Costa on the line and guarantee the debt if less than four songs were satisfactorily recorded, he agreed. What else was money for? He had already walked away from twice that amount during the concert tour.

A first-rate forty-three-piece orchestra comprised mostly of musicians from the New York Philharmonic was assembled. Mario, richly but casually attired, with his shirt open at the neck, worked swiftly and with the confidence he nearly always exuded in a recording studio. He took great comfort in the fact that a flub was recoverable. According to Richard Mohr, who produced virtually all RCA Red Seal recordings from the late 1940s to the mid-1970s, Lanza "was ready and able to discuss improvements . . . but he had been singing the music one way for years, and musically speaking one take was all he had."[4] He was in excellent voice, the timbre, range, and interpretation extraordinary by any standard.

The first selection was "Core 'ngrato" ("Ungrateful Heart"), a Neapolitan standard Mario sang with passion and abandon, delivering the definitive version so admired by José Carreras. Next was "Celeste Aida," sung with independent purpose and in a key higher than he usually risked in concert. Some classical music critics of the time regarded the result as unconventionally effusive; others praised it for its tone, beauty, and potential. Mario literally embraced the Neapolitan classic "Mamma mia, che vo' sapè," delivering what remains the definitive version. He completed the session in less than three hours, finishing with an impassioned, powerful "Che gelida manina," which was voted operatic recording of 1949 by the National Record Critics (the same people who would be at his throat in a few years for the same technique) and was added to RCA's selective Hall of Fame of historical recordings. Many consider it his finest recording. It would have brought down any house in Italy, where the patrons have been known to heave benches at tenors who are merely good and where sopranos keep a car and driver ready by the theater's side door.

It was an impressive session by any standard, let alone for an untried twenty-eight-year-old. As a conductor, Constantine was alarmed by Lanza's insistence on singing with his eyes closed during crucial sequences, tapping his internal wells and usually unerring instinct for guidance. He knew what was good for him and what would work. It was his baptism as a recording artist and the inception of his approach. Lanza sang as if his life depended on every phrase and note. When the session ended, Mario declared jubilantly, "Costa, we will both be famous."[5]

After the tour, Mario returned to Hollywood to prepare for the premiere of *That Midnight Kiss*. During rehearsals for his third and last appearance at the Hollywood Bowl, on what was billed as MGM night, he began an acrimonious relationship with Johnny Green, who was well established with the studio. When Green, whom Mario regarded as nothing more than an overrated bandleader, attempted to correct him, the tenor responded defiantly, "Green will conduct! Lanza will sing!"[6] The program that Tuesday, 16 August 1949, was eclectic. Frank Morgan, best known for his title role in MGM's *The Wizard of Oz*, was the master of ceremonies; Carmen Miranda, the Portuguese-born "Brazilian Bombshell" frantically danced while singing "Ca-Room Pa-Pa" from *Nancy Goes to Rio*; and Lanza performed the "Addio" from Verdi's *Rigoletto* with Mary Jane Smith and a solo rendition of "Celeste Aida." André Previn, who loathed Lanza, also appeared.

That fall the tenor recorded tracks from *That Midnight Kiss* and characteristically impassioned versions of "'O sole mio," "Lolita," and "Granada" at Republic Studios with Ray Sinatra, a distant cousin to Frank who had met Mario at MGM. Ray Sinatra and Lanza made dozens of recordings together. Some worked out well; on others, the lack of synchronization between singer and orchestra is glaring. Sinatra was well liked, not astonishingly talented, and wound up working as a house conductor in Las Vegas.

Lanza was the first to popularize "Granada," a previously under-valued composition by the prolific Mexican composer Augustín Lara

(1900–1969), who wrote more than six hundred songs. His perform-ance was remarkably spontaneous and serves—to this day—as the model from which other tenors develop their interpretations. It was nine-year-old Plácido Domingo's favorite song and is still a signature piece at his concerts. José Carreras, who attributes his love of the song to Lanza, does a commendable version while others have either under-sung it (Luciano Pavarotti) or been too ponderous (notably Mario del Monaco, the Met's primo Otello from 1952 to 1959). Augustín Lara visited the tenor at his Beverly Hills home in 1950. When Lanza played his recording of "Granada," Lara burst into tears, exclaiming that his composition had been graced with a rendition greater than he had ever envisioned.[7]

RCA was eager to time its release of Mario's first album with the premiere of *That Midnight Kiss*, resulting in a frenetic schedule of pro-duction, shipping, and promotion. Publicity for the film included a nationwide tour for Grayson and Lanza and a half-hour, coast-to-coast radio special on 29 September 1949. The tenor sang "Mamma mia, che vo' sapè" and "I Know, I Know, I Know" and was joined by Grayson in duets of "They Didn't Believe Me" and "Verranno a te sull'aure'" from Donizetti's *Lucia di Lammermoor*.

Grayson, no operatic soprano, was a detriment to Lanza musically. In the duet from *Lucia di Lammermoor*, she sang her solo portion with-out distinction. Lanza joined the performance on cue and sang his solo segment beautifully, the diction, spacing, and presentation all excel-lent. Then their duet began. As usual when she approached a duet with Lanza, Grayson did not keep to the form of the music or work with her partner to produce a pleasant union of harmony and sound. Instead she pitched upward, where no tenor should follow. Mario knew how things should be done but permitted filmdom to lead him astray, into singing that was distorted and unfocused.

That Midnight Kiss opened in September 1949, with Lanza and Grayson singing together before showings in several larger cities. When the tour reached Philadelphia, Mario and Kathryn were accorded a lav-ish welcome. Film footage of the motorcade shows a youthful, exuber-ant, and charismatic Mario absolutely enthralled by the reaction of the thousands who lined the streets of his youth. Mary Cocozza, still a res-ident of 2040 Mercy Street, sat beside her son in a Ford convertible. Betty followed in another car. After the last show, Mario and Betty joined the festivities at 636 Christian Street, where Salvatore Lanza filled the glasses and toasted his grandson, Freddy Cocozza, while a throng of admiring fans outside shouted and pleaded for a glimpse of Mario. Deeply and understandably proud of his grandson's accomplishments, he could not fully comprehend the change in Freddy's life.

A harried week followed, filled with parties, reunions, and adulation for the hometown boy who had made good. That the tenor had left Freddy Cocozza and Christian Street behind was clear when Eddie Durso, his shadow from high school days, visited him at Palumbo's, a mainstay for the Italian-American community in South Philadelphia. After a brief conversation, with Durso in awe of Grayson, Spadoni, and the rest of the entourage, Mario offered, "It is unbelievable. I'm recording for the same company as Caruso."[8] His successful friend invited Durso to his suite at the Ritz-Carlton, but Eddie had to return to his job on the Jersey Shore.

With regard to plot, direction, and production, the reaction to *That Midnight Kiss* was blasé, but the reaction to Lanza's own performance was more than even he expected. Bosley Crowther (*The New York Times*, 23 September 1949) called it a "launching of which any opera veteran might be proud." Harold Barnes of *The New York Herald Tribune* conceded that Lanza possessed a superb voice but cautioned that he had a long way to go as an actor. *Variety*, long the bellwether of the industry, predicted enormous success for the youngster: "His voice, when he's singing opera, is excellent. In addition, far from the caricatured opera tenor, he's a nice-looking youngster of the average American boy school, who will have the females on his side from the start."[9]

The moviegoing public loved him. Most had heard tenors sing arias without forming an attachment to opera. Lanza sang them differently. It was earthy, powerful, raw, and exciting. People who had been totally disaffected began to consider opera. Some critics hailed him as the find of the century; the more rigid sniffed that this was not how opera should be sung. Meanwhile at the Met, Peerce, Tucker, and Giuseppe di Stefano, whose lush tones and *pianissimo* were among the greatest ever, were singing to less-than-sold-out houses.

RCA's first Lanza entry sold briskly and *That Midnight Kiss* played to crowds in the United States and Europe. British music critic Dick Tatham recalled:

The start, for me, was late one afternoon . . . when there came an insistent ringing at my front door. It was Peter Grant (now of Sadler's Wells). He said, "I've just heard a fantastic tenor—absolutely sensational. Down at the Empire, Leicester Square. Know anything about him? His name's Mario Lanza. I'm going to see the film through again this evening. You'd better come along. You'll hear something out of this world."[10]

With the tenor's career soaring, the Lanzas quit Spalding Drive for an upscale Spanish-style home at 810 North Whittier Drive, within a few blocks of Sunset Boulevard and four blocks from Rodeo Drive.[11] The Cocozzas sold their house at 2040 Mercy Street and moved to Beverly Hills—to 810 North Whittier Drive. It was a neighborhood of gracious homes with lawns tended by gardeners and tennis courts made less conspicuous by shrubbery. Mario tore out the Oriental gardens, filled the pools, and constructed a boxing ring where he worked out with Robinson, Rocky Marciano, and others. He proudly created a Christmas wonderland on the grounds that December.

Mary Cocozza was forty-four years old and frankly quite frumpy when she arrived in California in late 1949. Shortly after, Terry Robinson convinced Mary, Betty, and the Weilers to join him and Mario in a regimen of regular exercise. Sam Weiler abhorred the idea of a sweaty brow and calloused hands and quickly abandoned Robinson's program. Selma and Betty soon followed. But Mary stayed with various programs to the end of her life, bringing her weight down and presenting the appearance of a woman at least a decade younger. "She got to looking like Gina Lollobrigida," Terry later mused. "When we had parties, the writers used to make passes at her. It got Mario real mad." [12] Mary later boasted that Mario duped the same reporters into believing that he was about to introduce them to the female lead in his next film. Then, as Mary told the story, she would be escorted into the room and Mario would, after a time, confess that she was actually his mother. It was a strange and unlikely source of pride. One thing was certain: Mary was overjoyed to be in Hollywood with her son and she was hellbent on making the best of "her career."

Tony Cocozza, the odd man out, seemed a part of a different generation. He was monumentally stubborn and still took his long, ritualistic walks or sat for hours in the garden with his dog, saying and doing little. It was as if he were a visitor, though Mary, to her credit, ensured that he was appropriately dressed and that he took part in most family activities.

The threesome of Mario, Betty, and Mary, or the twosome of Mario and Mary—nearly always driven by Terry Robinson—occasionally made the rounds. Mary sometimes introduced herself as Maria, later calling herself Mary or Maria Lanza for alleged convenience. Betty was blindly jealous of the attention her husband paid to his mother. Mary was not above sequestering herself on a loveseat with her son, forcing a seething Betty to sit apart from her husband. Al Teitelbaum, who described Mary Cocozza as "no bargain," remembers that the tenor would not buy a fur for Betty until he had presented one to his mother, explaining that it would "keep peace in the family."[13] But with mother and son under the same roof, Betty's chances for happiness had been dealt a knock-out blow. Like many things that work out badly, it seemed like a very nice thing to do at the time.

CHAPTER 12

The Toast of New Orleans

At my age, Caruso was nowhere, nohow, nothing. . . . At twenty-nine, Caruso used to crack on high B-flat. . . . Wait till I develop.

Mario Lanza, 1951[1]

Some were calling Lanza the biggest overnight success since Rudolph Valentino. RCA was eager to follow its best-selling Lanza album with another offering, and MGM rushed into his next production, a project called *Kiss of Fire*, on 20 October 1949. The title was changed to *The Toast of New Orleans* before it was completed.

MGM assembled another veteran cast for *The Toast of New Orleans*. Kathryn Grayson and J. Carrol Naish were holdovers from *That Midnight Kiss*. Richard Hageman; James Mitchell; Rita Moreno, the lovely Puerto Rican singer-dancer-actress who would go on to win an Oscar for *West Side Story*; and the versatile, always elegant David Niven completed the principal cast. Norman Taurog was again called upon to direct and keep Lanza within reasonable limits.

The prerecording sessions went well, though some selections are dated, showing a little too clearly that Lanza had emerged at the height of the post-opera and operetta tradition. Russian-born composer Nick Brodszky teamed with Sammy Cahn on two ballads ("I'll Never Love You" and "The Bayou Lullaby"). Neither song is memorable and Mario, as he frequently did, outclassed the material. At the end of the later recorded studio version of "The Bayou Lullaby," he hits a G that would have stirred envy in Beniamino Gigli, the master of *cantilena*.

Two more Brodszky-Cahn creations, "Tina Lina" and "Boom Biddy Boom," were the dumbest songs the tenor ever recorded—until they were swept away by his 1958 version of "Pineapple Pickers." Still he attacked them with gusto, and in the midst of a lark like *The Toast of New Orleans*, they actually fit. No singer of note—not Caruso, Crosby,

83

Sinatra, Garland, Cole, Tormé, nor Streisand—has escaped the igno-
minious fate of recording something absolutely dumb.

The operatic numbers, "The Flower Song" from Bizet's *Carmen*,
"O paradiso" from *L'Africana*, "M'apparì" from *Martha*; "Libiamo, libiamo" from *La Traviata*; and "Stolta paura l'amor" from *Madama Butterfly*, were aggressively and passionately sung. Lanza's role called for
him to play a rough fisherman whose magnificent but untrained voice
develops into an instrument of grand opera. Accordingly some of the
segments ("M'apparì" and "The Flower Song") were sung in an intentionally raw and undisciplined manner. The Love Duet from *Madama
Butterfly* was excellent, both visually and vocally, reflecting—as the
plot demanded—the singer's transition from a buffoon to an exciting
operatic performer. The tenor's detractors often focused on his intentionally unpolished singing as representative of his talent; some early
critics even charged that Lanza had never performed before an audience. He had sung in more than two hundred concerts and attracted
praise from critics throughout the United States and Canada—but
none of those performances were showing at the local theaters.

The last Brodszky-Cahn composition, "Be My Love," became
Lanza's theme song, though he could not deliver the finale (high B-flat
to high C) in his last years. In the film, Grayson sings the first verse, and
Mario joins in when the key moves from C to C-sharp major; the Lanza-
Grayson screamfest thrilled film audiences. The tenor also recorded an
innovative solo version of "Be My Love" in one take on 27 June 1950, at
Republic Studios with Ray Sinatra conducting and Sammy Cahn nervously pacing. Lanza's excellent taste and intuition made for a classic cut
that has never been matched. It sold well over one million copies before
a year passed and was a jukebox standard in its time.

Sammy Cahn, often called Frank Sinatra's private lyricist, was nominated for thirty Oscars; he won four. He declared that if you'd only
heard Mr. Lanza on record or tape, you'd never heard him at all. "No
mechanical reproduction could capture the startling brilliance of that
voice. It scared the hell out of you."[2] Metropolitan Opera soprano Re-
nata Tebaldi agreed; she said Lanza's voice "split the air."[3]

"Be My Love" was also sung, not too convincingly, by Richard
Tucker and Jan Peerce. Sergio Franchi's version is respectable, and a
wheezing Mario del Monaco's attempt, regrettable. José Carreras and
Plácido Domingo, great admirers of the tenor from South Philadel-

phia, frequently perform it in concert. Everyone backs away from the high-C finish, collectively validating how brilliant Lanza was on that recording. The tenor eventually resented his association with the song and the constant requests for it. He would substitute ribald lyrics during impromptu private concerts, derisively calling it "Be My Lunch."[4]

With *That Midnight Kiss* under his belt, Lanza became difficult, convinced that stardom was inevitable. He picked up where he had left off with the filming of *The Toast of New Orleans*. To provide extras and bit players with overtime, the tenor flubbed scenes and reported late. The problem was that he was just as motivated to spite authority as he was to help those he was now referring to as "the little people." Meanwhile, it was "the little people" who had to drain and clean the artificial lagoon on the set when he fouled it rather than trouble himself with walking to the restroom. December 1949 found him in poor health; he was absent on the 1st, 2nd, 3rd, 16th, 17th, 19th, 20th, and 31st.

One day he arrived on the set more than six hours late. When an enraged Taurog demanded to know why, Mario responded, "Oh, I was up all night listening to records. I'm tired." Taurog took some comfort in the fact that his temperamental star was learning something and inquired as to what recordings and to which artist he had been listening. Mario seemed annoyed. He regarded the question as idiotic and the answer obvious. He advised Taurog that he had been listening to his own recordings.[5]

He drank to excess and ate staggering quantities of food, causing Joe Pasternak to wonder if he could gain weight by simply swallowing air. Pasternak later wrote, "When Lanza was of a mind to eat, the secret service itself couldn't keep this trencherman in bounds."[6] The harried producer found that his unpredictable star would order meals for three from the commissary under different names, confounding his efforts to keep him from gaining too much weight. Lanza's voracious eating and regular weightlifting added to his naturally heavy-chested physique, resulting in a fifty-inch chest, a nineteen-inch neck, and seventeen-inch biceps. He stayed at around 200 pounds throughout filming, varying enough to be noticeable but not distracting.

Lanza got along well with David Niven and Rita Moreno, and he was smitten with Grayson, although there was never any romantic involvement. Once he offered to serenade her at her Brentwood estate; he scaled the fence, only to be chased away by guard dogs. Grayson, like many others, described Lanza's voice as "just glorious."[7] She also claimed he was often drunk before nine a.m. during filming, and she refused to consider another film with him, although nothing in the finished product hinted at the turmoil behind the scenes.

Unless his mother was visiting the set—in which case the son became obsequious and overly polite—Lanza's defiance of authority and fearlessness were unchanged from his earlier years. The difference was that Freddy Cocozza was expendable whereas Mario Lanza was, for the moment, irreplaceable: *The Toast of New Orleans* was nothing more than a vehicle for his voice, despite Grayson's contractual right to top billing. She sang but one solo to many by Mario; together they performed five duets.

Production concluded on 6 March 1950. The film premiered in September 1950, and Bosley Crowther (*The New York Times*, 30 September 1950) provided his typically definitive review:

> Following the musical trail it blazed some years ago with Jeanette MacDonald and Nelson Eddy, MGM has gone a step further in bringing grand opera to the screen . . . . *The Toast of New Orleans* . . . is a case where the track is triumphant, for the comedy-romance follows a formula that is devoid of novelty or sparkle. . . . But since the music is richly rendered and the scenery is lovely to look upon, *The Toast of New Orleans* comes off better than it has a right to when its story is so hackneyed.

Picturegoer (October 1950) found it mundane, just a story on which to build pieces from various operas.

The storyline parodied Lanza's life: Pepé Duvall, the rough-mannered protagonist the tenor played, emerges from an unlikely place called Bayou Minou and falters into New Orleans high society, courtesy of his great but untrained voice. Grayson, as lovely as ever, delivered an ingenue sort of performance. J. Carrol Naish was at times hilarious in his portrayal of an uncouth bayou fisherman and uncle to Pepé Duvall. Niven seems bewildered by it all.[8] Lanza? He projected considerable charisma and a burly, masculine charm. His acting had matured from *That Midnight Kiss*, and once again he displayed a natural facility for light comedy. He was occasionally overly bright-eyed or hammy, but not enough to overcome a sporting and energetic performance. The most prophetic line of the film occurs when Grayson berates him: "You know what you're doing! Don't you! You're trying to be difficult!" Lanza furrows his brow in an absurdly cocky manner, softened by the wonderful smile he had as a young man. "Me?" he meekly asks.

Lanza fever was in high gear. With his first album and two films, he had amassed a small but impressive collection of operatic recordings unlike those previously heard. An adoring public was struck by the startling beauty and freshness of his voice. Burt Solomon, who worked in the film industry for many years, eloquently expressed a view of his singing shared by many:

> I've read and heard much debate over Mario Lanza's talent and potential. However, I've never heard anyone credit him with bringing classical music to an entire generation of young urban males. I grew up in the Bronx and until *The Toast of New Orleans* and other Lanza movies I'd had little exposure to opera. Lanza, because of his earthiness, his personality, and his power, made it okay to listen to and appreciate opera—and I was not alone. It wasn't important at the time—or now, in retrospect—whether he ranked with the great tenors. I liked what I heard and I went on to del Monaco, Björling, Corelli, Pavarotti, and Domingo. But it began with Lanza.[9]

In his numerous interviews, Mario came across as a spirited, genuine, unaffected, and sometimes ribald young man who could not believe his rapid rise from anonymity. Again and again, he announced his intention to pursue operatic study in Italy and serve an apprenticeship before tackling his goal of performing at the Met. He stood firm against exploiting the voice before it was ready: it would not happen to him.

The twenty-nine-year-old tenor was the hottest star in Hollywood and the best-selling recording artist in the world. The money was rushing in and cascading out. He was paid $25,000 in salary plus a bonus in the same amount for *The Toast of New Orleans*, and his record royalties for 1950 exceeded $500,000. Sam Weiler and Mario formed an investment pool, MarSam (a combination of their names). Weiler acted with absolute autonomy and an absolute power of attorney. The arrangement would lead to bitter recriminations between the men.

From late 1949 through the spring of 1950, Mario dove into the muck that accompanies Hollywood stardom. He made the rounds at parties and set lavish spreads for weekend open houses, attracting the usual Hollywood leeches—agent, publicist, song-writer, tax attorney, entertainment attorney, voice coach, and so forth—until more than 35 percent of his gross earnings went for frankly questionable services. As Grayson later put it, with his success came "the hangers-on, the people that helped ruin his life, his marriage and everything."[10]

When his emotions were stable, the tenor pursued a vigorous program of road work, swimming, and weightlifting, bench-pressing 300 pounds and curling 150 pounds at his peak. His routine for breath control included swimming laps under water, which ritual he even convinced Jussi Björling to consider. The Swedish master admired Lanza's talent and visited with him at his Beverly Hills home, where the two tenors did battle with several bottles of Chivas Regal, Mario's favored drink for a time. The young American—who seldom hesitated to call himself greater than Caruso—occasionally stated that he was not Jussi's equal.

Mario maintained a frenzied pace, splurging on anything that remotely appealed to him. He became a regular at the Brown Derby, the Casa d'Amor (where a pizza, the Mario Lanza Special, was on the menu for many years), and other Hollywood nightspots. Fan mail arrived at the studio in sacks. Most of the letters were from women; some sent full-length, nude photographs and offered the proverbial good time. He was crushed by autograph seekers at the studio gates and at the entrance to his drive. Women screamed and mobbed him wherever he went. The last person to cause such a sensation was Frank Sinatra nearly a decade earlier. The next would be Elvis Presley, a decade later.

At home, it was too much attention to Mom from Mario. Mario, confused about his loyalties, made what Betty regarded as frequent mistakes. "You don't love me! You love her!" she sobbed.[11] Betty was unable to comprehend her husband's interior struggles or to endure her mother-in-law's advice about her husband's needs, dislikes, and likes. Lanza's imperfect solution was to rent a house for his parents at 204 South Crescent Drive in Beverly Hills; Terry Robinson became a permanent roommate of Mary's and Tony's.

South Cresent Drive was eight blocks from the Lanzas' home on Whittier; an amicable relationship between Betty and Mary would have started at five hundred miles. Mary and Tony were at the Whittier address for dinner every evening. They seldom missed a weekend. The situation was devastating for someone as dependent and vulnerable as Betty, and Mario could not protect her as he was inseparable from the problem.

Slowly but with growing momentum, Betty sought relief with alcohol. Drugs, in combination, soon followed. Unable to cope with a husband she no longer understood, a career that seemed to place her at the rear of the hall, and Mary, she took it out on the household staff of nine to eleven servants. Her orders were ridiculously autocratic and harshly given; her temper was mean and torrential. Household personnel, regarding their duties as domestic and not a turn at the pillory, left in droves. It would be nice to be able to say that Betty was a victim, but few things are that simple. She exacted her retribution from Mario and, despite her ordinary beginnings in Illinois, became an elitist. For him, Hollywood and success were merely props. For her, Hollywood and success were leading players.

It was a heady time for the tenor, and he rediscovered the one vice he had mostly forsaken upon marrying Betty: women. He found that Hollywood success included a brigade of willing women and pursued one-nighters, noontime trysts, flings, affairs, and whatever else came his way with a determination he otherwise reserved for food and drink. His liaisons included stars (Judy Garland); starlets (Inger Stevens); the not-so and not-at-all famous; and prostitutes. He had little regard for time of day or location—a closet would do nicely—and flagrantly displayed his promiscuity to anyone who happened to be nearby. He delighted in making cast and crew wait and listen while he carried on with a bit player or starlet in his dressing room. On other occasions, he left doors ajar or simply proceeded in spite of who might be nearby. Sometimes, he actually made love in a private setting. A favorite haunt was the Bel Air Hotel, where the tenor always ordered champagne and caviar from room service and startled the staff with one-hundred-dollar tips. In a town not long on restraint, he set a likely unexcelled standard.

Lanza bragged about his exploits to his cavalcade of spongers, claiming that those who were lucky enough to witness his methods had learned something that would make them better lovers and that his outside activities made him a better lover at home. Indeed Betty was again pregnant, and the rumors that raced through Hollywood inevitably reached her. When she concluded that some were true, her absolute admiration for Mario ended. She went from naive to disillusioned to bitter.

That spring of 1950 he and Betty vacationed with Tyrone Power and his wife, Linda Christian, the Weilers, and the Pasternaks in Hawaii. There Mario gave three concerts at the McKinley Auditorium, with Callinicos accompanying on the piano; although the tenor's contract with MGM provided him with six months for concerts and opera, these three concerts were Lanza's only such activity during the four-month break between productions of his second and third films. He wanted to do it all, and for a while, he did. He boasted that his career would continue to rocket upward as it had in 1950. For a while, it exceeded even his inflated predictions.

CHAPTER 13

MGM in Transition

When you have a rare orchid, you don't stick it in your lawn like a
dandelion—you give it special attention and it blooms. In the lawn
it would die. If I had stayed at my studio, the studio that I made
the greatest in the world, there would have been no trouble with
Mario.

Louis B. Mayer, 1952[1]

When Louis B. Mayer signed Mario Lanza to a seven-year contract
with MGM, he ran the most successful studio in Hollywood. Gable,
MacDonald, Rooney, and Garland were all under contract, and MGM
—with its roaring lion trademark, polished productions, and slogan
("More stars than there are in the heavens")—was itself the biggest star
in the show business galaxy. If Mayer is blamed for the prudish, anti-
quated views and lack of foresight that contributed to MGM's decline,
he must also be credited for its phenomenal success during the era of
his stewardship.

The mighty L. B. Mayer was in fact only an employee—albeit an
important one—at a studio that was but one of 124 subsidiaries of
Loew's, Inc., a multibillion-dollar concern headquartered in Times
Square. Mayer, head of production at MGM from 1924 to 1951, answered to Nicholas Schenck, an unimaginative, calculating man with a
penchant for meticulous attire. Louis signed the checks and contracts
on MGM's behalf, but every proposal for personnel or films had to be
approved by the New York office.

Mayer's theatrical career began in 1907 with a $600 loan and a run-
down vaudeville theater, the Gem, in Haverhill, Massachusetts. Reno-
vated and renamed the Orpheum, it showed the primitive moving pictures of the time. Vaudeville performers viewed film as a fad that would
not threaten their industry; many producers of silent films saw no threat

in the "talkies." Ironically, Mayer could see the future in both but was blind to the potential of television. He ventured into distribution and production, and prospered.

Marcus Loew began in 1905, with a penny arcade on East Fourteenth Street in New York. While Mayer was expanding his holdings, moving from Haverhill to Boston, Loew was buying up movie houses. By 1918, Loew's owned 112 theaters and paid ten thousand employees a total of $8 million per year. Ownership of a production company was the next logical step. As the system developed, each theater-holding group (MGM, Paramount, Fox, and RKO, for instance) produced its own features at its own studios. The positive side of such an arrangement was that the theaters had a guaranteed supply of product at a cost that could be controlled. The downside was that even mediocre and poor films were assured of an engagement and that independent producers had a limited market for their films.

Loew's target was Goldwyn Studios in Culver City, California, where Joe Godsol had forced Samuel Goldwyn out of his own studio. The facility included forty-two buildings and sets that replicated the streets of New York, Paris, the Wild West, and other locations. Film production had been concentrated in New York City, but the advantages of California's moderate climate, cheap, open land, long days of sunshine, and the ability to produce films for twelve months rather than seasonally were slowly being realized. Some diehards claimed that California sun was inferior to New York sun for photography and that Hollywood locations were mere fads.

Mayer's track record as a producer was marginal, with three films that showed minor profits. His fourth, *Pleasure Mad* starring Norma Shearer and produced by Irving Thalberg, was a hit. Still the Louis B. Mayer Company was hardly known, until William Randolph Hearst came along. Hearst had championed the career of Marion Davies, a pretty comedienne who was also his mistress, by forming Cosmopolitan Pictures. The company's sole purpose was the production of Davies' films. Hearst then mobilized the resources of his publishing empire to promote Davies and her films. Among the problems was Hearst's insistence that Davies play antiseptic, virginal roles when her true talent was that of a bold comedienne. Another problem was the public, as it easily spotted the difference between the overblown reviews in Hearst's papers and the quality of what was shown on the screen.

Hearst lost more than $7 million trying to launch Davies' career between 1919 and 1923, succeeding in making her little more than a national joke. Two decades later, Orson Welles would parody the relationship in his monumental *Citizen Kane*. Hearst deserved more than Welles delivered, but Marion Davies in no way resembled the broken-down soprano of *Citizen Kane*. She was captivating, liked by most, independently wealthy, and highly successful in business, after realizing that Hearst had cast her against type.

Davies knew that Hearst was mismanaging her career and urged that Mayer's company might help, as Cosmopolitan's films were distributed by Goldwyn. Hearst, ever the megalomaniac's megalomaniac, retorted that he would start his own distribution company and acquire the theaters in which to display her films. Davies realized that such a move would only exacerbate things. She knew that Hearst was willing to lose money, so she parlayed the one thing he could not bear to lose: Marion Davies.

Time and place were aligning for Louis B. Mayer. He won Hearst's trust by touting Marion's talent and feigning an interest in promoting her career; in return, Hearst offered him Cosmopolitan Pictures, Davies, and the support of his publishing empire. Mayer broke for New York for another round of groveling with Marcus Loew; if L. B. Mayer knew anything, it was that opportunity is the most perishable of all commodities. On 18 April 1924, *The New York Times* announced one of the biggest mergers in the history of the film industry. The new corporation would be known as the Metro-Goldwyn Corporation, combining the interests of what had been Metro Pictures, Goldwyn Pictures, and the Louis B. Mayer Company. Mayer brought the studio to glory and eventually got his name on the side of the building: Metro-Goldwyn-Mayer.

Much credit belongs to Irving Thalberg, the artistic genius who died at the age of thirty-seven and contributed to the studio's slick sophistication during the 1930s. But Mayer managed a nearly seamless transition to profitable, low-budget films and sequels (Mickey Rooney's *Andy Hardy* series and *Tarzan*) and glittering productions (*Boys Town*, *The Wizard of Oz*, and *The Philadelphia Story*). MGM never had a monopoly on the greatest stars or the most sophisticated films. It only seemed that way. What it did have was an army of cooks, carpenters, tailors, designers, workmen, dancers, and the most creative technicians in Hollywood. Its productions were technically excellent, though Mayer preferred maudlin or purely entertaining films, without grimness or a message.

After World War II, Mayer realized that public tastes had shifted. Young men returned from the war unwilling to live with their parents or in-laws. That desire for independence, facilitated by the GI Bill, resulted in tracts of affordable housing and the suburbs. Women were in the work place. Blacks, having tasted some semblance of equality, gradually sought more. Technology from the military build-up spun off into the civilian community. The changes were as swift and massive as the war effort had been, and 1945's *Adventure* ("Gable's Back and Garson's Got Him") did not attract many into Loew's theaters.

In 1941 Dore Schary—an urbane and literary New Yorker who with great difficulty might have acknowledged God as his equal—had been promoted, by Mayer, from the screenwriter's pool. Schary produced two dozen profitable, low-budget films during the easy market of the war years. In 1943 Mayer refused to permit more than one black soldier to appear in Schary's production of *Bataan*. Dore, regarding Mayer as nothing more than another employee of Loew's, Inc., tried to override his veto through the front office. Nick Schenck sided with Mayer. Schary next proposed a ponderous Western parody of the Nazi regime wherein Hitler, Goebbels, and the rest of the infamous were portrayed as gunslingers. He quit when Schenck rejected the picture. Mayer did not miss him. MGM grossed more than $166 million and *Gaslight*, starring Ingrid Bergman, tallied two Oscars in 1944.

In 1945 the studio won Academy Awards for Best Picture, Best Director and Best Actor (all for *The Lost Weekend* with Ray Milland) and Best Actress (Joan Crawford in *Mildred Pierce*). Attendance at movie theaters averaged eighty million each week during the war, but in 1946 profits tumbled; they fell even further during 1947. Seventy thousand television sets had been sold since the end of the war. Schenck, who never respected Mayer, blamed him for the decline. The studio lost money in 1948. David Sarnoff, the head of RCA, approached Schenck with a proposal for a joint venture into television. It was declined. Schenck felt certain that television was nothing more than a passing curiosity.

In 1950 one million television sets were sold. Ten million sets would be sold the next year. Weekly attendance at movie theaters fell to sixty-four million in 1949 and dipped even further in 1950. The last tile in the complex mosaic of the studio's demise was set in 1949. The United States Government's Paramount Decree meant that studio and theater systems would have to be separately owned. Loew's would have to divest itself of MGM, ending the guaranteed revenue the studio needed to function.

Schary returned to MGM as a producer in 1948. Mayer made a fatal error in misjudging Schary and overrating his position with Schenck. The two men battled over Schary's dull and unprofitable production of *The Red Badge of Courage*. Schary decided that his adaptation of Stephen Crane's short novel required narration. "The voice must be warm, intimate, and dignified. I may have to do it myself," he pontificated.[2]

The war between Mayer and Schary continued. Louis was at a great disadvantage as he saw himself and the studio as a single entity and fought for what he truly viewed as its best interests. Schary's goal was to remove all obstacles in his way; he cared nothing for the studio or its history. Mayer sent his resignation to Schenck, declaring that—if Schary remained—he would leave. It was a woeful miscalculation. Schenck wished L. B. Mayer a happy retirement. Schary was now chief of production at MGM. Mayer was not the man to lead MGM through the thicket that lay ahead; his ideas and methods belonged to a bygone era. It was equally certain, and proven by time, that Dore Schary was not the right man either.

What was significant for Mario Lanza was that Mayer understood and valued talent. He cajoled, demeaned, begged, and did whatever it took to get the most from those who had it. Mayer could have worked with Mario: "I understood him and he would have listened to me."[3] The tenor felt the same way about Mayer:

> I'd say I didn't dislike him but he and the studio were making me unhappy with the demands on my life and he'd say he'd do something about it and knew exactly what I was talking about. I'd explain it to him and he'd say again that he'd do something about it and I'd leave feeling a little better. Most of the time nothing was ever done but he knew how to handle me.[4]

When news of Mayer's firing reached Lanza, he called him and asked if he could do anything to help. He was touched by Louis' tears.

Schary pronounced Lanza's films worthless and assumed the reins at MGM with no regard for the singer's immense box-office appeal. He despised Mario Lanza and therefore *The Toast of New Orleans*; incredibly, he pronounced it a $3 million bomb even though it was MGM's most profitable film of 1950. Schary regarded Lanza as uncouth, foul-mouthed, arrogant, and of lowly origin. The idea of a talent like Lanza's, where the movie served as nothing more than a platform, was abhorrent to Dore and he cut the tenor no quarter. Ridding the studio of Mario Lanza was consistent with his bias: that talent meant nothing in comparison to his mission to bring his clumsy messages to the screen.

The tenor, frequently and mercilessly berated by Schary, lamented, "I'm doing as the studio says, but how can you cure a broken heart? Can Dore Schary remake me? What am I supposed to do? Take water and become a boy scout?"[5]

Mario Lanza is a strong contender for the title of the most truculent, morose, demanding star in the history of Hollywood. Still, his destruction was abetted by Schary, who did nothing to discourage or counter the tenor's eventual breakdown. Helping or salvaging an obviously troubled performer was, in Schary's view, beneath him. As with Weiler, the effort may have been futile, but who can make such a determination when no hand was ever extended? Dore Schary regarded Mario Lanza as trash and did nothing beyond see that he was hauled to the curb for morning pick-up.

Schary was driven to belittle Lanza and uninterested in the product he was capable of bringing to the studio. He never viewed the popular tenor as more than a novelty. Lanza, ever vigilant for a reason to be hostile and never able to evaluate his own behavior for its effect on others later did a masterful job—even by his standards—of rationalizing his battles as the cause of MGM's demise. When Schary was dismissed from the studio, the tenor boasted that he had at last emerged victorious.

Much has been written about Lanza, and Louis B. Mayer rates reams in the history of Hollywood. Schary? Whatever his triumphs and successes may have been, he was a loser in his dealings with Mario Lanza. It was not so much his reaction to the singer's behavior. Rather, it was a question of motive and a clear absence of humanity.

Lanza (the Great) at fifteen, in a photo inscribed to his pal Eddie Durso. Courtesy Eddie Durso.

Private Alfred Arnold Cocozza boomed his high notes from the stage at an empty Hollywood Bowl in 1944, three years before his triumphant debut. Courtesy Albert Teitelbaum.

Elizabeth Janette Hicks—soon to become Mrs. Mario Lanza—in 1945. Courtesy Albert Teitelbaum.

Betty and Mario on their wedding day, Friday, 13 April 1945. Courtesy
Albert Teitelbaum.

Mario and Betty run into "trouble" in Tijuana, Mexico, during the Bel Canto tour, 1947. Courtesy Albert Teitelbaum.

George London, Frances Yeend, and Mario take a break from the Bel Canto tour. Horses were a lifelong passion for the tenor. Courtesy Terry Robinson.

Lanza and Yeend during the Bel Canto tour, 1947. Photo Bruno, courtesy
Albert Teitelbaum.

Mario makes his selection from the Hollywood Bowl schedule, 28 August 1947. Courtesy Mario Lanza Institute.

Mario and Betty at the Hollywood Bowl before his concert, 28 August 1947. Courtesy Mario Lanza Institute.

Louis B. Mayer and Mario Lanza, 1947. Courtesy Albert Teitelbaum.

Lanza, Charlie McCarthy, and Edgar Bergen during the tenor's first appearance on their radio program, 14 February 1948. Courtesy Albert Teitelbaum.

Lanza, Jerry Lewis, Jack Benny, Don Ameche, and Red Skelton during the *Elgin Watch Thanksgiving Special*, 1948. Courtesy Albert Teitelbaum.

Tony and Mary Cocozza, Ellisa Lanza (the tenor's maternal grandmother), Mario, Betty, and Salvatore Lanza (the tenor's maternal grandfather) in front of the family store and home at 636 Christian Street in Philadelphia, during the tour for *That Midnight Kiss*, 1949. Courtesy Mario Lanza Institute.

Lanza and Constantine Callinicos, warming up before a concert during the tour for *That Midnight Kiss*, 1949. Photo James Abresch, courtesy Buddy Mantia, Vito Torelli collection.

Producer Joe Pasternak, Lanza, Kathryn Grayson, and director Norman Taurog set off to film *The Toast of New Orleans*, 1949. Courtesy Albert Teitelbaum.

Jimmy Durante visiting Kathryn Grayson and Lanza during filming of *The Toast of New Orleans*, 1949. Courtesy Albert Teitelbaum.

Kathryn Grayson, Mario, and Betty at dinner, 1949. Courtesy
Albert Teitelbaum.

And baby makes three —Betty, Colleen, and Mario, 1950. Courtesy Albert
Teitelbaum.

Tony and Mary Cocozza with their only son, 1950. Courtesy
Terry Robinson.

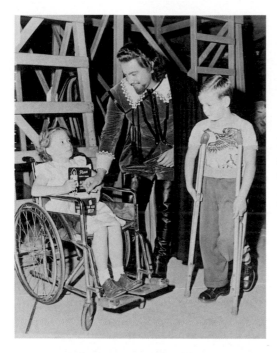

Lanza making time for special visitors, on the set of *The Great Caruso*, 1950. Courtesy Albert Teitelbaum.

Producer Joe Pasternak, Lanza, Elizabeth Taylor, and Vic Damone (partially obscured by Ann Blyth's hat) meeting with members of the Japanese consul during production of *The Great Caruso*, 1950. Courtesy Albert Teitelbaum.

Conductor Peter Herman Adler and Lanza during an operatic recording session for *The Great Caruso*, 1950. Courtesy Terry Robinson.

Lanza and Metropolitan Opera soprano Jarmila Novotná squaring off in *The Great Caruso*, 1950. Courtesy Terry Robinson.

Mario Lanza and Rita Moreno between takes for *The Toast of New Orleans*, 11 January 1950. Courtesy Albert Teitelbaum.

Mario and Betty arrive in Hawaii, where the tenor would give three concerts, spring 1950.

Betty and Ellisa pose for Daddy at 810 North Whittier Drive, Beverly Hills, 1951. Courtesy Albert Teitelbaum.

Lanza, with Costa at the piano, at Philadelphia's Academy of Music, 13 March 1951. Courtesy Albert Teitelbaum.

Andy and Della Russell, Ellisa Lanza, the priest who baptized her, and the proud parents at her christening, 1951. Courtesy Albert Teitelbaum.

Ricardo Montalban signs an autograph for Raphaela Fasano as Mario looks on, 1951. Courtesy Albert Teitelbaum.

Mario and Betty host a birthday party for Raphaela at their home, 1951.
Courtesy Albert Teitelbaum.

Lanza critiques would-be tenor James Whitmore during production of
Because You're Mine, 22 December 1951. Courtesy Albert Teitelbaum.

Lanza on the set of the film he hated most, *Because You're Mine*, 7 February 1952. Courtesy Albert Teitelbaum.

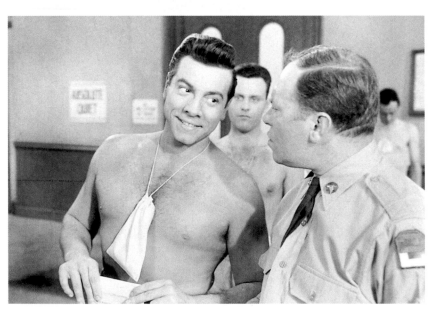

The tenor at 159 pounds, last day of filming *Because You're Mine*, 8 February 1952. Courtesy Albert Teitelbaum.

Lanza and Doris Day posing with their *Photoplay* Gold Medal Awards as the most popular stars of 1951. Courtesy Albert Teitelbaum.

Betty with furrier Al Teitelbaum, who managed the tenor's career from 1954 to 1957, and his wife, Sylvia, 1954. Courtesy Albert Teitelbaum.

Lanza faces friends and foes following *The Chrysler Shower of Stars*, 30 September 1954: Terry Robinson (upper left, looking into the camera), Betty (center), Al Teitelbaum (in striped tie, leaning right of Betty), and Nick Brodzsky (on Lanza's right). Courtesy Albert Teitelbaum.

Producer Henry Blanke, director Anthony Mann, Jack Warner, Mario, and Jimmy Stewart on *Serenade*'s first day of production, 1955. Courtesy Albert Teitelbaum.

Disembarking the *Giulio Cesare* at Naples, Italy, 28 May 1957. Courtesy Mario Lanza Institute.

Mario and the Italian Brigitte Bardot, Marisa Allasio, on location for *The Seven Hills of Rome*, 1957. Courtesy Mario Lanza Institute.

THE QUEEN GREETS MARIO LANZA...

Mario Lanza is greeted by Elizabeth II after his Royal Variety
Performance, 18 November 1957. Courtesy Terry Robinson.

Lanza in concert at Royal Albert Hall, 16 January 1958. Courtesy Buddy Mantia, Vito Torelli collection.

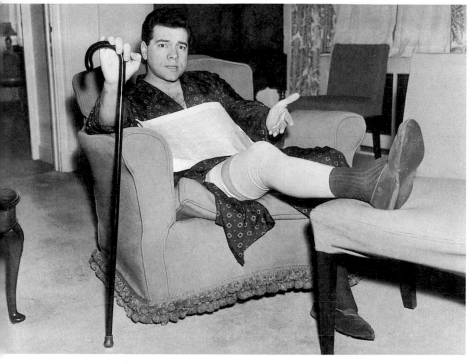

Lanza at the Dorchester in London, nursing his phlebitis, 3 March 1958.
Courtesy Buddy Mantia, Vito Torelli collection.

Lanza at London's Heathrow Airport, 15 March 1958. Courtesy Buddy
Mantia, Vito Torelli collection.

Mario and John Forsythe on the set of *For the First Time*, 1958. Courtesy Buddy Mantia, Vito Torelli collection.

Mario and Austrian actress Johanna von Koszian puzzling over the script of *For the First Time*, 1958. Courtesy Mario Lanza Institute.

Returning to Rome for a thirteen-day hospital stay, January 1958. Courtesy Buddy Mantia, Vito Torelli collection.

The Curse of Caruso

Caruso? You study that ridiculous legend? That guy could not even whistle properly.

Mario Lanza, 1958[1]

Few interested in voices would deny Enrico Caruso the adjective "great." Every tenor who made his debut after 1921, whether at the Met or in the shower, bore the burden of being compared with him. He was part reality, part protean myth, and an icon when Lanza went to Hollywood.

Caruso's was one of the greatest voices of the twentieth century, to be certain. But in an area where subjectivity effectively masquerades as objectivity, the view that Enrico Caruso was somehow leaps and bounds —even a galaxy removed—from all other tenors is absurd. All the best-known tenors have strengths, minor flaws, and outright weaknesses. Caruso is no exception. He was a great *tenore spinto* with a dark, baritonal quality. Dorothy Caruso, his widow, was correct in calling Richard Tucker's timbre the closest to that of her late husband. Tucker was a noteworthy performer at the Met, but few would accord him the status of possessing the greatest voice of his era.

The others? The list is long and each has a unique sound. José Carreras, a splendid *tenore lirico* at his peak, sounds nothing like Luciano Pavarotti, a wonderful technician who could probably deliver a high C in his sleep, or Plácido Domingo, whose baritonal qualities make his upper register seem more of an effort. What of Björling, whom many tout as the greatest of the century? If a grading system including tone, passion, and range were devised, he would finish high on anyone's list. What about Martinelli? Or Franco Corelli, whose stage fright rivaled Lanza's and whose high C, at times, seemed like the conclusion of a great inner struggle but whose overall performances were magnificent?

97

Caruso was great. Possibly, he was the greatest. But too much about him is mythical.

Gigli, hailed as his successor, begged that any comparison to Caruso was a desecration of something sacred and an insult to mankind. Martinelli, well beyond his prime at a party in 1967, responded to an opinion that Caruso's greatness rested more with his persona than his voice, as follows: "I grabbed the man by the lapel, looked him straight in the eye and said: 'You can take Gigli, Pertile, Lauri-Volpi, and me, roll us into one, and we would still be unfit to tie Caruso's shoelaces!'"[2]

Nonsense. An apt analogy is found in baseball: Babe Ruth was the first player to hit seven hundred home runs. Ruth was a demigod, legend, and icon. He was the first slugger, the so-called Sultan of Swat. Like Caruso, he was without a predecessor. When Hank Aaron overtook Ruth's record, he received death threats from some and jeers from many. But statistics are sacred to baseball, and Aaron hit 755 to Ruth's 714 home runs. Aaron's feat did not diminish Ruth's stature and effect on the game. Tenors do not accumulate statistics; everything about them is ultimately subjective, which makes for wonderful arguments.

Caruso had the unparalleled advantage of emerging as an original. He succeeded no one and set impressive standards for repertoire, diversity of major opera houses, and public acclaim, in large part because he was the first great tenor whose voice was recorded and therefore portable. The sounds made by the great singers who preceded him existed only in the memories of those who actually heard a performance. Reputations were built through reviews and by word of mouth, resulting in devoted but comparatively small and usually regional followings. Caruso's recordings were effective advance publicity. He was in demand wherever they were available, and they could be found wherever there was a major opera house or concert hall.

Of course, he possessed an impassioned voice and charismatic stage personality. He always gave solid-to-brilliant performances. His influence was immense, and he almost single-handedly put the Victrolas manufactured by the Victor Talking Machine Company in homes throughout the world.

Caruso's stature was also enhanced by the several decades through which excellent but comparatively less charismatic tenors reigned at the major opera houses. Gigli, a sometimes excellent technician whose presentation was more elegant that Caruso's, projected little of his so-called animal magnetism. John McCormack, who was quite popular despite a limited career in opera, was vocally inferior to Gigli and a woeful actor. Tito Schipa had personal appeal, but his refined sound lacked Caruso's masculine qualities. Martinelli was a great performer who came closer to Caruso's vitality than most. Björling was an exquisite tenor, somewhat unappreciated in his time, who also fell short in the area of sex appeal. All performed under the pall of being compared to Caruso.

Caruso was Rolls-Royce quality, Babe Ruth's most prodigious home run, the spectacle of the Empire State Building, and the grandeur of the Taj Mahal rolled into one. Even the poor recording technology of his time fueled his legend: many claimed that it was unfair to judge him based upon his recorded legacy, though it is possible to discern the quality of his voice from a careful review. The search for Enrico Caruso's successor was futile under such conditions. If the Great Caruso himself had reappeared, the public would have found him lacking.

When Mario Lanza starred in *That Midnight Kiss* and *The Toast of New Orleans*, the essence of his appeal was a thrilling and beautiful voice, a charismatic persona, and sex appeal in every quadrant. Even his critics agreed that he created more interest and excitement than any tenor since Caruso, making comparison inevitable. Worse, the publicity department at MGM saw nothing wrong with its reinventions of pedigree for those under contract.

First it was hinted that, because Caruso died and Lanza was born in 1921, God had passed Enrico's voice to Mario. Other mere coincidences were added to the mix: Mario was baptized by the Reverend Caruso; Giacomo Spadoni coached both singers; and Jesse Lasky, who produced Caruso's two films, acted as the titular co-producer on Lanza's next film. Some fans spout the rumors to this day. Mario, alternately rejecting and embracing the silliness, irrationally asserted that once in a hotel lounge, the great tenor had forbidden him to use "his" voice.[3] The comparison annoyed Lanza and, in truth, Caruso owed him the greater debt. The attention lavished on Mario and the numerous comparisons resulted in a reawakening of the Caruso legend. With the introduction of the LP in 1949, more of Caruso's recordings were sold after 1950 than for many years before.

The young tenor chafed under the constant comparison, nonetheless using Caruso as a yardstick. When he told Pasternak he was greater than Caruso, he was merely repeating what many others had told him. When he eventually failed to live up to his own promise, many critics were smug in trotting Caruso around the track again.

Both men were tremendously influential in their times, left enduring legacies, had magnificent voices, and sang with a vitality that excited their listeners. Caruso's venue was the opera and concert stage; Lanza excelled in film and on record. There is, however, little similarity in their voices. At his peak, Lanza ranged between a *tenore lirico* and a *tenore spinto*. Caruso ranged between a *tenore spinto* and a baritone. Enrico Caruso, Jr., had this to say regarding the man hailed as the American Caruso: "He imitated no one; his recordings of operatic selections are original interpretations. Let it not be forgotten that Mario Lanza excelled in both classical and light repertory, an accomplishment that was beyond even my father's exceptional talents."[4]

The curse of comparison with a demigod and myth would explode with Lanza's next triumph, MGM's grand spectacle, *The Great Caruso*.

CHAPTER 15

The Great Caruso

I can think of no other tenor, before or since Mario Lanza, who could have risen with comparable success to the challenge of playing Caruso in a screen biography.

Enrico Caruso, Jr.[1]

Jesse Lasky (1880–1958) had been everything from a Yukon goldminer to a Hawaiian bandleader before becoming a mostly successful film producer (notably, *Sergeant York*, 1941, and *Rhapsody in Blue*, 1945) and well-liked Hollywood man-about-town. He had produced two silent films starring Enrico Caruso. The first, *My Cousin*, was an improbable story of a sculptor who tells tall tales about his cousin, a supposedly great opera singer whom no one believes exists, until Enrico shows up to vindicate him. *My Cousin* caused a furor among exhibitors in the United States, forcing Lasky and his partner to pull it from distribution and refund rental fees, though it did reasonably well in England. His second Caruso film, *A Splendid Romance*, also did well in England. It was not released in the United States.

When *Rhapsody in Blue* premiered on 26 June 1945, at Warner Bros.' Hollywood Theatre on Broadway, Lasky was approached by Dorothy Caruso, Enrico's widow, who told him how much she had enjoyed the film. Lasky thanked her and mentioned that he intended to do a film about her husband's life, but that he had not yet begun research for the screenplay. Mrs. Caruso said he needn't bother; she had written a book, *Enrico Caruso: His Life and Death*, and would send him a copy.[2]

Lasky read the book and began negotiations, recklessly bidding $100,000 for a story in which the studios showed little interest. It was 1946 and opera had never been profitable in film, but the veteran producer, no stranger to creating a need for a product no one wanted, made the rounds. He dealt with a lack of a suitable star by stating that

Caruso's records would be used in the film with an unknown actor lip-synching the words, explaining that a widely recognized actor would make the project a harder sell and that audiences would readily embrace a newcomer.[3] Dorothy Caruso was convinced she should be played by Joan Fontaine. Lasky continued to peddle his concept to the studios, inspiring zero interest as no one could envision a marriage of plot, star, and voice.

Lasky heard Lanza's seminal 1947 concert at the Hollywood Bowl. He approached Louis B. Mayer, who eventually became interested in the project. In December 1949, MGM announced that it had acquired the rights to the Caruso biography and that Jesse Lasky would co-produce the film it intended to make.[4] Mario was enthusiastic about the project, and the studio began serious preparations within months. Dore Schary opposed the film, arguing that Lanza was too young for the role. Mayer pushed ahead, unaware that Schary was trying to undermine the project, behind the scenes, through Nick Schenck in New York. Schary's hatred of Lanza remains unfathomable. Truly, he was willing to sacrifice the best interests of his employer to thwart a man he personally loathed. The tenor was aware of the delays. He wanted the part very badly and angrily berated everyone but Mayer. "Who the hell do they think can play Caruso—Nelson Eddy? Nobody but me can play that role! I am Caruso!"[5]

In a move that must have been difficult for Lanza, he approached Schary and told him how much he wanted the part. Once again, the accuracy of the tenor's one-sided view was deadly: he was certain that the role would make him a great star. As usual, there was a downside to his thinking. Now that he was certain that he would become a great star, he demanded that he be treated like one. Schary explained that MGM could get along nicely without him. Finally, Schenck determined that the project should go ahead, even though its champion, Louis B. Mayer, had been dethroned.

The singer had been drinking and feasting, raising his weight to well above matinee-idol limits. Weight was a recurrent problem for the tenor. He looked his best at 170 pounds, but could soar to a chubby yet handsome 210, a frankly enormous 240, or a distorted and nearly unrecognizable 270 pounds plus. When the pounds vanished, it was always a sign that Lanza was ready to be productive. Conversely, weight gains were extreme, rapid—and harbingers of trouble.

When exposed to frustration or depressed, the tenor became hostile and overate to replicate what he knew, as a child, as love and for-
giveness. The situation was complicated by his belief that he needed
extra weight to record. He often refused to do more than one take when
slim and viewed himself as tireless when heavy. Obesity eventually
became a rationalization for failure, a means of escaping the anxieties
that came with the demands of stardom. He responded to routine pressures by ballooning, after he was expelled from high school, while in the
armed forces, and during nearly every year of his life after 1950. He
took great pride in his physique when slim and hated himself when fat.
He also had a great need to be accepted as he was, which was hopelessly
complicated by the rejection he experienced when heavy.

MGM rushed into production of *The Great Caruso* on 11 July
1950. *The Toast of New Orleans* had not yet premiered. Pre-production
activities included recording operatic selections ("Una furtiva lagrima,"
"Vesti la giubba," "Questa o quella," "La donna è mobile," "Recondita
armonia," "O tu che in seno agli angeli," "Parmi veder le lagrime,"
"Cielo e mar," and others) at Republic Studios for RCA with Constantine Callinicos conducting. The singer's career was moving so fast that
RCA released the album as *The Great Caruso*. It sold 100,000 copies
before the movie opened and became the first operatic LP to sell one
million copies. It remains widely accepted as the soundtrack for *The
Great Caruso* despite its containing no recording from the film and
only four titles sung during the movie. No recording featured in *The
Great Caruso* was released until 1998.[6]

Vocally, Lanza was at his peak, and the recordings for the film were
delivered with exceptional feeling. His musical instinct was extraordinary, his breath control something for any tenor to envy. It was the
young Lanza, freely demonstrating his wide range—producing pleas-
antly baritonal tones in his lower register—and vaulting effortlessly to
high C. Many find his aggressive approach to "Una furtiva lagrima"
incomparable, while others feel that he pressed too hard and lost the
poetic beauty of the piece. His "Cielo e mar" was fine and comparatively restrained, his "La donna è mobile" impassioned, and his performance on the famous quartet from *Rigoletto* unparalleled.[7] The
rest of the arias have seldom been sung with as much passion, vitality,
and sheer voice. Critics often lambaste Lanza for a tendency to force.
That he eventually did, but the young Lanza sang with a freedom of

range and original sense of interpretation that has seldom been equaled.

If there was a criticism to level at the album, it was that he strayed from his oft-proven ability to delicately shade his voice. He leaned toward Pagliacci on arias that called for Rodolfo and paid the price in some reviews.

Next, the singer had to lose weight. He rented a ranch owned by Ginger Rogers in Medford, Oregon, for six weeks of Spartan dieting and rigorous training, accompanied by the pregnant Betty, Colleen, a butler, Jack Keller (his press agent), and Terry Robinson. He was up early, ran, lifted weights, and cut back to a daily diet of three tomatoes, three hard-boiled eggs, and fruit juice, with an occasional steak. He also stopped drinking. When he returned to Hollywood, he was forty pounds lighter at just over 180.

Lanza prepared for the role by reading everything he could find about Caruso. He watched newsreels and earnestly questioned those who had known the Neapolitan tenor. When the cameras began to roll, Mario had adopted Caruso's habits, attitudes, walk, and mode of dress. He arrived at the studio in a homburg hat, spats, cane, and the broad stripes Caruso favored, though they were somewhat ostentatious even in his own time. Little touches, such as mounting a pocketwatch that supposedly belonged to the Neapolitan tenor on a wide, leather wristband, added a bit of whimsy to the scenario, but sporting such an outfit in July and August fell just short of ridiculous. The production became something of a legend on the MGM lot, with bystanders and the commissary abuzz about the tenor's latest stunt. If his name had been Brando, Dean, or Steiger, the behavior would have been ascribed to genius.

MGM assembled a good cast: Carl Benton Reid; Richard Hageman; Ludwig Donath, one of the few Lanza treated with respect and who was later blacklisted for alleged communist leanings; the dapper Alan Napier, cousin to Neville Chamberlain; and a gang of memorable character actors in bit parts. Richard Thorpe would direct. The leading lady? Ann Blyth, pretty, petite, and twenty-two years old, with a small but nice soprano was selected. She retired from films six years later and made occasional appearances in light opera and summer stock; she always spoke well of Mario.

Pasternak recalled it as the least troublesome of the tenor's films.

According to Lasky, "Contrary to all rumors and reports about his behavior, Mario Lanza cooperated beautifully and enthusiastically, displaying no unusual symptoms or tantrums."[8]

The crew, Mario's "little people," would not have agreed. He could be crude, arrogant, defiant, demanding, and hostile, berating some for imagined oversights and strutting as if his imminent stardom entitled him to behave as a despot. He overate and resumed drinking, again reporting to the set with the smell of alcohol on his breath. His weight fluctuated by twenty-five pounds through filming, causing costume department personnel to require oxygen. The onscreen gains and losses are noticeable but not troublesome.

The young star demanded that Peter Herman Adler, his old mentor from New York, be placed in charge of the operatic numbers; Johnny Green, whose scores were nominated for fourteen Oscars, directed the popular selections. Green considered himself upstaged and insulted by the newcomer, but it was another example of Mario's instinct for what would work best. Adler was worth his pay.

One morning Lanza was rehearsing with Adler and was unable to keep his voice from going sharp. Green, looking on from the control booth, abruptly activated the squawk-button and shouted for someone to get Lanza on key. The tenor's reaction was predictable. Green's retribution would be exacted during Lanza's next project.

Adler advised Pasternak that second-rate singers would make for a third-rate production and demanded talent from the Metropolitan Opera. The studio agreed and hired Blanche Thebom, the excellent mezzo-soprano; Jarmila Novotná, the fine Czech soprano; Giuseppe Valdengo; and Nicola Moscona. The studio also signed a second leading lady in Dorothy Kirsten, the beautiful soprano who was then at her peak.

The year ended with the birth of a second Lanza daughter, Ellisa, on 3 December 1950, and the elation of finishing the Caruso project. Lanza had sung fifteen solos and eight duets with one or more or the distinguished cast; even the chorus was comprised of singers from the Met. Mario regarded each performance as a physical challenge, not unlike a sparring partner trying for a knock-out of a champion. He used every bit of his range and correctly regarded the experience as the most important of his film career. Not long after, Adler pronounced Lanza the winner in his competition with the Metropolitan: "Mario made mincemeat out of them."[9]

Most of the Met stars praised him to his face, conceded his brilliance, and told him that he was advancing the cause of opera. Behind his back, some of them fumed about his late arrivals on the set and were aghast when he proclaimed, during playbacks, "Caruso never sang like that one day of his life!"[10] Dorothy Kirsten, who sang with and heard the best, recalled that he had to do multiple takes but always sounded magnificent. She described his voice as truly unique, a great gift, and was certain that he could have performed "in any opera house in the world."[11] She further remembered him as, at times, ill-mannered, and said that they never knew when or if he would show up on the set. (He missed two days in July, three in August, two in September, and two weeks in October because of a severely sprained ankle.)

The Great Caruso's storyline was weak: young tenor rises to international fame; falls in love; is rejected by the father of the woman he loves; marries; becomes quite happy; and dies at his peak while singing on an operatic stage. Frankly, any more story would have interfered with the gloriously exciting singing that was the movie's reason for being. Like Dorothy Caruso's book about her husband, it bore little resemblance to Caruso's actual life.

Enrico Caruso was born in Naples in 1873. His family was poor but not impoverished. Only three of the seven Caruso children made it to adulthood; the rest died young, possibly from causes related to the lack of sanitation in nineteenth-century Naples. Caruso's father was a mechanic who hoped that Enrico, who had a facility for the profession, would follow in his footsteps. His mother suffered from poor health and died in 1888.

Caruso was hardly an instant success as a singer. He performed at local cafes in his youth and seriously pursued vocal coaching. During his twenties, he avoided high C and routinely cracked on high B-flat. The young Caruso was described as exuberant, mirthful, and gentle, with infectious high spirits and animal magnetism. As late as 1897, the man who would soon become a millionaire could carry all his possessions in a brown paper bag. He made his Met debut in 1903, attracting only a decent review by Richard Aldrich in *The New York Times* (24 November 1903): "His voice is pure tenor in its quality of high range and of large power but inclined to take on the 'white' quality in its upper ranges when he lets it forth. In *mezza voce* it has expressiveness and flexibility, and when so used its beauty is apparent." He went on to tour the world and performed more than six hundred times at the Met.

Caruso's personal affairs were often in shambles. He maintained a long relationship with Italian soprano Ada Giachetti, who was the mother of Rodolfo and Enrico Caruso, Jr., forcing her to surrender her career in exchange for his company. He also had an affair with her sister, Rina, another soprano. In 1908 Ada Giachetti ran off with Cesare Romati, the family chauffeur, causing Caruso understandable disgrace. Enrico recklessly pursued several other relationships, never losing his status as the leading tenor in the world, whatever the scandal or however poor his judgment. He dodged marriage for most of his life and, when finally coaxed down the aisle at forty-five, did not choose wisely.

Caruso was burdened by a gift so great it was beyond his understanding. When he was not singing or promoting his career, it was difficult to keep him sensibly occupied. He alternated between generosity and extreme pettiness. He could be crude and embarrassing; kind, cordial and indulgent; or cruelly judgmental and temperamental over minor blunders. In many ways, Mario Lanza was well cast.

Dorothy Caruso married Enrico in 1918 and gave birth to his only daughter, Gloria, in 1919. She knew nothing of struggles and little of the triumphs of her husband's storied career. She met him when he was established and beyond his vocal peak and showed an innate capacity for spending his millions. When he died in 1921 from complications associated with pleurisy, she began the battle for his estate before his body reached room temperature. Dorothy was a young widow; though she married twice after Caruso's death, she retained his name, which opened many doors, and went on to live a handsome life with prestige that was pawned day by day. Much to her discredit, she assumed dominion over the story of her husband's life, though she knew very little about it, and wrangled with his sons to leave them as little as the courts would allow. Her book matched *The Great Caruso* for factual inaccuracy; its focus was the three years she spent with Enrico, eight months of which he spent as an invalid.

Dorothy Caruso later objected to the film, citing its inaccuracies and finding Lanza woefully inadequate in the role. Her criticisms can be discounted as the complaints of a woman with a borrowed identity and no independent claim to celebrity. Ultimately, she found it unbearable that the film dwarfed her book.

Where *The Great Caruso* absolutely succeeded was in conveying the rise, success, and excitement Caruso caused and experienced. The minutiae of his life was insignificant compared with his triumphs and influence—and for recreating the spirit of these things, the film was a masterpiece of its type. It premiered in Hollywood at the ornate Egyptian Theatre in April 1951 with Mario and Betty in attendance, dispelling rumors of a break-up over his extramarital escapades. The program announced "Caruso Sings Tonight" and the MGM pressbook touted Lanza as the only singer "who could capture the power and range of the voice of Caruso."

Now it was up to the audiences. At many theaters, people applauded after each aria and gave a standing ovation at the end. The film played at Radio City Music Hall in New York for a record ten-week run, grossing $1.5 million. It turned out to be MGM's biggest moneymaker for 1951 and one of its most profitable films of all time. Press releases reported that the American Caruso received $150,000 for *The Great Caruso*; studio records show he was paid $65,000.

As for the critics, most reviews were positive, calling Lanza's voice remarkable and the story weak. Comments on his acting were rare, which says a great deal about the thinness of the plot and the film's purpose as a vehicle for Lanza's singing. Bosley Crowther (*The New York Times*, 11 May 1951), pronounced *The Great Caruso* "perhaps the most lavish 'pops' concert ever. . . . Mr. Lanza has an excellent young tenor voice and he uses it in his many dramatic numbers with impressive dramatic power. . . . Something better—much better—as a story might have been contrived for the biography of Caruso, and something more subtle too." *Newsweek* (4 May 1951) wrote, "Lanza brings to the role a fine, natural, and remarkably powerful voice"; *Time* (21 May 1951) called Lanza's voice impressive but charged that the film was weak on facts and even weaker as fiction. John McCarten of *The New Yorker* (19 May 1951) sniped that Mario was "outgunned" by Met stars.

Enrico Caruso, Jr., a man with every reason to be less than objective, provided perhaps the most poignant critique decades later: "I can think of no other tenor, before or since Mario Lanza, who could have risen with comparable success to the challenge of playing Caruso in a screen biography."[12]

The film played to rapt audiences the world over. In the cultural exchange of 1960, it (along with *Marty* and *The Old Man and the Sea*) was sent to the U.S.S.R., where it played to huge crowds. It has weathered well, worldwide, in terms of rentals, exhibitions, and video sales. In Italy, where interest was understandably great, the Caruso family, offended by their lack of prominence in the film (his two sons were not even mentioned), claimed their reputation had been disparaged and sued, although they resented the free publicity their case provided. Thankfully, the family of Cesare Romati, the chauffeur who had cuckolded the great tenor, did not protest his lack of acknowledgment.

Tirenna Film Associata di Roma rushed into production with *Enrico Caruso: La Leggenda di Una Voce* (shown in English-speaking countries as *The Young Caruso*) starring Gina Lollobrigida, the curvaceous twenty-four-year-old Italian beauty, and featuring the voice of Mario del Monaco. If possible, the script was less factual than MGM's. Worse, it failed to convey any sense of Caruso's triumphant career. The film is long forgotten for one reason: in spite of del Monaco's long and illustrious career with the Met, his voice was no match for the other Mario's.

The Caruso family sought an injunction against both MGM and Tirenna. MGM was eventually ordered to withdraw all copies of the film from distribution in Italy and to pay the family 5 million lire (approximately $8000) in damages. The courts eventually relented and permitted *The Great Caruso* to be shown in Italy.

The Great Caruso brought excitement and a young audience to the stale venue of opera, which too often valued rigid form over individuality. Generations of opera fans can trace their initial interest to the film. Just as significantly, generations of singers have been influenced by Lanza's charismatic performance. Luciano Pavarotti has pinpointed his early aspirations to a sense of awe at hearing "Be My Love" and seeing *The Great Caruso* when he was a boy. Plácido Domingo, who saw the film as a youngster in Mexico, often cites it as a great influence on his career.[13] Even Roberto Alagna, the French-born Sicilian who has been touted as the king of the next generation of tenors, acknowledges Lanza as an early hero and initial source of his awareness of the heroic aspects of grand opera.

José Carreras, a seven-year-old boy in Barcelona when he saw *The Great Caruso*, willingly acknowledges Lanza's impact: "His wonderful voice and the charismatic appeal of his personality had a profound effect on my life, and I decided there and then that I too would one day sing the great operatic roles so persuasively portrayed on the screen by the young American tenor."[14] Carreras later struggled mightily to record *A Tribute to Mario Lanza* (Teldec 4509-92369-2, 1994), regarding the album as the payment of a long overdue debt and not wishing to discredit his idol in the process.

Hundreds of lesser known and thousands of unknown singers have been similarly influenced. *The Great Caruso* represents the zenith of Lanza's career. Through sheer momentum, his star would continue to soar.

CHAPTER 16

Triumphal Tour and the Coke Show

There is no chapter in my life entitled "My Struggle."
Mario Lanza, 1957[1]

The year 1951 began with incredible promise. *The Toast of New Orleans* continued to enthrall audiences, and by spring *The Great Caruso* began to pack Loew's theaters. "Be My Love" was an enormous hit, followed by "The Loveliest Night of the Year" from *The Great Caruso*. Remarkable recordings of "Serenade" (Toselli's as well as Drigo's compositions) and "Because," also from *The Great Caruso*, were well received. RCA's latest album was difficult to keep in stock; Lanza's record royalties would approach $1 million for the year.

Mario had surrendered the hardwon victory achieved at Ginger Rogers' ranch, feasting and drinking until his weight neared 230 pounds. He ate enormous breakfasts, often skipped lunch (rationalizing that to do so was a form of dieting), and then proceeded to consume evening meals that would have made a lumberjack cry for mercy.

Callinicos was scheduled to accompany Mario on a tour booked by Columbia Artists. It was scheduled to begin mid-February, but with Lanza still enormous in mid-January, another grueling diet and exercise regimen began, this time in a secluded, rambling home near Palm Springs. Weiler, sufficiently alarmed by the vast number of empty beer bottles left in his client's wake, joined Callinicos and Terry Robinson in overseeing the project. Once again, Mario followed a Spartan regimen, eating lightly and exercising heavily. His mood was elevated, and he actually enjoyed the torturous routine.

Terry Robinson pushed Mario. Lanza loved running into and up the hills around Palm Springs, correctly theorizing that it brought the weight down while improving his breath control. When the climb was finished, he absorbed the vista and sang toward the hills. He was fascinated with hearing his voice echo and reverberate. "This is the only way to live, Costa. The healthy road is the right road," Mario assured his friend.[2] They rehearsed daily, and when they left Palm Springs on 11 February, he was bullish and fit at just under 200 pounds.

Concerts were scheduled in Philadelphia, Pittsburgh, and Scranton, Pennsylvania; Utica, New York; Richmond; Columbus, Toledo, and Cincinnati, Ohio; Miami, Orlando, Tampa, and Daytona, Florida; Baltimore; New Orleans; Milwaukee; Chicago; St. Louis; Wichita; Kansas City; Omaha; Ogden, Utah; and Fresno, California. Lanza made twenty-two of the twenty-three scheduled concerts, often attired in the dreaded tuxedo and black-tie, and adhered to high artistic standards throughout. The opening date in Scranton, 16 February 1951, set the tone for the entire tour.

The five thousand seats for the concert had been sold out for a month and even the 567 standing room tickets went at a premium. Mario and Betty had driven down from New York; when they arrived at city hall, their car was mobbed by hundreds of fans and Mayor Hanlon presented Mario with the keys to the city. Then it was interviews, more jostling and tearing, and an autograph session at a local department store, where a riot nearly erupted. Women surged toward the store, crowded into the aisles, and stood on counters, washing machines, and furniture in order to get a better look at their idol. Some shouted requests for songs, others suggested that they were the answer to "Be My Love." They rushed forward, clutched at him, tore his clothes, or simply tried to touch him. The police were called to restore order. The concert itself was almost anticlimactic; it received rave reviews and remained, for decades, a warm remembrance for many in Scranton.

The program for the tour did not vary: four serious selections (Lamento di Federico, "Già il sole del Gange," "Pietà, Signore," and "Vesti la giubba"); three Neapolitan songs ("Marechiare," "'A Vucchella," and "La danza"); three popular songs ("The House on the Hill," "Softly, As in a Morning Sunrise," and "I'm Falling in Love with Someone"); a novelty piece ("Bonjour ma belle"); and six long piano solos by Callinicos. The encores, which were in truth what the audiences came to hear, usually included "Be My Love," "La donna è mobile," and "Because."

In Richmond, a sellout crowd of four thousand was thrilled by another brilliant performance. The thirty-eight hundred seats for the concert in Pittsburgh had sold out within forty-eight hours, prompting Edward Specter, the manager of the Pittsburgh Symphony, to offer tickets for the tenor's afternoon rehearsal. The two thousand tickets were quickly sold. Some ticketholders found other patrons willing to pay handsomely for the privilege of hearing a single aria. The audience at his afternoon rehearsal was loud and unruly. Many in attendance were the so-called bobbysoxers of the time. Conductor Vladimir Bakaleinikoff interrupted what was becoming an impossible situation, admonishing the audience to "shut up!"[3] The continued attention from his distaff fans fascinated the tenor.

Time (19 March 1951) pronounced the evening concert a success: "Mario proved to the cynics' surprise that he really has a voice. The ring and power of his high notes makes up for his lack of musical taste. Called back for cheer after cheer, Mario gave then as an encore his current best-seller, 'Be My Love.'"

The tour continued. Weiler and Betty dropped in and out, but Terry Robinson and Costa were along for most of the ride. The mild-mannered Greek, whose patience would have made Job seem like a blustering bully, coaxed the best performances from his friend, who still agonized over his upper register and worried about forgetting the words before every performance. Mario meant it when he beamed at Costa and said, "What a team!"[4]

Though his income exceeded $25,000 a week during 1951, Mario particularly relished the revenue derived from the sale of programs at each of his concerts. Terry Robinson usually recruited a boy scout troop to handle the task. Lanza plugged his latest RCA release ("Because") and the programs by dedicating the song to Terry in honor of what became his ever-recurring birthday. After each concert, the tenor emptied the canvas sacks of bills and coins onto his bed, giddy about the only money he earned from which no managers or agents exacted their percentages.

On 13 March 1951 Mario appeared at the Academy of Music in Philadelphia, where he was given a hero's welcome by a sellout crowd that included hundreds of standing-room patrons. Even the onstage seating, arranged especially for his concert, had been totally filled. The tenor, always acutely aware of the surroundings wherever he sang—be it an auditorium or a recording studio—spotted and acknowledged his boyhood pal, Eddie Durso. He gave a fine performance, delighting the hometown crowd.

Opera critic Max de Schauensee was in attendance. He chided the tenor for his informal, Vegas-style stage demeanor, but Lanza was performing within blocks of where he had been raised and the audience was out to have fun with a local boy who had made good. De Schauensee found minor fault with the tenor's lack of delicacy and excessive *fortissimo*, but admitted that the concert was an immensely entertaining experience and that Mario Lanza's fine tenor voice more than filled the Philadelphia Academy.

When the entourage arrived for the next concert in Miami, the singer was concerned about the heat in the concert hall, which was not air-conditioned. He took the stage, acknowledged the applause, and started to undo his tie. "You know," he began, "singing is supposed to be fun. I don't know why they insist we wear these things."[5] He urged the men in the audience to remove their ties and loosen their collars. Then he advised the ladies to adjust their corsets and relax. They loved him for it, but he received mixed reviews from critics, who wrote that they expected more from the great Mario Lanza.

The tour continued in Baltimore, where the concert was sold out seven weeks in advance; in Chicago, one thousand tickets were sold by word of mouth. The crowds rushed him, tore at his clothing, and made souvenirs of his handkerchiefs, ties, and scarves. Some critics took umbrage at his habit of acknowledging applause by clasping his hands together, above his head, in a pose not unlike that of a victorious boxer, and the shameless plugs for his latest record or film—but the frenzied audiences adored him. He sang without a microphone in large halls and drew good reviews for the power of his voice throughout the tour. Pronouncing Lanza's circuit the "hottest long hair draw" with "a $177,200 gross in 22 cities," *Variety* (9 May 1951) trumpeted, "No single artist has come anywhere near this box-office record."

The tour ended on 13 April 1951, the Lanzas' sixth wedding anniversary. Mario returned to California, where his wife had managed another complete turnover of household staff, save for the dignified Johnny Mobley. Mario rented a place to escape to, with members of both sexes, on Catalina Island, bought Terry Robinson a Chevrolet convertible, gave away watches like they were mints, and presented his parents with a fine home overlooking the ocean at 622 Toyopa Drive in Pacific Palisades. The immediate advantage was the fifteen miles it placed between Betty and Mary, though Terry, who still resided with the Cocozzas, quickly learned the downside with the increased drive. If things could go better, no one knew where the improvements could be made.

Though the press wrote them off as cheap publicity stunts, Lanza performed good deeds for no purpose beyond the pleasure he derived from them. He was a regular volunteer for bond drives and Easter Seal campaigns and always had time for the sick children who visited his sets. He spent enormous amounts of time and money on telephone calls to people who were hospitalized, responded to the volume of fan mail MGM refused to handle, and sent autographed photos to anyone who made a request. At first, Betty insisted that she manage the mail. When she began to hide sacks full of letters, secretaries were hired. The "autographed" photos posed a different dilemma. Mario signed many that were sent out. The tenor's signature is easily distinguishable, with its jagged "M" and Lanza's love of violet, green, or white inks. Mary, ever eager to share in her son's career, signed almost as many with her softer "M," in conventional inks.

Callinicos remembered that his friend could be moved to tears by the sight of a blind man begging for coins.[6] Later in his career, Mario insisted that extras and the crew on the set of one of his films be served the same meals as the cast rather than the hard roll and slice of prosciutto they were accustomed to eating: "What's the good of being a star if you can't do something for those poor suckers? At least I don't have to sit around choking on my food because everyone is sitting around hungry watching me eat."[7] The studio charged him for the extra cost.

Terry Robinson answered the phone at the Lanza home when Josephine Fasano called to ask if the singer would speak to her ten-year-old daughter, Raphaela, who was dying of leukemia. The young girl greatly admired the tenor, Josephine explained, and her dearest wish was to hear him sing. Robinson said that he would pass the message along. Mrs. Fasano assumed that was the end of it.

The next afternoon, Mario placed a person-to-person call from Hollywood to Raphaela in Newark, New Jersey. When connected, the highest-paid singer in the world delivered a ten-minute concert, raising the young girl's spirits considerably. To celebrate her eleventh birthday, he arranged for Raphaela, her mother, and a private nurse to be flown to Los Angeles. Raphaela spent five days at the Lanza home, attended a special party at the studio, and was showered with gifts and love by her idol. Mario called her nearly every Friday evening until 30 January 1953, when her father informed him that she had passed away. The tenor was genuinely grief-stricken by the news and remained so for several weeks. When the young girl was interred, one of Mario's last gifts— a sterling silver medal of the Immaculate Conception—was around her neck. There was much that was genuinely good about the man.

In June 1951, Lanza signed a contract with Diary Advertising, Inc., for a weekly radio show sponsored by Coca-Cola on CBS. He was paid $5300 per week; Sam Weiler received his 20 percent commission of the gross plus another $500 per week for phantom duties as producer. With his remaining $3740, Mario was responsible for overtime costs, which were substantial with a thirty-five piece orchestra, studio time, and engineering personnel. Lanza's net was often not much more, and at times less, than Weiler's guaranteed $1560 per week, demonstrating his lack of business acumen, naiveté, and unerring ability to gravitate toward the wrong management personnel.

Mario's gross earnings were always chiseled away by commissions for slipshod or nonexistent services and a payroll for people who advanced themselves rather than the tenor's career. He always rented homes, never realizing that his name did not appear on the deed of the one he claimed to own.[8] In addition, his operating costs for food, liquor, and household personnel were high. His gross was enough to support competent career management, a grand lifestyle, and a solid investment program. The spongers, the chiselers, and the bad contracts robbed him of the ability to invest, meaning that he lived his life with little surplus and frequent cash shortages.

Ben Barrett, a legend in the music business who touched the careers of everyone from Garland to Presley, was the contractor for the Coke Show. "Ben respected intelligence and talent," his widow Rita related, "and he thought Mario extraordinary."[9] Barrett assembled a first-rate orchestra comprised of some of the best musicians available in Hollywood. The Coke Show recording sessions took place in the Radio Recorder's Annex, a relatively small studio, during the evening. It was a side-gig for nearly all the musicians and the overtime came regularly; Harold Diner, a trombonist with the Coke Show orchestra, called an addition to his home the Mario Lanza Room, in honor of the man who "payrolled" its construction.[10]

Ray Sinatra was hired to conduct the sessions. Lanza eventually realized that the Sinatra-Lanza combination was less than ideal on the operatic and Neapolitan selections, resulting in a call to his old friend, Constantine Callinicos, after twenty-three shows. Ray Sinatra was not overly troubled as he continued to conduct the ballads and drew the same rate of pay. The tenor absorbed the costs of an extra conductor.

Fifty-nine broadcasts of the *Coca-Cola Radio Show* took place between 26 June 1951 and 22 August 1952. Typically the format included three or four songs by Lanza and two by a guest artist, usually popular Canadian singer-violinist Gisele MacKenzie. The show was transcribed with introductions and applause tracks added after acceptable "takes" had been recorded. The reason? Mario could not, with the time-consuming requirements of his film career, learn the score, work through each piece with piano accompaniment, and proceed to a live performance with reliability. Instead, he learned the arrangements prior to coming to the studio and, after arriving, used the three hours of recording time to get his approximately twelve minutes of singing down. Once all the pieces were in place, the unique Lanza artistry prevailed.

Harold Diner remembers Mario bursting into the recording studio shouting, "Fuck MGM!" He was always accompanied by Terry Robinson, who stood to the side of the stage and handed the singer a flask from time to time. When asked what was in the flask, Terry Robinson laughed and insisted the "thermos" contained something to soothe the tenor's throat, though he added that, if the whisky was missing, Mario would groan and demand, "Who's been talking to you—Robinson?"[11]

Diner, who played on recording sessions with Mel Tormé, Jan Peerce, Judy Garland, Danny Kaye, Milton Berle, Ella Fitzgerald, Kate Smith, Frank Sinatra, Plácido Domingo, Barbra Streisand, and many others, recalled that Mario was "a beautiful looking guy" but a poor musician. He acknowledged that Lanza had a great ear and could cue himself in and out of a song and usually remain on key, but said it was difficult for him to master a song and "get it right." Diner described a session where Lanza sang "Be My Love." Legendary trombonist Joe Howard turned to Diner when the song was finished. "Look at me," he shuddered. "I've been in this business for years and heard them all. I've got goosebumps!"

Diner explained that, in his experience, big band singers like Doris Day and Frank Sinatra recorded close to the mike while operatic performers like Jan Peerce sang well away from it. Mario moved in and out, depending on his volume, with natural instinct. Diner noticed that Mario's musicianship improved as the show progressed. Production values were high; he described the tenor as very concerned about the quality of the finished product, patient, and easy to work with. As an example, Diner remembered ruining what had been a good take by accidentally kicking a mute. It had been a long session and the sound engineers were livid, but the singer took it in stride.

"He always sounded beautiful," Diner said. "It was a glorious voice. Just beautiful. Usually, you can't hear the singer in the brass section. But I could hear Mario. He never sounded bad." When pressed to compare Lanza with Peerce or Domingo, Diner responded, "The voices were different. Mario had passion. I don't think of him as an opera singer. I think of him as a guy who happened to sing opera. He could sing an aria or a ballad, tunes an opera singer can't handle. . . . With Mario, there was a rush. It was just a beautiful voice to hear."

Diner recalled the rumors about the tenor's behavior at MGM but insisted he never saw it during the recording sessions. Diner's wife remembered Lanza as a handsome man who was bullishly built and acutely aware of who was in the studio and what was occurring: "He had beautiful, dark eyes, and he had a way of looking at a woman— undressing you with those eyes—that I never experienced with anyone else. Even today, when I think of it, it's eerie."[12]

According to Gerald Vinci, a violinist with a strong background in classical music and member of the Coke Show orchestra, "Mario was a jewel in the rough. It was a God-given, gorgeous voice. He was a bum— what we call a *cafone*. There was no class there." He too remembered Lanza's patience during recording sessions; he never blamed anyone for an error whereas Sinatra would blow a take, explode, and "blame it on everyone else."[13]

"Mario took advice," Vinci noted. "He was a lousy musician. He couldn't count and didn't know what a half-dot meant. That makes it tough to build a repertoire. There weren't any delays in recording though. He had a wonderful ear. Once he memorized the words, music, and tempo, he'd cue himself in and out." The violinist never forgot Lanza's coarse language:

> If it wasn't ["Fuck MGM!"] it was *"Viva la fica!"* [roughly trans-
> lated, long live the vagina] every three minutes, like we'd never
> heard it before. He was like a little kid. Sometimes he'd hide a
> pornographic picture in Gisele MacKenzie's sheet music and wait
> for her to turn a page and see it. Just like a kid!

But Vinci also remembered the voice:

> Pavarotti gets the most from what he has. Mario had a lovely
> instrument. A glorious voice. He owned his voice and knew what
> it would do to others. I used to watch the people in the studio and
> how disgusted they were with his behavior. When he sang, every-
> thing changed. They were in awe.

When asked about his best memory, the violinist described Lanza's
Coke Show rendition of "The Lord's Prayer" as "earth-shaking, just
earth-shaking," adding, "Mario had good taste. The producers wanted
a big finish. He would protest, 'This is a hymn. A high B flat doesn't
fit,' but that's what they wanted."

Vinci, who also recorded with Merrill, Peerce, and Tucker, opined
that all singers, even Caruso, have flaws. Like Diner, he remembered
Peerce as a great musician and described Tucker as a serious craftsman. "Mario had a simply glorious, passionate, Italian tenor, but he
wasn't a musician," Vinci ruminated, "but Mario's timbre was greater."
Vinci also recalled the flashy clothing, the tremendous weight gains,
and the tenor's occasional announcement: "I will not likely live long."

The Coke Show recordings were never intended for commercial
release. The variety of material was astounding, with everything from
Cole Porter to Giacomo Puccini, Romberg to Tosti, Rodgers and Hammerstein to DeCurtis. Lanza handled the shift in vocal styles with the
versatility that remains part of his unique legacy, producing many
exquisite recordings ("Non ti scordar di me," "Santa Lucia," "You'll
Never Walk Alone"), a variety of original interpretations ("And Here
You Are," "The Hills of Home," "La Spagnola"), and a few cuts that
were, for whatever reason, simply over the top ("Song of Songs,"
"Somewhere a Voice Is Calling," "Santa Lucia luntana"). Although the
productions were not second-rate, the orchestra was smaller and the
sessions more rushed than they would have been for an album. The
163 Coke Show recordings, made during Lanza's peak years of 1951
and 1952, represent a disproportionate percentage of his production;

his studio output totaled but twenty-five recordings for the same period and 203 for his entire career. But the compressed schedule demanded an entirely spontaneous approach, resulting in an ultimately splendid display that no other tenor has matched.

The Lanza home on Whittier Drive was always packed with a few friends and many moochers. As Gerald Vinci put it, "There were fifty guys on Mario's back every five minutes, and all of them wanted something." The money rolled in like the surf at nearby Malibu: steady, heavy, and seemingly endless. His earnings exceeded $1.4 million for 1951, making it a very good year for Sam Weiler and the Internal Revenue Service. The thirty-year-old tenor was proud of the fact that all bills, commissions, and his tax debt of $425,000 were paid in full. He loved his two little girls immensely, and for him, life seemed perfect.

In the East, Eddie Fisher was about to get the break of his life as Mario Lanza's replacement on the *Coca-Cola Radio Show*. Diner remembers that musicians called Fisher "Little Boy Lost" because he couldn't stay in tune or remain with the meter; the man he replaced would lose his way in more significant areas.

CHAPTER 17

Lanza and the Critics

I was one of the many opera lovers who seriously undervalued the
tenor while he was alive.

Robin May[1]

On 6 August 1951, *Time Magazine's* cover featured a caricature of
Lanza, Enrico Caruso, and a winding road of staffs, bars, and notes. Its
subtitle—"Would Caruso Fracture 'em in Scranton?"—gave a strong
hint of what was inside. The cover story on the hottest tenor in the
world, titled "Million Dollar Voice," was, in fact, vicious. While there
was much to criticize about the tenor's personal life and habits, it
demeaned even his voice, asking rhetorically if he was already headed
for failure. *Time* waged a merciless campaign to warn the public about
what it viewed as Mario Lanza's vulgarization of opera.

The story was devastating to Mario, chiding him for his reading
preferences, which included film and weightlifting magazines, and
accusing him of outright lying about offers from the Met. Rudolf Bing,
the manager of the New York Metropolitan Opera from 1950 to 1972,
hated the Hollywood Caruso; he felt that Lanza's films cheapened legitimate opera and regarded the idea of Mario Lanza at the Met as high
humor. In 1946 Bing's predecessor, Edward Johnson, had made inquiries about the young tenor. Lanza may have represented this interest as more current and formal than it had been, but Bing's outright
denial was less accurate than the tenor's exaggerations. It was now fashionable for classical music critics to disown Lanza. Many, including
Time, scoffed at the notion of Mario Lanza being courted by the Met.
Even today, critics unaware of Lanza's stature during the 1940s, jeer at
the suggestion.

Time admitted that even the critics were impressed by his vocal
power and breadth of range, but cautioned that their integration was

inconsistent. The magazine could not accept that Lanza had achieved so much notoriety without the painstaking training and discipline endured by singers such as Gigli, Tucker, and Peerce—all three lesser known and lower paid than the man portrayed in its pages as a bumptious delinquent from South Philadelphia. José Carreras called Lanza's achievement, at thirty, "an astonishing feat in itself and a pointed reminder to his critics, who felt he was shortchanging a God-given talent."[2] Even Caruso believed that a tenor, before thirty, possessed neither the emotional comprehension nor the technical competence to do great things.[3]

When asked if he had heard Lanza sing while he was training in New York during the 1940s, Maestro Julius Rudel responded, "No. But I wish I had."[4] He pronounced Lanza's voice excellent and observed that there was no reason the tenor could not have performed at the Met in roles compatible with his voice and "intuitive" musicianship. The Maestro, who conducted for or heard the great voices of the last four decades, also noted that Frances Yeend and George London, the tenor's Bel Canto associates, were "legitimate" talents with "substantial voices" and that Lanza had earned his spot: "They did not pull him along."

Time, and many critics, berated him for forcing his upper register. *Time* did not deny that the voice was big and expansive, rather that it was undisciplined and untrained. Neither Lanza nor his voice would ever be disciplined or trained, but his voice was settled, his phrasing and diction excellent (with a few noteworthy exceptions when he had been drinking or simply forgot the words), his range and timbre beautiful and wide, and his breath control extraordinary. Giacomo Spadoni remembers the tenor easily vaulting to the D-flat above high C and handling a low A that even some baritones fret over. Twenty-two years after the feature in *Time*, British critic Charles Osborne summarized the basis for the criticism leveled at the tenor: "It used to be fashionable to adopt a snobbish attitude to Lanza's performances of opera in films and on discs. As far as I know, he never appeared in opera . . . but he certainly could have."[5]

By August 1951, Lanza had completed the finest of his operatic recordings for RCA. He was at his peak, though he retained a magnificent voice and could produce memorable recordings even on his last day in a studio—when circumstance and his health and sobriety coincided. The excessive criticism, which the feature in *Time* typifies, shows the depth of the resentment over the tenor's rapid rise and sudden impact.

First, the critics charged that he was untrained. That Lanza failed to directly absorb musical theory is undeniable, and it is true that his legitimate training ended with his ascendancy in Hollywood. But his early influences, the sounds of great voices on records, remained indelible, and he did receive good instruction from Irene Williams and Rosati. He was not the totally untrained upstart of rumor. Further, everyone who worked with him found his natural instincts remarkable.

Second, many claimed that his voice was small, nothing more than the product of amplification, overdubbing, and electronic wizardry. That criticism is countered by remarks made by Robert Merrill, Sammy Cahn, Frank Sinatra, Dorothy Kirsten, Licia Albanese, Peter Herman Adler, Tito Schipa, Max de Schauensee, and others who heard him live. Arthur Cosenza scoffed at the notion: "Small voice? Not the Lanza I knew! He had one of the finest voices of the generation, though technically speaking, he left a lot to be desired. I never heard a clearer lyric tenor. Never!"[6]

John Coast, the European agent for Lanza and Louise Marshall, the exquisite Yugoslavian soprano, concurred. He commented—after hearing Mario well past his peak—that Lanza's was the most compelling and powerful voice he had ever heard. Coast also noted that Lanza could shade his voice with a magnificent, soft *piano*, that his ownership of the voice was complete. Like many others, Coast also expressed frustration at hearing such a superb voice holding an audience rapt but not put to its greatest use in opera. Nonetheless, the criticisms regarding a "small" or "amplified" voice are baseless. Home recordings from 1951 show conversation among Betty, Colleen, Mario, Mary Cocozza, and Constantine Callinicos at typical levels and Lanza blasting high notes with impressive volume. The same sound engineers who produced Peerce and Björling worked with Mario, using the same equipment and techniques.

The third criticism, that he made his records in bits and pieces, is a gross distortion based upon isolated circumstances, usually attributable to the singer's condition on the day of the session. Through 1951, when he approached the microphone in a recording studio, he was a "one take" recording artist; he resorted to second "takes" only later in his career, and then only seldom.

The fourth fault touted by some critics—that he lacked musical taste and forced his high notes—is the problem of a legacy so heavily weighted with Coke Show material. The worst examples of "forcing" were on his Coke Show recordings, usually at the request of producers; occasionally he finished with a note that would have made even a morning-shower tenor from Paducah wince. Retakes would have occurred during a more demanding album session.

Lanza's recording log contains a wide repertory, with many examples of restrained and tasteful singing, unmatched by any other tenor, in three mediums: romantic ballads, opera, and Neapolitan songs. Mario's recordings were often unconventional, but they were nearly always passionate and exciting. His style, unique and often unrestrained, has been a source of joy for many, though some regarded it as a tragic misuse of a great talent. Metropolitan Opera soprano Licia Albanese said, "He always sang with his heart on his lips."[7]

Lanza knew when things were out of control—and firmly believed that he remained within proper form and constraint. At times, he was intelligent and insightful about his voice and could discuss his shortcomings. He was also an astute judge of other tenors. He assessed Björling as masterful in his knowledge of how to use the voice; called di Stefano's lyric tenor beautiful; and wondered about del Monaco's success in view of what he regarded as terrible diction.

Lastly, many critics refused to consider the tenor because of his relative lack of operatic training and experience. That he never achieved a career in opera cannot be denied. He always intended to get to it next year, but that option ran out too soon. Peter Herman Adler, always a concerned friend, observed, in 1951: "There is still time. Ten years with the right opera company, and no one could compare with him. But who can expect him, after being a star, to go back to learning?"[8]

Mario Lanza portrayed an operatic tenor in his films so effectively that he was compared with or considered to be among those who sang on the great opera stages, which caused resentment with many critics. Much praised by his fans, peers, and some critics, he added to the situation by strutting, posing, and boasting. Lanza's venue was the recording studio and film; whenever the element of operatic experience is added to the equation, he must be discounted. But all we have by which to remember any singer are recordings and film, whether it be of studio sessions or live performances.

Mario Lanza left an adequate body of evidence from which to assess his artistry. As Maestro Julius Rudel observed, "I believe that talent finds its own direction, and that is what happened with him. You know, he is remembered beyond his contemporaries—those who had perhaps more legitimate careers—which is not a small achievement."

Time ghoulishly predicted that his voice would be ruined by mid-decade. They were only almost right.

CHAPTER 18

Because You're Mine

This is a piece of junk!

Mario Lanza, 1951[1]

Lanza handled the pressures of fame poorly, retreating to the defenses of obesity and hostile, antisocial behavior. His exceptional verbal skills made for volleys of obscene phrases that would have emptied the rowdiest saloon on the old Barbary Coast. He developed a coarseness of language that went beyond mere cursing, literally crafting obscenity with sight, sound, anatomy, and scent in a manner that degraded both him and the listener. The target of his tirades was often a mythical mother-in-law or sister-in-law; once a woman was identified as a "mother" or a "sister," he immediately became chivalrous.

Betty grew more and more resentful of the attention her husband received and retreated deeper into the defenses of alcohol, drugs, and wholesale firings of household staff. She was absolutely taken with her status as the wife of a film star. She had the misfortune of equating marriage with stardom and was inevitably disappointed when fans rushed by her to get at Mario. She berated him for getting all the credit, hurled vicious insults about his relationship with Mary, shrieking that a psychiatrist would find it enough for a conference, and demanded a life of chauffeurs, upstairs and downstairs maids, a private masseuse, and nurses for the children. Betty had come a long way from her days in Chicago, and not much of the journey represented an advance.

Her husband was drinking more than ever and carelessly bedding everything that came his way. He developed the expensive habit of promising film parts to or procuring silence from his consorts, dropping thousands of dollars in a round robin of cheap hotels and faces without names. His pace was too hectic for secrecy, leading to bitter accusations from Betty. Their arguments became violent, with lamps, dishes, furniture, glassware, and bric-a-brac smashed or thrown. The outcome was usually another retreat to the bedroom for Betty and a night on the town for Mario. He had mixed feelings about his wife's increasing periods of incapacitation. On the one hand, he realized that much was being neglected in his home. But with Betty in a stupor, he was free to pursue women of negotiable virtue without interference or incessant nagging.

Surrounded by lackeys and sycophants who told him anything he wanted to hear, Lanza began to disavow responsibility for his voice, claiming that it was a gift from God, that he was merely its caretaker, and that it simply passed through him.[2] Amidst such heady views, and supported by those well paid to pad his ego, Joe Pasternak proposed the project Mario hated more than any other endeavor of his career.

When MGM signed the tenor, he was a concert artist on the way up, a favorite with the critics, and a man whose goal was the Met. But now, in his view, with two introductory films and *The Great Caruso* under his belt, he had arrived as an operatic film artist. Once again, Lanza was right: it was time to follow *Caruso* with another heavyweight dose of opera folded into a grand costume musical. Pasternak was not interested in the path Mario had been traveling when he signed with the studio. He agreed that *The Great Caruso* needed a quick follow-up, but his idea was weak: a tale "about a singer who is drafted into the army, doesn't like it, and finally is a better person for learning to be human like everybody else."[3] Mario exploded. "This is the worst piece of shit I ever heard. . . . You can make the goddamn picture without me!"[4]

Pasternak made things worse by telling the tenor that MGM had taken him from nothing, nurtured him, and made him a star. The singer—through whom God supposedly passed—exploded again, sharing credit with no producer, director, studio, or deity: he was the star.

It seemed to escape him, but MGM had scraped bottom with cruel parodies of his life and habits in *That Midnight Kiss* and *The Toast of New Orleans*. Now Pasternak wanted him to replicate his experiences by portraying a pop singer whose career is interrupted by induction into the armed forces, which Lanza regarded as the lowest period of his life. The singer had made no secret of his hatred for the military, and the role seemed like nothing so much as an expression of a screenwriter's animosity toward the star, a quick, low-budget follow-up to *The Great Caruso*. Even Sam Weiler disliked the part, though he again failed to function as a manager by representing his client's interests with the studio. If the irate star had approached Pasternak in a rational manner, a compromise might have been reached. Then again, if he had taken a logical approach, he would not have been Mario Lanza.

MGM was stunned by the inroads from television and was slow to react to the changes it brought to the world of entertainment. It responded by trimming costs and continuing to denigrate what it viewed as a fad. The studio had a roster of aging, high-priced stars who were no longer paying their way, and the word from Nick Schenck was that everything and everyone must operate at a profit—even Clark Gable would be released in 1954. That directive, combined with Dore Schary's hatred of Lanza, meant that the studio would not reconsider its plans. When MGM stood firm against the star, humiliating him with a role written to accomplish that end, the singer reacted with the hatred and rebellion against authority he had developed during childhood: he would make the film but endeavor to become the most difficult star in the history of Hollywood. Records of such things are difficult to quantify, but he was named the most uncooperative star of 1952 by the Hollywood Press-Writers Association. If and when a lifetime award is given, he merits strong consideration.

The production—originally titled *The Big Cast* but renamed *Because You're Mine* in order to capitalize on a marginal Brodszky-Cahn composition that Lanza turned into a big hit—was scheduled to begin on 15 May 1951, to coincide with the excitement caused by the nationwide premiere of *The Great Caruso*.

The casting was disastrous. The Korean conflict was in full swing and the World War II veterans were still young men, so sappy GI stories were viable. But Lanza was thirty, which was too old for a newly conscripted private. It figured that the studio would not grant him the dignity of playing an officer, making the concept all the more a waste of Lanza's surefire, box-office appeal. Finding a leading lady to star opposite the temperamental tenor was not unlike trying to solicit letters of endorsement for Adolf Hitler from responsible citizens. His reputation for vile conversation and crude behavior caused even actresses down on their luck to shudder and refuse. Kathryn Grayson was available, but she wisely stood by her vow. Mario wanted Lana Turner. Pasternak rejected her; the part called for someone who could sing. Joe selected Doretta Morrow, a New York City–born singer-actress whose stage credits included a successful stint in *The King and I* at the St. James Theater in 1951. She had never appeared in a movie—and she had been educated in a Venetian convent.

The tenor took an immediate dislike to Morrow, complaining that she was not sexy enough and that no one would believe her as the woman who lured him away from someone else.[5] He also complained about her incessant smoking, finding her stale, tobacco odor intolerable during their intimate scenes. Pasternak again held firm. Instead of making the best of the situation and trying to contribute to the production of a decent picture, Lanza's behavior toward Morrow would have been enough to make the fiercest wolverine scamper for cover. He later claimed that his Hollywood outbursts were geared to upgrade the finished product.

MGM presented Alexander Hall (notably, *Here Comes Mr. Jordan* and *Bedtime Story*) with the unenviable task of refereeing its recalcitrant star and protecting the rest of the cast, which included durable actor-pitchman James Whitmore, Paula Corday, Jeff Donnell, Spring Byington, and Bobby Van. Johnny Green was the musical director and veteran cinematographer Joseph Ruttenberg, who regarded Lanza as the biggest pest of his seventy-nine-film career, handled the lighting and photography. Ignoring his own rollercoaster weight gains and losses during filming, the singer later berated Ruttenberg, claiming it was his faulty camera angles that made him look heavy in *Because You're Mine*.

The tenor had been cooperative during the production of *That Midnight Kiss* but, during the filming of *The Toast of New Orleans*, began to view himself as another Cecil B. De Mille. Some days, he could be meddlesome, with a barrage of ideas and suggestions that Pasternak simply tolerated. During *The Great Caruso*, his more productive demands resulted in talent from the Met and the wonderful scene where he sang the Ave Maria with a boys' choir. His demands for *Because You're Mine* resulted in changing his role from that of a pop singer to an opera star who is drafted, leading to the addition of several arias and "The Lord's Prayer." Still, for every viable suggestion he made, there were ten that were absurd or impossible.

The prerecording sessions went well until Lanza and Doretta Morrow were scheduled to sing a duet. Johnny Green had assembled a seventy-five-piece orchestra and, shortly after the number began, the tenor demanded that his co-star become more sensual. He insisted, in vile terms, that she come closer so that he could feel her vagina against his groin. Morrow bolted from the soundstage in tears, threatening to revoke her contract and initiate a lawsuit. Dore Schary spoke with Mario and advised him that such language would not be tolerated. The tenor again ranted about her not being sexy enough and again demanded that the role go to Lana Turner.

The next day, Green and his seventy-five musicians were back. Several bars into the duet, Mario told the orchestra to stop playing and launched into a volley more obscene than that of the day before. Morrow fled once more and communicated through her agent: she wanted a release from the contract.

Schary claimed that he hired a huge stuntman to pose as Morrow's brother, a soldier who was assigned to a nearby post. The stuntman visited the tenor and advised him to behave around his sister or he would sing in a higher range for the rest of his life. Allegedly, Mario provided a meek apology and promised never to behave like that again. Schary claimed that, with the exception of Lanza's weight, the picture proceeded without difficulties.

Dore Schary's version of a cowardly Lanza reflects an abject misunderstanding of the troubled star. While it is true that Mario tried to run Morrow off the set, he knew nothing of the word fear. The stuntman, if confronted by an angry, powerful, and intoxicated Lanza, would have found that this was not easy money. If the singer acted with remorse, it was because of status, brother to sister, rather than the stuntman's empty threats. Furthermore, Schary's claim that Lanza behaved properly during the rest of the production is disputed by nearly everyone who was on the set.

Lanza's studio antics included tearing his dressing room apart, board by board, panel by panel, and chair by chair in search of a microphone allegedly planted to spy on him and smashing furniture in Joe Pasternak's office when he did not get the hairdresser of his choice. Away from the studio, he rammed his Cadillac into the mailbox in front of Pasternak's home, spewing vile oaths and insults as he sped away. He was convinced there were plots to undo his stardom and steal his money. In a word, he was impossible.

But his singing was excellent, including several operatic selections ("Addio alla madre," "Questa o quella," and "Addio, Addio" from *Rigoletto*; and "O paradiso" from *L'Africana*), another run with "Mamma mia, che vo' sapè," a memorable rendition of "Granada," "Because You're Mine," "The Song Angels Sing," an insipid composition called "Lee Ah Loo" that was listenable only because it was sung by Mario Lanza, and a powerful though ill-placed performance of "The Lord's Prayer."

The tenor's wildly fluctuating weight, drinking, and temperament made filming disastrous. In June he was ill nine days. He was absent on the 2nd, 7th, and 10th of July, resulting in a suspension of his contract from the 16th to the 29th. August found him in poor health again; he was absent from the 7th to the 12th, leading to another suspension of his contract as well as the entire production. His weight reached more than 240 pounds that month. It seemed that the similarity of filming *Because You're Mine*—in which he wore a military uniform, was berated as a private, and regarded as an interruption to his operatic film career—to his actual air force experiences triggered an identical cycle of depression and weight gain. Mario returned to Palm Springs, rented a home, and began the familiar punishment of dieting and exercise. He lost the weight, though production did not resume until 3 December. The film was completed on 8 February 1952, with Lanza absent seven more times.

Because You're Mine was severely flawed by the singer's weight fluctuation through the picture. Scenes shot at different times—a fit 160-pound private entering a chapel and approaching the altar at an immense 230 pounds—should have been scrapped. Mario refused to do retakes, claiming that the studio was attempting to make inroads into the six months reserved for concerts and opera (he made no appearance in either venue in 1952). Strangely, it was a rare review that mentioned the distraction of what looked like three different men playing the same role.

In England, where the tenor's popularity was and remains great, *Because You're Mine* was selected as the Royal Command Performance film for 1952. Not surprisingly, Mario was aghast at the selection. The film was a box-office success, but the critics were tepid about what was a corny though bearable light comedy. As *Picturegoer* (29 November 1952) noted, "You could argue that *Because You're Mine* is hardly a worthy follow-up, but it is not so far below par as to warrant a wholesale trouncing—purely on its merits as a musical—of course."

Other critics were at odds about Doretta Morrow, with some pro-

nouncing her impressive and others finding her short on the appeal
necessary to carry the part of leading lady. Doretta Morrow had come
to Hollywood fresh from success on Broadway, presumably full of hope
for a film career. Those who saw her on the stage found her to be bright
and attractive. It did not translate to film in *Because You're Mine*. She
seemed timid and, true to her co-star's prediction, not up to the task of
seduction. Doretta Morrow never appeared in another film.

Newsweek (13 October 1952) wrote that the film contained "a good
deal of music not worth his voice," while *Time* (13 October 1952) called
the musical undernourished and Lanza's voice "distinguished for its
sheer volume." In fact, most critics found the acting—with the exception of James Whitmore—ordinary, the story pointless, and Lanza's
singing, much of it tasteful and restrained, the only reason for the film,
which won the November Blue Ribbon for outstanding merit in family
entertainment. "Because You're Mine," a big hit for Lanza, was nominated for an Academy Award as best song, losing to the memorable
theme from *High Noon*.

Mario's performance was amiable and charismatic, though he had
little to work with. He was made the butt of barracks's jokes, forced to
peel mounds of potatoes with a "Sad Sack" theme in the background,
and assigned to walk a fenceline in the foulest weather. Pasternak's
claim that the studio wanted Mario to be considered an ordinary fellow
was disingenuous; MGM was in the business of making stars, not mor-
tals. Mario Lanza had been put in his place, and circumstance, politics,
and motive pointed to one source for the directive: Dore Schary.

Johnny Green had achieved his revenge for being replaced on *The
Great Caruso*. There was no Peter Herman Adler nor singer from the
Met in *Because You're Mine*. Mario repeated, to anyone who would lis-
ten and then some, that he knew it was a lousy concept from the start:

> For a year, I screamed about not wanting to do *Because You're
> Mine*, and delayed it as long as possible. In it I was made some-
> thing of an idiot. It was not the kind of picture to follow Caruso
> and foisting it on the public wasn't fair. I was right. Critics the
> world over said, "This is no vehicle for Lanza."[6]

He was right. But once again his course had been destructive. Another
man would have adapted and moved along. For Lanza, being forced to

portray an army private in an often-demeaning role was a personal attack from which he would not recover.

Studio records show that he was paid $40,000 for *Because You're Mine*. Another notation suggests that MGM got what it paid for: "10-8-51: he paid us $50,000."[7]

After production closed, Mario ballooned again, Betty attacked and retreated. The tenor's hostility was directed toward new targets. During violent rages, he did considerable damage to the home at 810 North Whittier. Then he turned against what made him and his mother so proud: "her" career.

CHAPTER 19

The Student Prince

They all need help. How can we possibly give in to one man's temperament? You must understand one thing: MGM is a factory . . . the product comes first.

An MGM executive, 1952[1]

MGM had found that trying to tame its box-office bonanza was time-consuming, costly, and a guaranteed source of stress for everyone, from the men who swept the sets to Dore Schary. The next Lanza project, *The Student Prince*, reverted to some of the personal considerations and concerns for quality demonstrated during the making of *The Great Caruso*. The tenor was familiar with Romberg's score, having sung various selections on *The Celanese Hour* and the Coke Show. He was excited about the prospect of playing Prince Karl Franz in the sentimental operetta, and the studio consented to his request that Constantine Callinicos be hired as his personal music director. Lanza was convinced that MGM had made a mistake with *Because You're Mine*, and its attempt to grant him latitude in *The Student Prince* only reinforced that view.

Finding a leading lady willing to endure Lanza was again a challenge. Jane Powell, whose career needed a boost (she had not yet scored a hit in *Seven Brides for Seven Brothers*) implied that Devil's Island would be preferable. The studio chose the safest course available by casting Ann Blyth, with whom Mario had worked well in *The Great Caruso*, as his leading lady. The tenor, obviously buoyed by what he considered the studio's recognition of its errors in *Because You're Mine*, anticipated another great success.

Everyone close to the singer knew that his personal life was spiraling downward, but they were either powerless to intervene or uncaring. Weiler was concerned, but too close to assess the immensity of the problem or devise a solution. Friends, like Al and Sylvia Teitelbaum, Andy and Della Russell, and Ray and Prima Sinatra, usually saw the Mario and Betty Lanza who were energetic and fun, desperately in love with one another and generous with and affectionate toward their two daughters.

One evening, Mario and Betty joined the Teitelbaums for dinner at the legendary Mocambo. When a flower girl approached the table, the tenor asked her if she was having a good night. She said business was terrible. Mario replied that he would correct that and personally took her from table to table, explaining that her mother was sick and that the poor girl needed help. The patrons, impressed by an approach from a famous star, invariably but gladly overpaid. On another occasion, the Lanzas dropped by the Teitelbaum home and Mario, upon spotting their daughter, Juli, and a group of young friends by the pool, left the adults and spent more than an hour entertaining the children, using his natural skills as a mimic to imitate popular cartoon characters.

Once the Lanzas rented a yacht, the *Celestine*, and hosted the familiar trio of the Teitelbaums, the Russells, and the Sinatras, among others. The group cruised toward Catalina Island, drank champagne, and planned to hear a broadcast of the tenor's *Coca-Cola Radio Show*. When someone suggested that Mario sounded like Caruso, he at first agreed, but after reconsidering the remark, he glowered and began to hurl glasses against a bulkhead. Everyone wrote it off to the pressures under which the tenor lived. The family physician, Dr. Reimer, did not help as he provided a slowly increasing supply of barbiturates to Mario and Betty. Incidents where Mario would do "stupid and brutal things" while under the influence of alcohol or drugs and "have no recollection of what he had done when he recovered" were becoming more frequent.[2]

At the studio and in Hollywood, Mario was friendly with Red Skelton, Vic Damone, Ricardo Montalban, Jimmy Stewart, Jerry Lewis, and Jimmy Durante. The others—Lanza's leeches—saw him as a pay envelope and encouraged the self-proclaimed "Tiger" to roar back at the studio. His salary, $2500 per week at twenty weeks, would total $50,000 for *The Student Prince*. Monthly record royalties exceeded that, with an album of brilliantly interpreted and passionately sung Christmas standards and continued demand for the *Caruso* album. Even the Coke Show paid him more for ten weeks of part-time work than he would earn for twenty weeks of hard work making another film. Though the films provided a great showcase for his voice and fueled his massive record royalties, he was underpaid and seething with resentment.

Lanza and Doris Day won *Photoplay*'s Gold Medal Awards for 1951. Mario dazzled the crowd at the presentation banquet when he explained that he would not join the other winners on the dais, but rather would prefer to sit in the audience with his parents, who were uncomfortable among strangers. When the award was presented, he thanked Frank Sinatra, Hedda Hopper, and Joe Pasternak for their contributions to his career. The veteran producer was thrilled. Lanza also won the Independent Film Journal's Award as the most popular male star for 1951 and 1952. When he failed to personally accept the second award, many in the press labeled him unthinking, conceited, and temperamental.

Sam Weiler began to distance himself from the Lanzas, finding their incessant demands and childish need for attention so stressful that in the spring of 1952 he and Selma packed their bags and headed for the Poconos to recuperate. He complained that Mario kept him on the phone for more than six hours each day, playing recordings, or insisted that he come to the house, at three o'clock in the morning, to look at his collection of wristwatches. While the Weilers rested, Betty resorted to Dr. Reimer and took to her bed over the crisis of having to run the house without Sam. She was in the first trimester of another pregnancy.

Nick Brodszky and his crew, any one of whom could have given the best neighborhood gossip a run for the roses, began to occupy more of the singer's time. They fed his ego, assuring him that MGM would collapse if he left. Unfortunately, Mario believed them. Betty thought it wonderful that her husband was taking such a serious approach to his career by spending so much time at Brodszky's apartment rehearsing. For Mario, it was nothing more than a place to drink beer and bring his women. His sexual encounters were rough at times, and he pushed at boundaries he respected only a few years earlier. Once, when Brodszky refused to play a request, a drunk and irate Lanza destroyed his piano. When other acquaintances learned that a drunken Mario was headed their way, they locked their doors to prevent one of his furniture-smashing melees. On at least one occasion, suspecting that someone was in, he simply knocked the door down. He rationalized everything as being fine because he was willing to pay for whatever was damaged. The singer's behavior was erratic, but many stood by and cheered him on while the money rushed out of his coffers and into their pockets.

The prerecording sessions for *The Student Prince* found Mario in good spirits. Romberg's score delighted him and Nick Brodszky, in successful collaboration with lyricist Paul Webster, added "Summertime in Heidelberg," "I'll Walk with God," and "Beloved," which compositions seem like part of the original score. Callinicos and Weiler claimed that the prerecordings were a series of one-take efforts, which contradicts the MGM recording log.

On the first day, the tenor recorded "I'll Walk with God," "Summertime in Heidelberg," "Serenade," and "A Mighty Fortress" in single takes. "Beloved," which was also done in a single take, caused the first explosion on the set. Curtis Bernhardt, who had been assigned to direct *The Student Prince*, viewed Prince Karl Franz as a man of breeding and restrained emotions. Mario saw the prince as a rogue, a man who would snub his aristocratic background to marry a barmaid. Given the fact that MGM so often selected experiences from Lanza's life for his film scripts, his personalized interpretation should not have been surprising.

Whenever Mario Lanza stood before a microphone in a recording studio, all his considerable torment vanished. He poured his unique combination of voice, emotion, physical commitment, and passionate interpretation into every note. His "Beloved" was a particularly impassioned plea. His voice and artistry would silence anyone. It did not silence Curtis Bernhardt, who coldly dismissed the tenor's interpretation during a playback, exaggeratedly waving a baton to emphasize his sense of annoyance.

Mario could barely listen to criticism about his acting, singing, or weight, never truly accepting any of it. Criticism of his singing was an intrusion on what he regarded as sacred land. He demanded that Bernhardt be fired from the film. Pasternak refused. The singer was unaware that Dore Schary was monitoring activities on the set through, among others, Lanza's leeches. He later explained that Bernhardt's view of Prince Karl was at odds with his voice and interpretation. A song is not merely thrown into a film for good measure, and Lanza felt his interpretation was consistent with how the character and the romance would develop.

Two days later, Mario did two takes of "Golden Days" and "What's to Be," which was not used in the picture. Five days after that, he recorded "Drink, Drink" in a single take, parts of "Gaudeamus Igitur" in two takes, and "Ergo Bibamus," which was not used on the RCA soundtrack, in a single take. The final session was troublesome; Mario did seven takes of "Deep in My Heart, Dear," a song he had easily mastered for a Coke Show broadcast. Overall, his singing was tasteful and passionate, the tones glorious and fluid. The recordings remain a daunting standard for any tenor who approaches the role of Prince Karl Franz.

Now that the soundtrack was complete, it was time for a familiar routine: the tenor had to lose forty pounds in six weeks. Once again, he exercised, dieted, and brought himself down to film weight.

The Student Prince was a grand costume film with a large cast of extras. Terry Robinson drove Mario to the studio on the first day of principal rehearsals, 24 June 1952. Mario asked if Curtis Bernhardt was going to direct. The response was "Yes." Mario asked Robinson to get the car; the tenor's first day at the studio was over. He sought refuge at the ranch of John Carroll (a handsome raconteur and leading man from the 1940s) in Chatsworth, where Betty—three months pregnant—joined him. Lanza felt that the studio had betrayed him by keeping Bernhardt on the picture. He thought nothing of the huge number of extras that had been kept waiting, were paid, and then dismissed. He failed to report on the 25th, 26th, 27th, 28th, and 30th.

"Is anything wrong, son?" Pasternak asked. The tenor insisted over and over that he would be in tomorrow. [3]

The standoff continued. Weiler claimed that he brought Bernhardt to the Lanza home, where discussions lasted for six hours. Then Mario kept Sam up all night long, gushing about how wrong he had been: Bernhardt was a truly wonderful fellow. As the days passed, the tenor's moods continued to swing between euphoria and depression.

He did not appear at the studio on 8 July. He also broke with Sam Weiler, demanding to see the corporate books for MarSam. Betty added her customary jabs, berating Weiler for having access to their home with none in return. Weiler retorted that he did not need Lanza's money, that he could buy and sell him ten times over. Mario grumbled about how the buying would involve his own money. The barbs flew but it was pointless. Weiler had grabbed the tail of a meteor that was burning itself out.

Friends interceded and tried to facilitate a truce with Weiler. Sam,

who once believed he could develop Lanza's talent, now called Mario
and Betty "sweet children who needed help. . . . Success completely
changed them . . . life is too short to put up with all that."[4]

There was no singer present on the 9th, 11th, or 12th of July. MGM
suspended his contract on the 14th. Mario asked Terry Robinson to
take his parents to the studio. He was certain that Schary and other
executives would change their positions when they met Tony and Mary
Cocozza: "Let them see the kind of stock I come from. Let them know
I'm not one of their bums."[5] Mario Lanza was an outsider, the son of a
former seamstress and an ineffective, disabled veteran. Such a belief
would have been marginal in a typical family setting, but it was pathos
in this situation. The meeting accomplished nothing.

The press was having a field day with the ongoing crisis. MGM had
kept reports of Lanza's antics from the public and had even closed the
sets to exclude onlookers. Now it began to divulge information in what
Lanza viewed as a campaign of whispers. Hollywood was not short of
people willing to sell stories about Mario Lanza, including former
household personnel who had fled in fear of the tenor's drunken rages.
He hid at his parents' home in Pacific Palisades, occasionally returning
to the secluded rental he and Betty had moved to at 500 Bel Air Road.
MGM reinstated his contract on 28 July.

Negotiations were sporadic as the tenor was without a manager and
usually uncooperative when contacted. He never showed up at the studio, and on 20 August his contract was again suspended. Dore Schary
finally realized that his reluctant star was ill and suggested that he seek
psychiatric treatment at the Menninger Clinic. Lanza agreed to see a
psychiatrist at the UCLA Medical Center, but nothing resulted from
the few sessions he attended. It seemed that the physician, Dr. Augustus Rose, was thoroughly charmed by his celebrity client and entirely
sympathetic to his plight. He pronounced that Mario suffered from
megalomania, a euphoric state characterized by feelings of grandiosity.[6]
Dr. Rose attributed the tenor's troubles to difficulties with handling
Hollywood success, labeling him conceited and vain. He was incorrect.
It was not the last time Mario Lanza would be misdiagnosed or inade-
quately treated.

The lag time between production and the release of a film made the
saga all the more fascinating to the public. The furor from *The Great
Caruso* had not yet waned, *Because You're Mine* had not been released,

the Coke Show was attracting good ratings, and the tenor's albums were bestsellers, which made his apparent self-destruction seem surrealistic.

The Diary Advertising Agency jumped on MGM's suspension of the tenor's contract. The following announcement appeared in *Variety* (21 August 1952):

> Metro yesterday notified the Diary Advertising Agency, which handles The Mario Lanza Show for Coca-Cola, that Lanza, in failing to report, was in default of his contract and would not be permitted to appear on his weekly show either personally or via taped program.

Diary Advertising was eager to dump Lanza. His erratic behavior had not been restricted to MGM, and his drinking had made production difficult. If MGM wanted him leveled, cooperation was theirs for the asking.

The tenor—having retreated to the comfort of his old friend, food—was now too large to play the dashing prince. MGM would not give up. Mario reported to the studio on Friday, 22 August, and promised to return on the following Monday. He did not appear or explain his absence.

On 28 August, MGM threatened to sue its defiant star. One week later, Loew's, Inc., notified him that it had canceled *The Student Prince* and warned that it considered him to have breached his contract. After another week, Lew Wasserman, Mario's agent and the powerful head of MCA, met with Schary. No progress was made. The tenor met with Schary on 14 September. The meeting was acrimonious; Schary called him a bum and a disgrace to MGM, and Lanza responded with one of his classic tirades.

MGM filed suit in the U.S. District Court on 19 September 1952, seeking $4.5 million in general damages (lost profits, goodwill, etc.) and $659,888 in special damages (actual losses). The studio also sought, and was granted, an injunction in accordance with Paragraph Four of the contract, which provided that Lanza could not appear in operatic, radio, and concert venues or record music if "he was in default hereunder."[7] The provision was onerous in that MGM, in seeking general damages, should not have been entitled to injunctive relief.[8] Nonetheless, the court enjoined the tenor from engaging in any form of employment related to acting or singing, reducing him to income from past recordings until the lawsuit was resolved. Again, it was MGM's town, though Lanza's emotional state made the pursuit of any form of employment questionable.

He responded to the allegations in a letter, declaring that he was "now ready, willing and able to perform all of the terms and conditions"of his employment contract.[9] The letter was typed on standard eight by eleven inch paper. His signature was five inches high, indicating a great deal about his state of mind and willingness to be conciliatory.

He retreated to his home, more stunned about the fact that he was prohibited from working than he was about not working. He refused to see anyone. When Lew Wasserman dropped by with a check for $50,000, the despondent singer sent word to leave it with the butler.

His financial situation was dismal: a net worth of less than $100,000 and a tax bill in excess of $250,000. The tenor blamed Weiler, citing bad investments and outright embezzlement. He fired his agent, lawyers, and press agent. The third Lanza child to be born in the month of December, a son named Damon (Mario was fond of Damon Runyon's work) arrived on the 12th. Mario drank, ate, and raged in his Bel Air home without prospect or interest in work as the year ended. Hedda Hopper interviewed him and asked why he had declined to respond to the serious allegations and rumors circulating about him. The tenor explained that he had done nothing wrong, which made a response unnecessary.

With the new year, the Lanzas looked forward to better times. In January 1953, the owners of the house they had rented at 810 North Whittier sued for $17,000, alleging considerable damage to gardens, furnishings, and the home. The matter was later settled for $9000.

It would prove easier to repair the house than it would to rebuild the career.

CHAPTER 20

Standoff

Exploited? I don't understand the meaning of that word. What do you mean when you say that Mario Lanza was exploited?

Gerald Lipsky, 1996[1]

Lanza's inability to apply himself to the rigors of filming *The Student Prince* was solely attributable to his poor mental and physical condition. Nevertheless, there were rumors, some traceable to the tenor through Robert Kapp, one in a series of attorneys who found Mario to be an impossible client, that Lanza had intentionally scuttled *The Student Prince* in order to close off his enormous income until he devised a way to remove Sam Weiler from his payroll. It was a sorrowful attempt to make positive a situation he had misread and mishandled. Mario could not stand the idea that, once again, someone had ordered him to pack and leave. As evidence of his immature thinking, he saw his suspension as nothing more than an unjustified expulsion over his stance against injustice. If he had intentionally reduced his income to thwart Weiler, it cost him eighty cents for every twenty it took from his former manager. In addition, Weiler had hired MCA, at half his 20 percent, to handle the career side of his duties—which left him with little to justify his considerable income.

For a long time, Weiler had been limited to a haphazard role as Mario's surrogate father, lackey to Betty's unreasonable demands, and funnel for revenue. Sam was a stranger to the worlds of film, recordings, and concerts, and he accomplished little in that regard for the world's highest-paid tenor. Lanza's concert tours during 1949 and 1950 were arranged by Columbia Artists, with whom he had signed while at Tanglewood in 1942. His recordings were planned by RCA as a consequence of the contract he signed in 1944, before he met Weiler and while still in the armed forces. Even the contract with MGM was

Mario's achievement, the result of his brilliant and well-timed performance at the Hollywood Bowl; Weiler was in New York peddling real estate when the tenor called for help with negotiations. He helped all right, agreeing to a film contract that bound the tenor to entry level salaries for his first three films and gave the studio the right to transfer or terminate the agreement without notice.

If Lanza, or any other player under contract, were going to succeed, it would be during the first three years. If that occurred, the studio had a money-making star at bargain rates. If it did not work out, MGM was free to abandon the contract. Worse, the onerous Paragraph Four was nothing short of enslavement. Lanza was earning more money as a concert artist than the contract provided during its first three years, and films accounted for just over 10 percent of his career earnings.[2] Common sense dictates that the inducement should have been greater, causing one to wonder about Weiler's penchant for side-agreements from which his client derived nothing.

Mario drifted between Bel Air, his parents' home in Pacific Palisades, and a house he rented in Palm Springs as the controversy unfolded. It was typical that he was right about so much (Weiler, the compromise of his art, and the contract) but so confused about how to achieve resolution. One thing was certain: MGM did not want to lose Mario Lanza. The suit was nothing more than a desperate attempt to bring him in line. He owned no property or substantial assets, and MGM was hardly interested in collecting installments on a debt for a failed movie project.

The studio used the courts to prevent the singer from working, wrongly calculating that a loss of revenue would subordinate him to their demands. They failed to reckon with the vast royalties from recordings already in production and the trove of unreleased Coke Show performances. More importantly, MGM failed to recognize Lanza's inability to differentiate independence from defiance or constructive criticism from unwarranted rejection. Harry Gershon, the attorney who represented the studio in its battle with the tenor, said that MGM was holding firm in its view that Lanza was obliged to make three more films. He went so far as to predict that production on *The Student Prince* would be restarted in April 1953 and that Mario Lanza would fulfill the terms of his MGM contract.

Mario went into seclusion and failed to inform his advisors or friends of his intentions. He continued to train with Callinicos for the day he would return to his public. Home recordings from that period and somewhat beyond show him engaged in some interesting, powerful, and quite tasteless singing devised for destroying a great voice. In one segment, he repeatedly searches for a high C while singing the last phrase in "Celeste Aida" ("vicino al sol!") though the aria calls for a high B. The upper register shows signs of abuse and wear. In fact, he had occasionally cracked on high B-flat and high C since the production of *The Great Caruso* was completed, but he bristled at suggestions about his methods. Even when his upper register rarely failed, he had worried about approaching a high note and holding it; now he was terrified of an occasional failure before a live audience and refused to consider offers for a lucrative concert tour. Worse, he intermittently smoked cigarettes and even appeared in advertisements for Camels, extolling their benefits to his voice and overall singing.

In the spring of 1953, the tenor, who was veering toward depression, said that he hoped to complete *The Student Prince*, make two or three more films, and then "take off for Europe and operatic study in Italy," with the goal of becoming "the foremost tenor the Metropolitan Opera in New York has ever presented to the world."[3] He was moving fast, but the Met was only receding in his rearview mirror; he would eventually say of the institution, "That dump! I wouldn't be seen dead there!"[4]

Joe Pasternak, a basically good man who was torn by his sense of awe at Lanza's talent and capacity for self-destruction, desperately wanted to make *The Student Prince* with Mario Lanza in the leading role. Pasternak had made money for the studio, but he was considered second-rate to Arthur Freed—who produced such films as *Babes in Arms*, *Meet Me in St. Louis*, *Easter Parade*, *Show Boat*, and *Kismet*— in terms of artistry and sophistication. He correctly evaluated Lanza as a star who could enable him to combine profits with artistic achievement and began to circulate rumors that Deanna Durbin would come out of retirement to star opposite the tenor. Most felt that such a prospect would drive an actress to retire rather than undo the decision. Pasternak later described his disappointment:

> The incident was in many ways the most upsetting I had known. I had been . . . harsh with Mario, but always *con amore*, with love, as a father is harsh to a son whose inner fineness he would never

doubt. To the end, I thought well of him. I would always think of him as a friend . . . even though his stubborn refusal to work in a picture in which I was so deeply committed seemed to me unfair, to say the least.[5]

Some progress was made in March, but Lanza's vacillating mood convinced the studio that the war was not worth the battles it would have to fight. MGM terminated its contract with the tenor on 10 April 1953. He was now free to work.

In May the studio dismissed its suit against the tenor in exchange for the right to use his prerecordings in any film it chose to make. The settlement also required him to return to the soundstage to record another version of "Beloved." Curtis Bernhardt's victory was a bitter form of submission for Mario. Again overweight and badly out of shape, Lanza appeared on the MGM soundstage on 20 May. Word spread throughout the lot, and many gathered to hear the last recording Mario Lanza would make at the studio. He did one take and four ten-second retakes of bar 28. Then he left the studio.

Lanza's voice darkened more quickly than most. It was relatively settled by the time he was twenty-nine, which is uncommonly young for a tenor. By thirty-two, his voice was dark and rich. The difference between the prerecordings done in May 1952 and May 1953 is dramatic; the real tragedy was the ensuing silence from a voice that should have been at its peak.

The public could only surmise that Mario Lanza had been ruined by financial success. He remained inactive but speculated to one reporter that he would return to the recording studio, be back on radio by fall, and star in *The Vagabond King* for Paramount with a possible follow-up in *La Bohème*. His plans were quite specific:

> [I'll] finish 1953 by going out on the concert tour I've hated to delay for so long. In concerts, I can be completely serious about the masterpieces in music. It's a medium of expression that is a total contrast, but it's the one I began in, and I want to make a three-month tour a part of my future pattern.

More than two years would pass before his next film production; his next and last concert tour would be five years later. To a question about grand opera, he responded, "Opera on stage? Yes, when I'm older."[6]

The thirty-two-year-old singer had six years left to live.

CHAPTER 21

Wasteland

My personal plans? For the first time, I am experiencing the thrill
of being able to do what I've dreamed. At last there are so many
things I can start in the way I wish. Each morning, I wake up
quickly, eagerly.

Mario Lanza, 1953[1]

Lanza was free to approach any studio about a film contract, appear at
a dozen concerts each week, perform on radio twenty-four hours a day,
or record around the clock. Callinicos, now the musical director of the
Highland Park Symphony, continued to coach the tenor. Two years
earlier, Costa had drawn a $2000 advance for a composition, "You Are
My Love." Lanza had often promised to record it and now, in the spring
of 1953, seemed eager to follow through.

When Constantine dropped by to rehearse, he was informed that
Betty did not think the material was good for Mario, whose studio work
during the past year had been limited. Betty was extremely jealous of
her husband's prospect of a return to active work and even more concerned that Callinicos might share the glory.

Betty stuck with Mario through plenty of less than glamorous times,
but she often failed him at crucial moments, berating him when he
needed praise or to be left alone and wagging her barbed tongue in an
"I knew it!" tirade whenever he failed. Like everyone else who knew her
husband, Betty was incapable of understanding that his demons were
internal. Al Teitelbaum remembered that, when he first met her, Betty
was "a simple housewife, sure that her husband would be an opera
singer." When he turned toward films and soared to stardom, Betty felt
threatened and often, with the best intentions, interfered and caused
problems.[2] Whether "You Are My Love" was "good" for Mario or not,
a return to work was what he needed—even if it meant singing "Three
Blind Mice."

Mario overruled his wife and recorded four songs with Callinicos at Republic Studios on 17 June 1953. "You Are My Love" was reminiscent of Nick Brodszky's work for the tenor, forcing him through the pointless swings into the stentorian singing some critics found tasteless. It was not very good, though it became a minor hit. Mario, feeling grandiose, mused that with the recording, he had provided Costa with "an income for life."[3] They also recorded "If You Were Mine" and "Call Me Fool" (another minor hit), but the jewel of the session was a powerful and tasteful interpretation of Johnny Mercer's lyrics to Rimsky-Korsakov's "Song of India." He had been in good voice throughout the session, but this was a masterful performance that ranks with the finest of his career. The word tragic can easily be overworked when it comes to Mario Lanza, but the fact that he would not successfully record a single note for another two years is at least that.

In July, MGM announced that Edmund Purdom would star in *The Student Prince* and lip-synch the tenor's recordings. It was a big break for the British actor, whose third wife was Tyrone Power's widow, Linda Christian. Purdom's Hollywood career proved brief, however, and he was soon back in Europe making low-budget films. The studio announced that it would spend $25,000 on a three-day production-quality screen test with Ann Blyth and Purdom to see if he could handle the role. Lanza saw it as proof that he had been underpaid and scowled that the public would never accept his voice with another man's face.

In August, a suit setting forth a demand for an accounting, alleging illegal use of funds and seeking $241,459.80 in damages, was filed against Sam Weiler in the Santa Monica Superior Court. The singer alleged that the good investments went to Weiler and the bad to his accounts, which was not entirely incorrect. For example, Weiler acquired an Orange Julius stand with $11,500 of his own money. When the investment went bad, he transferred it to Lanza's account. Other investments that went well were transferred from Lanza to Weiler. The tenor also correctly asserted that double or excessive commissions had been assessed, that loans remained unpaid, and that Weiler charged personal and private business expenses against his accounts. Mario sought to void the contract by its own terms, which would leave Weiler with the right to 5 percent of his gross earnings in perpetuity.

Weiler, strident about the hardships he had endured as "Lanza's keeper" during the last year of their relationship, received tenacious representation from attorneys Guy Ward and David B. Heyler, Jr.[4] Conversely, the lawyers who represented the tenor were lacking a necessary ingredient for success: a rational and cooperative client. When it became apparent that he was unable to conform his behavior to time, circumstance, and place with predictability, the matter was settled with Weiler forgiving $58,157.70 in past commissions in exchange for his perpetual right to 5 percent of the tenor's gross income. It proved to be good pay for his brief stint as the tenor's so-called keeper.

Betty was devastated to find herself pregnant for the fourth time. She wept, took to her bed, and resorted to Dr. Reimer for an accelerating combination of sedatives, barbiturates, and alcohol. She took insufficient nourishment, resulting in malnutrition and occasional hospital admissions. The harm done to the unborn child was substantial.

Mario ate and drank to excess and refused to receive nearly everyone who stopped by. He made exceptions for boxer Rocky Marciano and George London. His old friend from the triumphant Bel Canto days was shocked by Mario's emotional and physical condition. The tenor was drunk, tearful, and depressed. "You're my only friend," he told London, who was touched but deeply disturbed to see him in such a condition.[5]

In December 1953, the tenor returned to the recording studio with Callinicos to rerecord the songs from *The Student Prince* for an album RCA planned to release concurrent with the release of the film. Ann Blyth was under contract with a different label, necessitating the substitution of soprano Roberta Sherwood.

Lanza had been drinking heavily and smoking. After a few poor attempts on "Summertime in Heidelberg," the tenor's chauffeur arrived with several cans of beer. Costa canceled the session. Two days later, Mario's singing was even worse. Realizing that he could not remain on key and that his pride—his wondrous breath control—was nonexistent, he said nothing and slowly left the studio. A third session was scrapped, and Callinicos returned to New York.

RCA substituted the takes done by yet another soprano, Elizabeth Doubleday, over Ann Blyth's voice on the original recordings. The "gift from God" had failed him and, with 1953 coming to a close, his outlook and mood banished any prospects for a quick return to a productive existence.

With the new year, Lanza continued to drift. He drank well into the night, often until he lost consciousness; raged at cooks while hurling food and plates against walls over an imagined underseasoning; and again began to destroy the home he rented. He often lamented that no one understood him, never realizing that he did not know himself. Like most who drink until sleep comes and have no place to go come morning, he awakened late and remained lethargic until the nightmare repeated itself. Some days, Callinicos was waiting to coach a man who could barely talk. Costa more than proved his loyalty to Mario, facing embarrassment or left stranded without payment—having sacrificed risk-free engagements in order to help his old friend. Callinicos was pragmatic: if Lanza was willing to pay him for waiting on a sofa, he had no objection. When Costa was not waiting, the singer took his place on the sofa and stared out the window for hours.

Where he had once enjoyed setting out lavish decorations for Christmas, a forlorn tree, now brown and nearly bereft of needles, was still in the living room in late February. At the end of the month, the Internal Revenue Service filed a lien in the amount of $169,153 for delinquent taxes. An immediate fallout was the reduction of household staff and the defection of what was left of Lanza's leeches. Callinicos remained for a while and attempted to interest Mario in interesting arias from obscure operas. The tenor tried to work again; at least it was something.

The fact that he did no public singing or recording did not mean that the voice was coddled. He often locked himself in his music room and listened to his own records for hours or emptied his emotions into song after song with destructive, top-of-the-lungs singing. Occasionally, he would light up at three or four in the morning and phone Costa, demanding that he come to the house so that he could sing. Whatever singing he did during those months went up into the night and vanished in the air. The sporadic elation soon passed, and Mario, more depressed than ever, hunkered down to a familiar pattern that took him to 250 pounds and rising.

He was without competent management. His income was limited to royalties for past performances and, lacking any desire to enhance his prospects, he found that the IRS had curtailed his ability to live in the wasteful manner to which he had become accustomed.

Mary was concerned and suffered when her son's career disintegrated, but she could not reach him. At times she blamed Betty for driving him to drink and gain weight. "Look at what you're doing to yourself, what you mean to so many people," she begged. But nothing could shake him from his depression. He sat for hours at a time—completely unresponsive to anyone—with his eyes cast downward and his expression immobile.[6]

Expenses were not met when services were provided, leading to arrearages and discontinuations. Where deliverymen once found a call at the Lanza household a privilege because of an opportunity to sample a well-prepared Italian dish, they now refused to leave orders unless a check was already prepared.

One afternoon, the local representative for *Photoplay* phoned Al Teitelbaum and informed him that Mario Lanza was at his office at Doheny and Santa Monica in Beverly Hills which, during better times, had been one of the tenor's favorite haunts. The representative was concerned; Mario was too drunk to drive and needed help. The tenor, terribly overweight and barely recognizable, was wracked with sobs as he complained about how his career had been sabotaged by people out to get him.

Teitelbaum arrived and took the tenor to his home. Dr. Clarence Agress was called and, after examining Lanza, ordered that he be admitted to the Cedars of Lebanon Hospital. The tenor objected out of fear that publicity would result. Also, his financial status was such that he could not afford treatment; their landlord was threatening to evict them. After a great deal of discussion, Teitelbaum loaned Mario and Betty enough money to pay their rent and operate for a while. The tenor was admitted to Las Encinas Sanitarium, where his physical condition improved despite his repeated attempts to bribe the nurses into providing him with liquor.

If the tenor's behavior had staggered his career, the lack of effective management leveled it. Al Teitelbaum, who had known Mario since 1948, was smooth, urbane, and successful. He billed himself, not surprisingly, as "furrier to the stars" and operated from a prestigious location at 414 North Rodeo Drive in Beverly Hills. He had no intention of becoming Lanza's personal manager, but events led him to precisely that role.

Teitelbaum, realizing that the tenor needed work, approached Lew Wasserman and Dore Schary. The results were predictable.

Mario and Betty were floundering without the attention once provided by Sam and Selma Weiler. They pressed Teitelbaum for an agreement as Mario's manager and, effective 1 May 1954, the relationship was formalized. The contract was unusual in that Teitelbaum was obliged to find no work for his client and became immediately and irrevocably entitled to 10 percent of the singer's gross earnings.

Teitelbaum quickly assembled a team of well-known Hollywood attorneys and management personnel. The first to come aboard was Gregson Bautzer, the dapper, handsome, and utterly ruthless prototype of a Hollywood entertainment attorney. Bautzer was charming; the first of his four wives was actress Dana Wynter, and he squired everyone from starlets to Marilyn Monroe. The contract between him and Lanza provided his firm, Bautzer & Grant, with a perpetual right to 5 percent of the tenor's gross income. Next, well-respected tax attorney J. Everett Blum was brought on through a contract that provided him with a perpetual right to 2.5 percent of Lanza's gross income but guaranteed no services to the singer. Lastly, Business Administration—a competent organization headed by Myrt Blum, Jack Benny's brother-in-law—signed on for a guarantee of 5 percent of the singer's gross earnings. When the settlement with Sam Weiler and an arrangement with MCA was added to the equation, Lanza was paying 37.5 percent of his gross income for an array of real and phantom services. Worse, even if he had fired the whole lot the next day, they would have been entitled to receive 27.5 percent of his gross income in perpetuity—which is precisely what occurred for nearly four decades.

Incredibly, Mario Lanza was without a recording contract. His affiliation with RCA was terminated when he foolishly rejected a $1 million guarantee for one hundred recordings, claiming that it was the same deal offered to Dinah Shore and that he was worth twice that amount. A new contract was fashioned—not negotiated—wherein there was no guarantee and some of the singer's material was released through RCA's Black Seal division at reduced royalty rates. Then, there was the matter of his inactivity. RCA had nothing in its vaults, and Lanza was in no condition to record.

The problem was solved, and not entirely in the singer's favor, through an advance against royalties for RCA's right to use the 163 titles and numerous outtakes recorded for the Coke Show. Mario owned the material outright and had paid for production and overtime but received nothing, beyond the advance, for RCA's release of material in which it had invested nothing. In spite of his lofty talk about high standards, he permitted the release of Coke Show recordings he knew to be inferior to his studio work. Worse, he signed over all rights to the Coke Show tapes to Al and Sylvia Teitelbaum for value received. Ownership of the Coke Show tapes was transferred to the Lanza heirs as a result of litigation decades later.

The immediate advantage of the new arrangement with RCA was that Lanza was presented as an active artist through releases of Coke Show material on several albums (*A Kiss* and *The Magic Mario*). Lanza recorded nothing in 1954, but it was not because of a lack of interest at RCA.

On 19 May 1954, the Lanza's fourth and last child, Marc, was born. The next day, MGM held a press showing of *The Student Prince* on Stage 16 followed by a meal featuring German cuisine at the Rheingold in Beverly Hills. Most of the reviews made little mention of the dubbing of Lanza's voice.

The formulaic film lacked the ingredient to which it owed its inspiration: Mario Lanza. Ann Blyth delivered a respectable performance as Cathy, the barmaid adored by every student and loved by one prince in Heidelberg, and the stable of MGM character actors filled in adequately. But Edmund Purdom was against more than insurmountable odds. He was handsome, slim, and woefully unconvincing when he mouthed the words to Lanza's memorable recordings. The film needed Lanza's fire and charisma, and Edmund Gwenn's final words, "Let us rejoice while we are young," might have been directed at the film's absent star. The film never escaped its need of Lanza as a centerpiece.

Time, still vigilant in its perceived duty to warn the public about the excitement Lanza had brought to opera, decried "I'll Walk with God" as a song to avoid and cautioned that the excessive volume of Mario Lanza lurked behind his substitute's lip synching. John McCarten of *The New Yorker* (26 June 1954) panned it as "claptrap," and *Newsweek* was similarly unimpressed. The film was not successful at the box office.

Sales of the soundtrack passed the three million mark in the first decade after its release and volume remains impressive. A video is available, and it seems certain that sales are not enhanced by the performances of Ann Blyth or Edmund Purdom. Once again, the tenor was right—and the biggest loser.

MGM released several successful films in 1954, though the studio did not show an overall profit. The only part of the scenario that mattered to Mario was that the studio lost money, which he attributed to its handling of *The Student Prince*. He claimed a mighty victory while doing little more than diminishing his career, body, and voice. The tenor never saw *The Student Prince* or, for that matter, *Because You're Mine*, and the mention of either film made it a bad day for all who had to be around him.

When summer came, he stirred from his depression and inactivity and began to entertain again—firing one destructive note after another at a new round of moochers. He chafed under the notion of an allowance from the IRS, though it did not restrict his access to liquor, food, and women. He courted more than his share at several odd places, not the least used of which was an office at the rear of Al Teitelbaum's fur salon.

He was eager to work but no studio would touch him. He counted on starring in *The Vagabond King* for Paramount and even the female lead, Kathryn Grayson, was willing to consider working with him again. The studio demanded a psychiatric examination and proof that he had not lost his voice, but Lanza saw no reason to submit to the indignity of seeing a doctor or to spend an afternoon in a recording studio. The part went to Oreste, the Maltese tenor, and the film, which proved to be Grayson's last, did not show a profit.

MGM was still standing, and although Mario Lanza was decidedly down, no one could convince him that he was not a winner.

CHAPTER 22

The CBS Hoax

My answer to the television offers is—no, thank you, but not for me yet. When I can present what I can in a theater, on a wide screen, then I will be anxious to take that step. I won't settle for less, meanwhile. Not for any amount of money.

Mario Lanza, 1953[1]

Despite this earlier caveat, Lanza settled for considerably less. His first engagement since *The Student Prince* was a television special. The Chrysler Corporation had signed with CBS in a then-daring move to introduce its new line of cars on *The Chrysler Shower of Stars*, a series of variety shows. L. L. Colbert, the controversial chairman of Chrysler, greatly admired Lanza and wanted him to appear in the first show.

Negotiations were tense as the singer, happy to receive $40,000 and two new automobiles for singing three songs of his choice, balked when he learned that the $40,000 would be applied to his tax arrearage. Not surprisingly, he viewed it as working for nothing. After being placated with assurances about the publicity value of showing studio executives that he still had it, he became enthused. But the deal almost slipped away again when the IRS demanded that both autos be sold and the proceeds applied to his taxes. It was finally agreed that Mario could present one of the cars to Betty. His only motivation for accepting the project was to "show 'em." He had no desire to work for the sake of the art he had until recently regarded as so precious.

The summer of 1954 found Betty confined to her bed and receiving her children as a queen receives her subjects. Back at home, Mario, at 270 pounds and taking no exercise, continued to assault plates of food, alcohol, and the four walls that surrounded him. He talked in grandiose terms about his plans for recordings, film, and opera, but made no move to secure such work. If ever the moment was right for

154

attention to a career in opera, it was in 1954. He had the time, a voice, and enough notoriety to interest any opera house in the world.

In August 1954, Mario conceded that he needed help to prepare for the show. His weight was up, his blood pressure dangerously elevated, and his temperament such that he was unable to sleep or concentrate. Like his grandfather Salvatore, he was also moderately diabetic. The disease would play a role in his overall health during the last three years of his life. After being assured that the media would not learn of his decision, Mario again checked himself into the Las Encinas Sanitarium to dry out, lose weight, and stabilize himself emotionally. With close monitoring in a locked setting, he managed to lose a bit of weight and avoid alcohol. He was placed on a diet and began an exercise program. Though the situation was far from ideal, it appeared that Mario was improving.

Giacomo Spadoni tried to coach him daily, often without pay, in preparation for the great comeback. His daughter Colleen mused, "He was forever rehearsing for something, which is strange now that I look at the record. I mean, nothing was going on."[2]

Nervous, withdrawn, and depressed, Mario listened to his own records or sang to himself for hours on end. None of the studios wanted him on their lots and even Lew Wasserman, head of the powerful MCA, was unable to arrange a film. Howard Hughes considered making a film with Lanza, whom he greatly admired. Negotiations were sporadic and, in keeping with the Hughes tradition, maddening. The reclusive billionaire and tenor had several long telephone conversations, which turned out to be nothing more than an opportunity for a famously eccentric fan to satisfy his curiosity. Mario insisted on the right to select his own leading lady; he did not want to costar with Jane Russell, whom he feared was Hughes' choice. A contract was drafted and signed by the tenor, and presented to Hughes. He never responded.

As the date of the Chrysler show approached, it was obvious that Lanza, despite being in good voice, was not up to a live performance. Three days before the show, it also became obvious that he was unable to prerecord his numbers as co-star Betty Grable had done. Chrysler and CBS had plenty riding on the outcome. Mario Lanza had not performed in more than two years and curiosity about whether or not he could still sing was running high. If he failed to appear, his detractors would see it as proof that he never had a voice. Time was running short and several alternatives, including cancellation, were considered. Everyone associated with the production finally realized that Lanza was emotionally incapacitated; even a complex comedy skit was scrapped. Indecision added to the tension, and the opportunity for a graceful bail-out slipped away.

The worst decision of the two available—cancellation or the use of recordings done several years before—was made. The old reliable, Constantine Callinicos, began to work with Mario on the technique of lip-synching to RCA recordings of "Marechiare," "Vesti la giubba," and a Coke Show rendition of "Be My Love." Teitelbaum later blamed Callinicos for the singer's deficiencies, but the simple fact was that Lanza was emotionally incapable of singing or lip-synching. In addition, too many people—from sound engineers to stage hands—knew about the plan. Leaks to the press were inevitable.

The tenor weighed 230 pounds and his season as a young man was over. He was enormous but chubbily handsome at the same weight in *Because You're Mine*. Now, with no significant exercise and too much abuse, he was fat and dissolute when *The Chrysler Shower of Stars* aired on 30 September. His attempt to lip-synch to old recordings was unconvincing, but the mere fact of lip-synching was irrelevant; Betty Grable's technique was far from perfect. It was the use of old recordings that would make a great story in a country that is sadly drawn to toppling icons.

Hundreds of media representatives had been treated to unlimited drinks and were seated to one side of the stage. After the show, they surrounded Lanza, cheering him as he entered and calling out rapid-fire questions: "Where have you been? What are your plans? Will you do another movie?" Then Lanza's purported friend Jim Bacon—no stranger to the underbelly of a story—began his clever set-up: "When did you prerecord your numbers?"

"Just a few days ago," Mario replied.

That response was all that Bacon needed, but he cruelly persisted. "Isn't it true that these were some of your old recordings?" A comparison of tape-to-record would have been necessary for Bacon to make such an accusation, but the truth was that he had been tipped off and was miles away from being above skewering the hapless tenor. The singer, unaware of the leaks, painted himself into a smaller corner: "Hell no! I told you! I just did them!"

Bacon simply smiled and left the room to cable his story.

Lanza, no more up for a hostile press conference than he had been for singing, was rushed from the room, pathetically protesting, "My voice is as great as ever!"[3] Many reporters who had come from the East Coast and Europe were left without an interview. Lanza's sudden departure—combined with his failure to sing, the use of old recordings, and the attempted cover-up—led to brutal accusations of fraud. CBS, left to clean up the mess, only made matters worse when it denied, the next day, that old recordings had been used.

The New York Times (1 October 1954) called it "zombie TV," which was among the kinder things said. The next day CBS admitted that old recordings had been used. It was a story with an amazing life. The press battered Lanza for his lies and proclaimed him finished. He had become a laughingstock. Then, in one of the surprising rallies the tenor could muster in the midst of ruin, he decided to invite the press to his home for a concert. His motivation—an intense desire to prove his accusers wrong—was an improvement over his ongoing paralysis.

Four days after *The Chrysler Shower of Stars* aired, Jim Bacon, Hedda Hopper, Erskine Johnson, Bob Thomas, Sheila Graham, Max de Schauensee, and other writers, photographers, and press agents crowded into the music room at the tenor's Beverly Hills home. He offered a cordial greeting and in his typical stance—collar open, legs apart, feet firmly planted, and buckle loosened—sang "Be My Love," "Vesti la giubba," and "Che gelida manina" with Giacomo Spadoni accompanying on the piano. The reaction was positive; he had sung well. Bacon, eager for a new angle, was disingenuously sympathetic and claimed that he had been misled. De Schauensee raved. The consensus was that Mario Lanza could still sing.

Six days later, CBS and Chrysler, not wanting to lose the momentum, announced that Lanza would sing live on a second *Shower of Stars* to be aired on 28 October. He would receive $40,000 for singing two songs of his choice. Trendex reports showed that 46.3 percent of the viewing audience had watched the first show, cutting the mighty *Dragnet*'s ratings by 26 percent.

Given Lanza's emotional and physical state, no one could safely predict that he would appear or sing on the second show. Only one motivation drove him: to show the public that he still had it. When the second show aired, he insisted that Betty stand in the wings where he could see her. He sang "E lucevan le stelle" from *Tosca* and "Some-day" from *The Vagabond King*. His tones were powerful and round, the singing impassioned. Between the two songs, he offered thanks for the many kind letters he had received. He was obviously nervous and stiff, but the quality of the singing on 28 October 1954—and it was a magnificent tenor voice on display—is proof of what had been lost by his silence. A third *Shower of Stars* was planned, but the momentum waned. His point proved, the singer returned to his reclusive, destructive ways. The show was never done, though Lanza was paid $50,000.

On 21 December, Warner Bros. announced that it would sign Lanza to star in a film version of James M. Cain's controversial novel, *Serenade*. He would receive $150,000 plus a percentage of the profits with an option for a second picture. Jack Warner knew it was a gamble, but he was sympathetic to the singer's plight.

The year came to a close with two things certain. First, things would get better. Second, they would get much worse before that happened.

CHAPTER 23

Vegas

I'd sooner go bankrupt.

Mario Lanza, 1953[1]

The year 1955 began with an advance from RCA that eased the restrictions imposed by the IRS. Lanza was amazed by the generosity, never equating his release of the Coke Show recordings with value received by RCA.

Al Teitelbaum continued to practice an alchemy that the tenor did not question. Like all things and people in which the singer invested his trust, Lanza's confidence in him was total at the outset and only later eroded by suspicions. Teitelbaum's priority was money but he, like many, genuinely liked the troubled tenor. He wanted Lanza to succeed and labored, subject to his limitations, to secure him work.

A radio series incorporating the Coke Show recordings and new material was proposed but failed because of union objections, and the production of *Serenade* was slowed by Lanza's adamant rejection of the novel's homosexual theme. After lengthy discussions, Warner Bros., eager to accommodate the tenor, finally agreed to eliminate the controversial aspect of Cain's novel. Anthony Mann (*Winchester 73, The Glenn Miller Story*, and, later, *El Cid*) was assigned to direct; Nick Brodszky and Sammy Cahn were brought aboard at Lanza's request and expense. The studio advanced him $1000 weekly, and he moved his operation to a mansion in Palm Springs at $3000 a month, leaving another wrecked rental home in his wake.

Filming was months away, and the Lanzas had no place to go when their lease on the Palm Springs property ran out. Worse, Mario's reputation as a one-man wrecking crew was widespread, and many property owners would sooner have set fire to their homes than rent to him. When Teitelbaum told him that a Las Vegas hotel would pay him a record $50,000 a week to sing, Lanza angrily denounced "their money."[2] But the amount worked on his mind: $50,000 was an enormous sum of money in 1955. Mario decided to accept the offer in order to acquire his first home. He and Betty were as giddy as honeymooners.

The engagement, two weeks at the New Frontier Hotel in April 1955, would pay him $100,000. After the percentages for his management team and the confiscatory tax rates of the time were deducted and his travel expenses were paid, he would net less than $25,000. The view that the engagement would pay for the house of their dreams was as childish as everything else they did.

Mario began the torture of working himself into shape. He trained hard, physically and vocally, and seemed at ease in Palm Springs. When sober and free from anxieties, which was not often enough, he could be effusive, earnest, and likable. He played with his children, took Betty to an occasional movie, and lived something close to a normal life. During the evening, Mario and Betty often ate their meals from TV-tables and watched television. Ellisa and Colleen were occasionally permitted to join them, which meant staying up past their bedtime. The tenor's diet mode meant a repetitive evening meal of steak, cooked very rare, and sliced tomatoes. At those moments, the doting father laughed, hugged his children, and often shared his steak with them.

But just as often, a "friend" would interrupt the idyllic setting by dropping by, whispering to the "Tiger" about prospects he had located for the evening. The scene would then become wrenching. Mario would hurry from the house with Betty screaming after him.

The tenor swore off of drink more often than he changed his ties, but he was as hopelessly addicted to alcohol as Betty was to anything that altered her mood. She too was admitted to Las Encinas Sanitarium; when she had gone through withdrawal, Mario "rescued" her. They played on one another's weaknesses, alternating their roles according to their needs. The destructive tugging at one another was paramount. During this time, Al and Sylvia Teitelbaum learned the painful lesson taught to Sam and Selma Weiler: dealing with the Lanzas was initially seductive, always time-consuming, and ultimately futile.

During his last month in Palm Springs, Mario's weight dropped below 200 pounds for the first time in years. Betty's mother joined them for two weeks, forcing a cease-fire in the household. Ray Sinatra commuted from Los Angeles to work on the arrangements, and Mario, given complete freedom to develop his own program, was eager and fresh. Ray Heindorf, who won Academy Awards for arranging and conducting the scores for *Yankee Doodle Dandy*, *This Is the Army*, and *The Music Man*, also worked with Lanza in preparation for *Serenade*. Ray enjoyed his liquor and made the mistake of having it available when the tenor dropped by at his bungalow, which Mario viewed as a refuge from the pressures of home life. As usual, the furniture and walls absorbed a beating. Heindorf, shocked at the damage a drunken Lanza could inflict, quit stocking liquor. The visits tapered off, but the music for *Serenade* had already been selected and discussed.

Mario was brimming with ideas and boasted that, once he began to roll again, "a million bucks will seem like small change."[3] Ben Hecht, the prolific screenwriter, novelist, producer, and raconteur; Ray Stark (who later produced *Funny Girl*); and Harry Saltzman (who produced the James Bond series) met with Lanza; although Hecht in particular regarded Mario as a phenomenal talent and an interesting character, the trio concluded that what he needed was a keeper, not a director. Regardless, Mario looked great and Hollywood was showing interest. Lanza, who had not filmed a single frame of *Serenade*, was convinced that a second film was in his future.

Teitelbaum located the Lanzas' dream house at 355 St. Cloud in Bel Air. Built by Harry Warner at a cost of $750,000 in the 1920s, the house was completely furnished, with a custom, $40,000 living room carpet, an ornate marble foyer, twelve bedrooms, fireplaces in each of the main rooms, and a theater, with a kitchen and private bar, that sat eighty people. The complex was gated and included elaborate gardens and a huge swimming pool. Mario and Betty were overjoyed with their new address. They did not see the mansion as a relic from a bygone era. To them, it was a grand home much deserved by a great movie star and a great movie star's wife. Louis B. Mayer was among their neighbors.

The cost of upkeep for the old mansions of Bel Air was such that they glutted the market; the house had been for sale for some time. The elderly owners, realizing the diminishing returns that came with the payment of heavy taxes and maintenance and their inability to enjoy the home, practically gave it away. A deal was struck on 18 March: the Lipperts would sell the property on a land contract for $115,000 with $15,000 down and vacate before the commitment in Las Vegas, set to begin on 4 April, was finished.

Mario Lanza's Las Vegas engagement had been planned as a two-week grand opening with the highest-paid singer in the world, not unlike Elvis Presley's more than a dozen years later. Both men were booked at record fees and interest from the press and fans all over the world was unprecedented. Every seat for all the tenor's shows had been sold weeks before the New Frontier Hotel was scheduled to open and were being resold at hefty prices. Sammy Lewis, who managed the complex, was overwhelmed by the demand. "Would Mario consider six or eight weeks?" he asked, offering that the singer could earn millions if he stuck with Vegas.[4]

The New Frontier cost a then-princely $20 million to build. The Venus Room, a big, terraced showroom built around a revolving stage, was billed as the finest theater-restaurant in the world. The decor included rocket ships, space platforms, and other Vegas-style visions of space, the new frontier—the theme upon which the hotel was designed and named.

The Cloud Nine Lounge, with its customary assortment of blackjack, crap, and roulette tables, was across from the Venus Room. Mario, like any other entertainer, was expected to draw enough customers to fill the casino. It was not a mission that sat well with him.

The Lanza entourage—a personal hairdresser, Ray and Prima Sinatra, the children, three nurses, Al Teitelbaum, and enough others to fill an entire Pullman car—left Los Angeles and arrived in Las Vegas on 31 March. A throng of reporters awaited the tenor as he disembarked from the train. It was a cold and windy night in Vegas, though it did not stop the reporters and photographers from living up to their reputations by pushing and shoving for position, nearly trampling the children, and vying to outshout one another. Lanza—trim, tan, and toned, his nerves as taut as ever—enjoyed the attention from the reporters and remained on the platform until the questions ebbed.

Lanza and his legions left the station and found that the largest suite in the hotel, though attractive and spacious with a living room, several bedrooms, and a private kitchen, was too cramped for their party of nine (Mario and Betty, the four children, and the three nurses). Betty's rage only worsened when the manager explained that the hotel was overbooked, their party was larger than anticipated, and after all, they had arrived earlier than anticipated. She played her role well, causing her already overwrought husband to pace and join in denouncing the treatment as shabby. She succeeded in goading him into regarding it as a personal insult.

Friday came and went without Mario leaving the crowded suite. As usual, he did not inspect the stage and showroom. Most artists want a feel for the size and layout of the stage and room before a performance, but Mario frequently saw the place where he was scheduled to sing, for the first time, when the concert began. The empty hall would loom as a specter and haunt him if he saw it in advance. That he missed rehearsals was somewhat more troublesome, but again not unusual for the tenor. Ray Sinatra knew he was familiar with the arrangements and had an intuitive ear for the cue. Nonetheless, Sinatra compulsively drilled the orchestra and fretted about whether or not the string section was ready.

Saturday came and went the same way. Lanza complained of a sore throat. A doctor was summoned and advised him that he would be fine. Sylvia Teitelbaum flew in from Los Angeles the next day. Mary Cocozza, Terry Robinson, and Tony drove in from Pacific Palisades and visited with Mario in the suite. Otherwise, Sunday was a rerun of the two preceding days.

On Monday, 4 April, the tenor tested his voice. He told his wife that his throat was still sore, he might not be able to appear—and the mean chemistry of their relationship took over. If Betty had consoled her nervous husband and offered that he was always tense before a recording session or concert, he might even have laughed at himself. Instead, she tore into him for always behaving that way before a performance and coldly dismissed his complaints.

The situation was tense. Lanza exploded and swung at Betty; according to some, he missed. When Teitelbaum checked in, Lanza was agitated and still complaining about his throat. A doctor was again summoned. He examined the singer's throat, wrote a prescription, and recommended that the performance be delayed for a day or two. It was as if the situation preceding the *Shower of Stars* debacle had been duplicated, but lip-synching to old recordings was not an option. Teitelbaum was in a quandary. The only certainty was that Mario was taking safe harbor in the doctor's advice; he now felt justified about not having to confront what had paralyzed him since arriving in Vegas—taking the stage in the Venus Room.

The tenor paced while Teitelbaum pondered a way to salvage the situation. The children, bored with their lot in the suite, became loud and unruly, which caused Mario to erupt again. Sylvia Teitelbaum wisely suggested that she and Betty take the children shopping. Shortly thereafter, Nick Brodszky and Ben Hecht arrived. Lanza ranted about his terrible luck and complained—not too convincingly—about his disappointment over not being able to go on. "Lanza's luck" had never diminished. Rather his increasing paranoia and capacity for self-destruction forced him to turn away from it. For him, good fortune was a thing to smash, like the glass after a toast.

Brodszky, sensing that the tenor had been cooped up for too long, suggested that he and Teitelbaum come to Hecht's apartment at Sands Hotel. Teitelbaum agreed, but pulled Brodszky and Hecht aside and told them that no liquor was to be made available. They agreed, though Brodszky believed that a drink would relax the singer.

Lanza then bolted from the suite, crossed the Strip, and found an iced bottle of champagne waiting at Hecht's apartment. A distraught, nervous, or even happy Mario could down a magnum of champagne faster than most could a glass. He took his first drink since leaving Palm Springs, and it was off to the races. Lanza's capacity for alcohol, though not in the legendary class of Bogart or Flynn, was amazing; he continued to drink when incoherent and nearly unconscious. Showgirls came and went from Hecht's apartment. More champagne was delivered and empty bottles were taken away.

The tenor continued to complain about his terrible luck in not being able to go on and explained that, since his condition would not matter that evening, he could drink. Louella Parsons arrived in response to an invitation from Nick Brodszky and was startled to find a highly intoxicated Mario Lanza.

Lanza was a talented mimic. During his days at MGM, he occasionally caused problems by calling various personnel and, in a perfect imitation of Joe Pasternak's soft Hungarian accent, countermanded orders for the next day. His best imitation that day was of a man with laryngitis, and he delivered it many times. Parsons was so taken in that she agreed to appear with Mario onstage at the Venus Room, where both would explain that he was unable to perform. The scheme mushroomed into the realm of the ridiculous with the props of a thick scarf, covering the singer's neck, and an exaggerated hoarseness decided upon.

Lanza was scheduled to do two shows that evening and, with his introduction for the first only hours away, personnel at the New Frontier were checking bar stock, preparing salads, arranging tables, placing flowers, and readying the kitchen for what would be a busy evening featuring the most heralded Las Vegas debut to date.

Teitelbaum and Lanza left Hecht's apartment. During the walk back to the New Frontier, the tenor decided that he could not withstand another debacle; he repeated, again and again, that he was fearful of more rumors that he had lost his voice. He would appear, explain his dilemma, and sing a few less demanding songs. Teitelbaum remained indecisive; certainly the new plan, that Mario would attempt some easier material, was better than advising Sammy Lewis that the grand opening was in jeopardy. Besides, he desperately clung to a hope that Lanza would rally and appear as scheduled.

When they arrived at the New Frontier, Betty launched into an accusatory tirade about his condition and timing. Mario, slurring his words, assured everyone that he would be fine; he needed to rest. Betty again left with the children so that the suite would be quiet. The singer then swallowed what were later estimated to be ten of Betty's Seconal tablets. When Teitelbaum discovered what had occurred, he called Sammy Lewis, who rushed to the suite.

Lewis, accustomed to drunken entertainers, ordered that the singer's stomach be pumped and that an oxygen tent be brought to the suite. It was pointless. Mario's depression and paranoia had provided him with a successful retreat from a situation he could not confront. The money he would lose meant nothing to him. Word spread fast on the Strip: some of the gambling houses were offering three-to-one odds against Mario Lanza appearing at the New Frontier.

The lobby of the hotel was electric with the excitement of Mario Lanza's debut. Lavishly dressed patrons arrived in limousines and were escorted to their tables in the Venus Room, where they ordered drinks, shrimp cocktails, and champagne. The murmur in the room grew as showtime approached.

The scene in the suite was far from pretty. The aggressive attempts to revive the singer were destined to fail. He had consumed something on the order of a gallon of champagne, and any decent voice required sobriety for an acceptable performance. Minutes seemed like hours and showtime arrived with Mario barely stirring. Jimmy Durante, an old pro who greatly admired what Lanza could do when things were right, entered the room and sized up the situation. After a few minutes, he headed for stage. "I have a very painful announcement to make. Mr. Lanza is ill and will not be able to appear tonight."[5]

Boos and catcalls erupted from the audience, and the media, more than a thousand strong, went into action. Durante tried to explain that the singer was quite ill, that he had just left him in an oxygen tent. The commotion continued. Sammy Lewis took the microphone and announced that drinks and dinner were on the house, but the crowd would not be quieted.

The hall outside of Lanza's suite was jammed with hundreds of reporters and onlookers. The fact that he was unavailable to make a statement was not well received. It did not seem possible, but the mood was more hostile than it had been after the *Shower of Stars* telecast.

The tenor was still unconscious when the second show began with performers sent by other hotels. The audience went along with the routines by Durante, Ray Bolger, Mindy Carson, and Edgar Bergen, but no one was buying the story about the singer's illness. After the debacle of *The Student Prince* and the CBS embarrassment, Lanza was without credibility. Mario's latest agent, Arthur Parks, and a crew from Warner Bros.' publicity department flew in from Los Angeles to ease the public relations aspect of what was already an unsalvageable situation.

On 5 April, Lanza awakened, unaware of the ongoing crisis. His lips were bruised from the pressure of the oxygen mask but he was otherwise recovered and seemed contrite about what he explained as an inadvertent overdose of Seconal. A press conference was scheduled for ten o'clock that morning. The tenor would not make an appearance. As always, he left the torturous task of offering explanations to others.

Nothing could quell the press or management at the New Frontier. Arrangements had been elaborate and many had flown in from Europe for Lanza's much publicized Las Vegas debut. What should have been a triumph had degenerated into a disgrace, a waste of time and money. Teitelbaum and Parks explained that the tenor might be able to appear in a few days. The press responded with jeers and accused them of lying. Sammy Lewis, grandstanding for the media, shouted, "Lanza sings tonight or he's fired!"[6] The press corps cheered. Mario's failure to appear had become a bigger story than a successful show would have been. Bulletins and headlines ran for days, none of them kind to Lanza.

At eleven o'clock that morning, the Lanzas were presented with an order to vacate their suite and a bill for room service and lodging. Phone service was disconnected. They remained in the suite that day and made arrangements to return to Los Angeles the next morning.

Mario could not avoid direct questions from reporters as he made the agonizing walk toward his train. A reporter asked how he was feeling. He whispered that he was not well and pointed toward his throat, but as the interview progressed, his voice became loud and clear. He expressed amazement at so much publicity over a simple case of laryngitis and wondered how anyone could suggest that he had intentionally squandered $100,000.

He was indignant at the suggestion that he had disappointed the New Frontier and his fans, demonstrating his customary lack of introspection and rationalizing everything away as the fault of anyone but himself, going so far as to claim that he had lost a hundred thousand badly needed dollars while the New Frontier had doubled that in the value of the free publicity he provided.

He then boarded the train for Los Angeles. Other hotels, all too aware that Mario's emotional state would prevent him from ever appearing on their stages, taunted him with offers of even more money. The offers always came in the form of publicity releases and were usually nothing more than cheap stunts. The Seville Hotel in Miami, for example, offered $20,000 for one rendition of "Figaro" from the *Barber of Seville* on the evening of its grand opening. Lanza did not respond.

When the train reached Los Angeles, the media was waiting. One reporter asked him if he felt guilty about disappointing his fans. Mario turned to the man, incredulous at such a suggestion, and snapped, "Guilty? If I felt guilty, it would be a feeling of guilt toward God!"[7]

Meanwhile, serious discussions about canceling *Serenade* were underway at Warner Bros. The publicity stayed white hot, convincing Jack Warner that it was worth the risk. One Warner executive explained that Mario would become the hottest box-office attraction in the country simply by at last appearing when he was supposed to.

The Great Caruso had premiered only four years before. The devastation to person and career since was harrowing. It was enigmatic that Lanza, a man who could be so proud of his voice and appearance and sensitive about how others viewed him, could place himself in so many disgraceful situations. Most attributed his behavior to stage fright or temperament, but it was far more sinister than that. A part of Mario Lanza wanted to do what was right, to pursue the higher calling, to display his voice properly. The greater part of him—the part he could not understand or defeat—compelled him to pursue an antisocial course of behavior, to grow fat, and to fail to meet the simplest obligations of life.

In subsequent years, Lanza claimed that a voice like his did not belong in a Las Vegas casino, though Richard Tucker and Jan Peerce, who successfully adhered to the higher calling their art demanded, saw nothing wrong with earning handsome fees there.

By 1955 Swedish tenor Nicolai Gedda had already debuted at La Scala, the Paris Opéra, and Covent Garden; Carlo Bergonzi was with the Chicago Lyric Opera; and Franco Corelli had made an impression at the Spoleto Festival. All were destined for the Met. Mario Lanza was headed for 355 St. Cloud Street.

CHAPTER 24

Serenade

Why didn't I sing? I couldn't! It was not a physical thing. The voice was always there. But a man must be free in order to sing, or there is no will to sing. For three years, there were obstacles. Now they are gone—and I am singing again.

Mario Lanza, 1955[1]

Mario and Betty settled into their new home in April 1955, thinking themselves rich, while the New Frontier Hotel scrambled to find replacement acts. The tenor was now blaming Caruso for his most recent failure, solemnly asserting that God had sent him to intervene.[2] Within weeks, Lanza was bored with life at the Bel Air compound. He and Terry Robinson drove to Tijuana, still the dusty bordertown of legend rather than the quirky metropolis it has become. Robinson parked the Cadillac at a filling station, and he and Mario, disguised in a hat and dark glasses, wandered the streets and took in the risqué sights. After a few hours, the singer suggested lunch at a cantina Robinson remembers as dark and undistinguished, a true hole-in-the-wall. Not long after the two men were seated, a young Mexican wandered in, positioned himself at a table, and began to strum his guitar. Mario's eyes were riveted on the young man's instinctive movements and chording.

"Look at that," the tenor whispered. "Probably never had a lesson in his life. That's a real musician."

Then the guitarist shifted to a few chords from "Granada." Lanza threw down the hat and glasses, stood, and burst into song. The tenor was popular in Mexico, and the crowd in the cantina quickly overflowed into the street as the man who only weeks before walked away from a $100,000 engagement sang for nothing; in fact, he paid for the privilege, since he tipped the guitarist $300. The difference between Vegas and Tijuana was that in Tijuana, the tenor honored his own rule rather than what he was expected to do.

169

The crowd surged forward when Mario finished, begged for more, and tried to touch him. An old woman managed to grasp his hands; when he looked into her eyes, he saw that she was crying. The police were called to restore order and escort the men from the cantina. During the drive home, the singer reflected. "Did you see that old woman? The tears in her eyes? My singing touched her heart." He gazed out the window. "That's what it's all about. It isn't the money."[3]

In May 1955, at 8:30 one morning, a process server tossed a summons and complaint toward a bathrobe-clad Lanza as he hurriedly ordered a maid to shut the gate. The papers flew back over the wall as the process server left—becoming very expensive litter. On 13 June, Mrs. Norman Kaiser, owner of the house Mario and Betty had recently vacated, provided extensive testimony before the Superior Court in Los Angeles. She testified that the property was left in shambles. Lanza failed to respond to the complaint, so a default judgment in an amount exceeding $40,000 was entered. Another suit, filed by Noah S. Andrews, alleging $17,000 in damages to yet another rental home the tenor had pummeled, was pending.

On 22 July, Mario appeared in the Los Angeles Superior Court and denied receipt of the Kaiser pleadings. He was somewhat heavier than three months before in Las Vegas, though not obese. He drew a surprisingly artful diagram of the St. Cloud estate on a blackboard and testified that, because of its configuration and the fact that he never left his chambers before midday, he could not be the person at whom the process server threw the documents. The judgment was set aside. Lanza's attorneys settled the matter for $12,500. The Andrews case was settled two months later for $3000.

The New Frontier Hotel also filed suit, seeking $14,800 for accommodations, rehearsal costs, and advertising; $10,121 in advances; and $100,000 for loss of good will. The case was later settled for $13,900. A quick boost was needed if 1955 was to be an improvement over the wasteland of 1954.

Recording sessions for *Serenade* began in July and continued, sporadically, through the fall with Ray Heindorf conducting. The sessions went well, though Constantine Callinicos' patience no doubt would have contributed to an improved score. Heindorf, long curious about whether or not Lanza's voice was big or electronically enhanced, was impressed by his power and musical instinct. But despite some very good work, he let too much pass in deference to the singer's prideful one-take stance. The prerecordings, filming, and editing of *Serenade*—all expensive undertakings—were rushed at the expense of the overall product.

Lanza's voice had darkened considerably, through maturation and abuse, since his last operatic recordings more than three years before for the *Caruso* album. In addition, he selected a program of demanding, complex arias that serious artists add to their repertoires only after years of serious study. Lanza's work in *Serenade* was all the more remarkable since he was, as Coke Show trombonist Harold Diner observed, "a singer who happened to sing opera as opposed to a trained operatic performer."[4] Still, he tended to force as if to show that his voice was still huge and his high C, though resonant, did not come with its previous ease, consistency, or control. His voice wobbled occasionally and cracked twice (while running through the scales and in the last version of "Serenade").

"Amor ti vieta" from *Fedora* was tastefully sung with appropriate restraint. "O soave fanciulla" (with soprano Jean Fenn) from *La Bohème* was also well done. "O paradiso" from *L'Africana*, an aria he had sung beautifully in concert and on the *Caruso* album, was forced. "Torna a Surriento" was exciting but, in part, also forced. He was excellent in the Lamento di Federico, bringing tears to the first-chair violinist. Howard Keel, then just beyond his heyday as the star in a string of memorable musicals (*Kiss Me, Kate*, *Rose Marie*, *Seven Brides for Seven Brothers*, *Deep in My Heart*, and *Kismet*) was present during a replay. He remarked that only a man out of control could emote in that manner—not realizing that Mario was seated behind him. He was treated to a vintage Lanza barrage.

The tenor was also excellent in a difficult fourteen-minute segment from the third act of *Otello*. His partner in "Dio ti giocondi" was Metropolitan Opera star Licia Albanese, who had sung with the greats of several decades. As with so many of those who actually sang with him, she too was in awe of his talent: "This boy has, to me, a greater voice than Caruso. He has the greatest voice I have ever heard."[5] The inclusion of such a long operatic sequence was daring. It remains the finest operatic scene ever featured in a non-operatic film.

Voice critic Robin May later reviewed the soundtrack:

[*Serenade*] includes two pieces with piano accompaniment, in one of which, the Love Duet at the end of *La Bohème*, [Lanza] sings very sensitively with Jean Fenn. Even better proof of what a good artist he could be is his "Amor ti vieta" . . . sung with poetic feeling. . . . [He conveyed] considerable vocal character and much feeling in the long sequence from Otello . . . [and] could colour his voice much more than his detractors would admit. . . . . He deserved every bit of his popularity.[6]

The score of *Serenade* also included "Di quella pira" from *Il Trovatore*, with a forced high C that is barely controlled, and a compelling "Nessun dorma." Critic Charles Osborne later wrote:

Had he lived in another time or in another place, or both, he might have been a serious rival to Corelli or Gigli, or for that matter, Caruso. I've certainly heard in some of the world's leading opera houses less well sung performances by famous tenors of "Nessun dorma" . . . and "Di quella pira."[7]

The lemons of the prerecording sessions—and they could sour the Nile—were a couple of Brodszky-Cahn compositions, "Serenade" and "My Destiny." Nick Brodszky was still trying to recapture the magic of "Be My Love," taking Lanza through his paces to an enormous finish, but Cahn's lyrics were uncharacteristically awful. The tenor, obviously at the end of a long battle, labored through both songs. The unsteady, reedy high C at the finish of "Serenade" would have driven St. Patrick out of business; the snakes on the Emerald Isle would have fled to the sea voluntarily. Neither song was worthy of release.

Unfortunately, the studio tapes were vastly superior to RCA's treatment of the material. Prior to the development of electronic amplification systems, acoustics were even more vital than they are today. In a good hall, the sound carried, echoed, and built; risers, which echoed and projected the sound toward the audience, were commonly used. In the primitive 1950s sound technology, echo enhancements were overused in an attempt to bring this concert hall sound to the living room. Singers like Johnny Ray and Elvis Presley exploited the echo with great effect, but it was a detriment to Lanza. A good example is "La danza," which the tenor sings to a group of laborers in an open field. The release features a thundering echo that detracts from and is at odds with the setting.

Lanza's overall singing on the operatic pieces was uneven. Retakes, which Pavarotti, Domingo, or Carreras would gladly have done, could have made for an extraordinary result. Those opportunities, like so many others with Lanza, fall into the category of what might have been. For now, the studio had to contend with making a picture to justify its soundtrack. As for the tenor, he mused that the Met would be calling after hearing the recordings. The phone remained silent.

Warner Bros. assembled a decent cast for the film. Two leading ladies vied for Mario's attention. Joan Fontaine, then thirty-eight, played an icy patroness who discovers the singer in a vineyard, brings him to the brink of fame, abandons him for a sculptor, and then tries to reclaim him. Sarita Montiel, the torridly beautiful Spanish actress, played the Mexican woman who nurses the emotionally devastated singer back to health, marries him, and triumphs over Fontaine. A bemused Vincent Price rounded out the list of major players. Vince Edwards, later to strike gold in the *Ben Casey* television series, landed a minor role at Mario's insistence. Their tastes were similar, and they got along well.

Filming began in the beautiful town of San Miguel de Allende, Mexico, in September 1955. The month marked the 145th anniversary of Mexico's independence from Spain, which provided colorful fiestas and crowds as a backdrop for the film. The local populace flocked to see Lanza, causing occasional security problems; the tenor was fleetingly happy to see that the fans were still with him—here.

But back in Hollywood, a new brigade of actors was emerging in Hollywood. The list was long, including an unlikely Tab Hunter, Rock Hudson, and Tony Curtis. James Dean died that month on a lonely road in Pasa Robles, California, but he had left his mark, and durable leading men like Kirk Douglas and Burt Lancaster were establishing themselves. Marlon Brando had become a social and creative force. Lanza was losing his teenaged audience to a new breed of heroes. Time was slipping away, and he could not afford to lose much more of it.

The tenor occupied what was once the count's master suite in the Institute de Allende, which had been the palace of the Spanish counts of Le Canal. Built in 1734, it is set amidst fifty acres of lush gardens with sweeping views from every room. Lanza weighed over 220 pounds when shooting began and, with the rock 'n' roll pompadour he had adopted, looked more like a union enforcer than a man who would be at the center of a duel between Montiel and Fontaine.

Lanza took an immediate liking to Sarita Montiel, who treated him with great respect. They attended a bullfight together and spent a great deal of time talking on the set—until her romance with Anthony Mann, whom she later married, occupied center stage and, in many ways, distorted the film. The tenor was certain that Mann was favoring her in their scenes, and their relationship chilled. He was also convinced that Joan Fontaine, who was terrified of him and loathed his crude and childish antics, was trying to outshine him. He resorted to an old tactic of chewing garlic cloves before scenes in which they had to kiss or embrace. Likely the dignified Fontaine found it among the more tolerable things he did.

Mario was different with Licia Albanese. He treated her with immense reverence from the moment they met and told anyone who would listen that he loved her. They remained friends, and the tenor occasionally phoned her during his darkest hours. The soprano later recalled, "He was a terribly sick boy and tortured by a lack of true understanding. . . . Every day after I left him, I prayed for him."[8]

The troubled star drank heavily on and off the set, and the results were noticeable to viewers and those who had to work with or around him. Feeling as embattled and defiant as ever, he retreated to his dressing room, sneering about people being out to get him. He also found time for the local women and barely avoided a scandal.

Production was somewhat more orderly back at the Warner Bros.' studio in Burbank, where the set sequences were filmed in October and November. The tenor's weight ranged from 210 to 230 pounds, which difference, though noticeable, was not as distracting as it had been in *Because You're Mine*. The wardrobe department eventually assembled three collections of clothing for the tenor.

The part of Damon Vincenti (Mario insisted on the name in honor of his oldest son) was a departure from the tenor's previous light comedic roles, with a script that called for a dramatic portrayal of an emotionally tortured man. Mario was a novice in such a role—on film. He sensed that the part was too downbeat for him and the interior scenes too dark, but he gave it an earnest effort. If he could learn to sing by listening to records, he would learn to act by watching movies. Marlon Brando had launched an armada of imitators who engaged in exaggerated motions, furrowed brows, stooped and slowly nodding heads, and overly intense stares into nothing, and Lanza seemed to have taken the method to heart. The effects of his explosive mood swings were captured on the screen.

Serenade was poorly edited and ran just over two hours. The basis for the attraction between Vincenti and Kendall, the part played by Fontaine, was hazy. The transitions from song to speech were often ineffective and ponderous. As filming progressed, Mann—obviously enchanted by Sarita Montiel and absolutely confounded by Mario Lanza—expanded her role. The result was more and more Montiel in what became a parallel story that made the film disjointed and tedious. What began as a Lanza film wound up as a confusing, three-part story featuring Mario, Montiel, and the colorful celebrations in San Miguel de Allende.

Serenade opened at Radio City Music Hall over Easter Weekend 1956, to mixed reviews. Contrary to press releases, Lanza did not attend the premiere. While allowing that the tenor delivered "a better acting display than ever before," *Picturegoer* (2 June 1956) further noted, "The trouble with Lanza is that he can never forget he is Lanza. When he does—as in the magnificent Otello aria—he comes very close to being sensational." *The New York Times* (24 March 1956) observed that *Serenade* "served to bring Mario Lanza back to the Screen. . . . [He] was never in better voice."

It went downhill from there. According to John McCarten of *The New Yorker* (31 March 1956): "Mr. Lanza finds his pipes a bit rusty . . . Mr. Price delivers the jokes. They are no good." *Time* (9 April 1956) seemed to forget that Lanza was playing the part of an opera singer, not acting in an operatic role. Its review began with a boorish ethnic reference:

He looks like a colossal ravioli set on toothpicks . . . the face aflame with rich living, having the appearance of a gigantic red pepper. . . . In his acting, the tenor seems desperately afraid he will not be noticed. His eyes flash, his lips twitch, his nostrils flare, and great shudders run through his body as he mutters hoarsely to a fellow he has just met, "How do you do?" On the lifting of an eyebrow, Lanza expends as much energy as might be required to lift a piano through a tenth-story window. This is not, as the tenor seems to think, operatic acting. It is just smarm.

Sounds a lot like Brando or Dean trying to say "No"—and *Time* fell all over itself about them. But the magazine was half right about one thing: "The big voice is just as big as ever. Lanza can still rattle a teacup with his 'C' and with this picture he seems sure to rattle the cash registers all over the land."

Serenade never showed a "profit" that translated to payments to Mario Lanza. The film enjoyed an early burst at the box office but quickly tapered off, grossing just over $3 million in its initial theater run, nearly $2 million of which came from markets outside of the United States. Lanza's box-office appeal in the American market had considerably eroded during his lengthy period of inactivity.

The studio was entitled to recoup its production costs, a 30 percent distribution fee, and associated distribution costs, both fixed and actual. Though Warner Bros. never spent more than it realized from *Serenade*, the picture would show a "loss," which is borne out by its present (30 June 1997) status of a $694,519 deficit, with $1,584,807 attributed to distribution fees. The tenor's happiness with a contract that provided him with 50 percent of the "profits" was understandable, but the fine print was such that he was again duped.

Late in 1955, prior to retakes for *Serenade*, the singer had been distraught, even by his extreme standards. Mario, who had once before talked of suicide, brought it up again, and spoke nearly incoherently about plots and attacks against him. Terry Robinson and columnist Lloyd Shearer, concerned about their friend, talked him into going to New York to consult with a psychiatrist. The time frames described by Robinson and Shearer vary slightly. The important thing is that what they independently described is identical and that it really occurred.

Robinson and Shearer accompanied him on an overnight plane to New York. He was drunk and behaved outrageously during the flight. Once in New York, the trio retreated to the apartment of Lanza's former Hollywood secretary, Kathryn Reitzle. Lanza was glad to see her; he told her that his life was in danger and that he was at the breaking point. Later the celebrated tenor, his 260 pounds clad in ill-fitting clothing, spoke at length with a psychiatrist at the Payne-Whitney Clinic. When the session ended, Lanza was furious. He fumed at Shearer, "Where did you find that phony doctor! He's a nut and so are you! This is no hospital! This is a nut house and the Tiger's breakin' out! You hear me? The Tiger's breakin' out!"[9]

Mario huffed down the hall, exited the hospital, and entered a cab. He fought with Robinson, accused him of being out to get him, and refused to allow him into the cab. He relented when he realized that Terry had all the cash between them. The scene was loud, and a crowd gathered. The cabbie, figuring that this was just another day in New York City, knew that his fare was Mario Lanza.

The trio wound up at Nathan's Restaurant in Coney Island, eating hot dogs and drinking root beer as the wind blew in the salt spray from the Atlantic. Mario, now calm, talked and laughed about life and family. If he had looked due east, he would have been staring at the country where his parents were born and where production on his next film would begin—after two more troubled years.

CHAPTER 25

Casting About

I will go to Europe rather than so debase my voice.

Mario Lanza, 1957[1]

Two days after Christmas 1955, Al Teitelbaum, deeply in debt, staged a robbery at his fur salon. Lanza was dragged into the sordid mess by circumstance and association. His fortunes were not advanced by the publicity that resulted.

Terry Robinson and Mario went to the salon early in the evening of 27 December, accompanied by Arthur Walge, a bit-part actor nearly seven feet tall who later testified that he was employed as the tenor's chauffeur, and a "nurse" named Esther Collins. Walge, Collins, Robinson, and Mario approached the rear entrance to the store. The singer knocked on the door. No one responded. Teitelbaum's car was parked in the lot, and the lights were on in the salon. Lanza, convinced that someone was inside, pounded the metal rain cover above the rear door with a palm frond. Walge walked to the front of the salon and rapped on the window. He returned to the car, and all four drove to the front of the shop.

The tenor, apparently eager to show Collins around Teitelbaum's office, persisted. They were finally admitted by Al Stan, an employee, and met by Teitelbaum, who showed them tape marks on his meticulously tailored suit and announced, "We've been robbed."[2] The police arrived, and Lanza, not wishing to be interviewed, left.

The robbery did not withstand investigation. The tenor was called to testify before a grand jury in February and March 1956. His testimony, pitched to protect his manager, was damning in that it enabled the prosecutor to narrow the time between his banging with the palm frond and Teitelbaum's sounding of the alarm to between three and six minutes, which was not enough time for a theft involving 241 furs.

As might be expected, publicity was extensive because of the prestigious North Rodeo Drive address and the tenor's involvement.

Teitelbaum and two associates, Claude Wilson and Clifford Weiss, were indicted for conspiracy to commit grand theft and filing a false and fraudulent insurance claim for the theft of 241 furs in the amount of $244,510.90. Teitelbaum was convicted and sentenced to one year in prison. His appeal was denied on 26 August 1958, and petitions for rehearings were denied on 15 September and 22 October that same year. Shortly thereafter, the sentence was imposed.

After a nearly three-year absence, Lanza reentered the recording studio in 1956. The results ranged from brilliant to unlistenable. In May, he recorded twelve Broadway hits with Irving Aaronson at the Warner Bros. studio. Selections for *Lanza on Broadway*, ranging from "September Song" to "My Romance," were the type of composition he had always sung beautifully. That did not occur with Aaronson at the baton. Rodgers and Hammerstein's "You'll Never Walk Alone," a song he had sung beautifully on Coke Show recordings, was uneven and labored. Unfortunately, that version was included on the soundtrack of the 1994 film from New Zealand, *Heavenly Creatures*.

Mario still drank and smoked heavily. His voice lacked coloration, with flat and labored tones, a restricted range, and little evidence of musical taste. The sessions were difficult and should have been rescheduled, but Aaronson, whose career was floundering, pressed ahead. He was leery of postponing anything with Lanza, fearing that he might not return. In truth, the tenor had agreed to work with Aaronson out of sympathy for his situation. That same situation left Irving without the option of taking extra time—and spending more of RCA's money—to strive for a decent product.

RCA processed the material in New York, adding an echo to what already approached bellowing on a few selections. Jan Peerce, who heard playbacks, was aghast and asked why anyone needed to do such a thing to Lanza as release the material. The tenor himself can be heard calling it, after one take used on the album: "That's not it."[3]

The album was released under the title *Lanza on Broadway*, featuring an elegantly gowned model, but no Mario Lanza, on the cover. It sold several million copies upon its initial release and more than a million during its second life, as *Mario Lanza: Pure Gold*.

Some critics were surprisingly kind to the performance. *The New*

Musical Express apologized, offering that he had too much voice for such songs and that he might have been reaching for standards beyond those of other singers who had already recorded the songs. In fact, it was the worst Lanza material ever released by RCA and did much to fuel rumors that he had lost his voice. It also provided his detractors, the most virulent of whom implied that he carried a tune as if he were lugging a barrel of beer, with an indisputable basis for their claims that he forced his tones and lacked musical taste.

The singer was eager to work on another film, but no studio shared his zeal. Lew Wasserman of MCA, exasperated with the tenor, claimed that no studio would touch him with his track record. During the first few weeks of work on *Serenade*, Lanza and Anthony Mann had entered into a joint venture known as Cloudam Productions; two motion picture projects, *The Golden Boy* and *The Golden Voice*, were under their consideration, but after the struggles on the set during the production of *Serenade*, Mann refused to discuss the projects further. Leo McCarey was shopping a script called *Marco Polo*, proposing a cast that would have included Lanza, Orson Welles, and Ann Blyth—a combination that did not have directors lining up at the studio door. Terry Robinson encouraged the tenor to sign up for *Marco Polo* but was voted down, and McCarey's concept never sold, with or without Mario Lanza.

Teitelbaum approached Colonel Tom Parker, Elvis Presley's manager, and proposed a film starring Lanza and Presley, the former Hillbilly Cat who had left the Louisiana Hayride and was soaring toward an international orbit. Parker accepted the proposal but set terms and conditions that were impossible to meet. Three decades later, Teitelbaum protested, "You just couldn't deal with that man."[4]

In August and September 1956, the tenor recorded twenty-three songs with Henri René's Orchestra and the Jeff Alexander Choir at Republic Studios in Hollywood. He was in better voice, and the recordings included eight beautifully sung Christmas carols and two songs ("Earthbound" and "Do You Wonder") that became moderate hits. Henry Hill, who wrote "Do You Wonder" and spent his career in the shadow of his famous brother, Victor Young, was the first-chair violinist on most of the sessions. Hill found Lanza's instincts and abilities first-rate, though he gruffly pronounced, "He isn't Caruso."[5]

The tenor also recorded a selection of songs from musicals and operettas made famous by singers like Allan Jones ("The Donkey Serenade") and Nelson Eddy ("Will You Remember, Sweetheart" and "Rose Marie"). He breathed new life into the material; the voice was dark, controlled, and impassioned, with solid approaches to the high B-flats. In addition, the arrangements were more intricate and contemporary than any featured on Lanza's earlier recordings.

The collection, A Cavalcade of Show Tunes, is one of two severely underrated albums in RCA's vault of Lanza material and has been unavailable for years. His versatility, from a dramatic "Yours Is My Heart Alone" to a light and lyrical "Gypsy Love Song" and a boldly committed "Only a Rose," was a vocal tour de force that few singers have matched. The album is invariably a favorite with those familiar with the Lanza catalogue, which makes its unavailability all the more incomprehensible.[6]

Producer Mike Todd (Around the World in Eighty Days) was a regular at 355 St. Cloud, talking about a thousand projects for every one he ever launched. Todd, who began life in Minnesota as Avram Goldenbogen, wanted to link his Todd-AO widescreen process with a series of all-star opera films. His theory, developed as he chomped on his ever-present cigar, was that the public attended the same operas year after year with no great voices in the cast. His films, with great singers from the diva to those carrying the spears, would supplant live opera. Clearly, Todd did not comprehend what attracts an audience to live performances of opera. Mario was excited about the concept. Such a series would be timeless, he thought, and he saw himself as the star of every opera. The project was still on Todd's cluttered agenda when his private plane, "The Lucky Liz" (named after his wife, Elizabeth Taylor) crashed in March 1958.

Movie work was not to be found, and Lanza needed the combination of films and recordings to generate the income necessary to support his lavish lifestyle and brigade of moochers. His behavior, on and off the sets, had offended too many. Many now saw him as fat, crude, and offensive. The lackluster box-office performance of Serenade convinced the studios that he was no longer the 500-pound gorilla who could stalk the sets as he pleased. The combination of his difficult behavior during the filming of Serenade, its disappointing performance, Mario's troubled private life, and a vile outburst against Warner executive Harry Cohn resulted in the cancellation of plans for a second film. No matter how much Mario rationalized the situation, another studio had sent him packing.

Life at 355 St. Cloud became, if possible, more difficult. Mario and Betty quarreled violently. His drinking was more uncontrolled than ever. At times, he combined alcohol with uppers like Benzedrine, resulting in behavior considered erratic even for him. His language and behavior toward women could silence a crowded restaurant, and he was banned from more than one, earning a reputation as an unwanted bum. He continued to bed women in his peculiar, more and more public way, and occasionally, when drunk, was too rough. A scandal seemed imminent. Betty slept for days on end and woke only to eat.

The new year began without resolutions or promise. On 31 January 1957, Mario turned thirty-six and was sued by thirty-two-year-old cabbie Seymour Maslow, who charged that the singer was clearly unaware of his circumstances when his car collided with his cab on Laurel Canyon Road. Lanza's creditors were pressing, from the $8900 owed on his advance from the New Frontier Hotel to the more than $16,000 owed to various merchants and grocers for foodstuffs and alcohol. More than $13,000 was owed to various physicians and more than $5000 to Schwab's Pharmacy, evidence of the enormity of the Lanzas' drug and health problems. If that was not enough, the Lanzas still owed $10,000 to Norman Kaiser for damage done to a rental home and $25,000 to Lew Wasserman and MCA. The tenor was also supporting his parents. Mary had developed Hollywood tastes and was aggressive in her demands for money. When it was unavailable or slow in coming, she berated Teitelbaum and accused him of stealing from her son. All in all, Lanza's debts totalled nearly $120,000, not including a substantial tax arrearage. David Martin of Business Administration spent hours of each day juggling funds and playing one creditor against another.

Lanza's luck had run out in Hollywood. It was time to cast even further for work. After much discussion between Teitelbaum, Greg Bautzer, and Lanza's tax attorney, J. Everett Blum, a plan was developed. Lanza would accept an offer from Titanus Films for a project in Rome—a joint venture with MGM. His contract with RCA was restructured so that royalty payments would be characterized as advances during the next three years, eliminating his tax arrearage. In addition, he would undertake a European concert tour, in order to discharge a debt exceeding $17,000 with Columbia Artists, Inc. The proposal was that Columbia Artists would recoup its debt through 50 percent of the commissions earned from the tour. Not a single concert had been booked.

The singer rallied himself from his sloth and depression, seeing MGM's involvement as proof that he had been right all along. Even if that were untrue, the plan served to rejuvenate Mario and Betty. Franco de Simoni, an executive with Titanus, came to Hollywood and worked on a what bore a vague resemblance to a script with his future star. Other preparations included storage of personal items, closing the house at 355 St. Cloud, saying good-bye to what friends he still had, and furloughing household help. As he pondered a first visit to the country where his mother and father were born, the tenor was convinced that a return to the heights he had hit during 1951 was inevitable. It turned out to be something less than that.

CHAPTER 26

Farewell to America

La vita è breve; la morte vien (Life is brief; death is coming).[1]

Transporting the Lanza household to Italy was as hysterical and over-blown an enterprise as anything else Mario and Betty worked on together. Terry Robinson was concerned, correctly fearing that neither were in sound emotional states. He was also alarmed by Mario's physical condition: "He looked bad. Too heavy. Not like a movie star."[2] Robinson suggested they wait six months, during which time the singer could resume physical training and work himself back into shape. But despite his poor physical condition, Mario was eager to start anew, make films, and study opera in the great houses of Europe. Robinson persisted until Betty, whom he had nursed at her worst after combinations of alcohol, Milltowns, and Seconal, sneered, "Yeah. You just want to be seen with Mario Lanza. That's why you want him to stay."[3]

Betty complicated things by buying and packing enormous amounts of clothing and supplies that could easily have been purchased in Rome. And there was a last-minute rush to schedule baptisms for the boys, Damon and Marc, despite their pending journey to the most Catholic of all cities. Al and Sylvia Teitelbaum stood in as godparents as Father Paul Maloney, a young priest who would shortly be transferred to Rome, presided.

The tenor bid farewell to his father and Terry Robinson before being driven to Las Vegas; none of the men could know the good-bye was final. Betty boarded a train in Los Angeles with the children and a single attendant. Her husband planned to board in Las Vegas, thereby avoiding reporters and interviews. While he waited, Lanza dined with friend and conductor Ray Sinatra, promising to give thought to another try in Vegas. Both men knew it was idle conversation.

Once aboard with his family, the singer settled back and wondered about his decision as the train rumbled across the heartland of America. Every mile traveled put one more between him and the city he hated more than any other. Hollywood had produced several grand musicals (*Show Boat*, *Kismet*, *Oklahoma!*, *The Desert Song*, and *The Vagabond King*) in which the tenor could have starred if his career had gone otherwise. He had desperately wanted the role of Billy Bigelow in *Carousel* but had to pay admission to watch Gordon MacRae deliver a memorable performance. More and more, he seemed to require a collision with nearly final ruin to rally himself against the black rages, the overeating, the endless drinking. Now it was harder to lose weight; the body did not regain its tone or bullish physique. The drinking was harder to kick, if he could stay away at all. He saw the Italian venture as a proverbial new lease on life, vowing to restore his career, train his body and voice, and pursue healthy habits. He also swore to stay away from other women, reluctantly leaving another behind in California. A lack of opportunity would hold him to that promise for the moment.

Betty too was happy to leave Hollywood and experienced her own form of rejuvenation. Her life, and the marriage, had become a nightmare. While she desperately needed Mario and her sinecure as a Hollywood wife, neither situation was gratifying. She did not understand her husband, and the fact that Hollywood shared her confusion made public life unbearable. The retreats to drugs and alcohol meant days in a stupor, frequent falls, and an alarming number of hospitalizations for a woman who was only thirty-three years old.

RCA officials met the train in Chicago. Mario declined invitations to meet with the local press, insisting that they devote their short stay to Betty's family. It was a strange tradeoff, as the tenor frequently complained he could not stand more than a few minutes with his in-laws.

The long rail journey ended in New York, where the singer was again uncooperative with the press, refusing all interviews. If he hoped to revive his career in the United States, he was going about it in a peculiar fashion. Sadly, he saw his departure as a rejection and his only defense to such a perception was defiance. He believed that leaving Hollywood had freed him from something—but Europe would expect just as much of him.

When the Lanza family arrived at the Waldorf-Astoria, it was another moment in a hotel accustomed to celebrity comings and goings.

Lee Berthelson, now vice-president of the Marcus Hotel and Resort Group, was a bellhop at the Waldorf in the spring of 1957. He considered himself Lanza's greatest admirer and paid another bellhop for his shift, hoping to assist the family with check-in. When the Lanzas arrived, Berthelson froze and could not leave the baggage room. Another bellhop delivered the family's luggage to their suites. He told the tenor the entire story. Lanza was adamant: "You tell him to come here, and I'll sing anything he wants to hear!" To this day, Berthelson regrets that he could not muster the courage to call on his idol.[4]

Lanza said good-bye to Art Rush, who had originally signed him with RCA, Mannie Sachs, and other Victor officials. That evening, 16 May 1957, he dined at the Waldorf with Salvatore Lanza, aunts, uncles, nieces, and nephews who had come up from Philadelphia. He treated them to the finest wines and cuisine and accepted room service charges exceeding $500.

The next day, he would depart the United States and the city where he had appeared in *Winged Victory*, courted Maria Margelli, trained with Robert Weede and Enrico Rosati, met Sam Weiler, filled in for Jan Peerce, and lived—very happily—with Betty less than ten years before. How so much could happen, and change, in such a brief period was unfathomable.

He offered his favorite toast during dinner, *"La vita è breve; la morte vien"*—Life is brief, death is coming.

CHAPTER 27

The Seven Hills of Rome

When I walked down the gangplank at Naples and set foot in Europe for the first time, I knew that a new life awaited me. Hollywood is six thousand miles away—little more than an unpleasant dream.

Mario Lanza, 1957[1]

On 17 May 1957, the Lanzas boarded the Italian liner *Giulio Cesare* at pier 84 and settled into the four staterooms they had reserved. The ship cast off, passing Ellis Island, where Mario's parents had entered the United States, and the Statue of Liberty, and headed into open water, bound for the earthy port city of Caruso's birth, Naples, Italy. The voyage was uneventful, as most tend to be, though Mario suffered from occasional seasickness. The family traveled in a style the first-generation Lanzas and Cocozzas could not afford, but it did not mean that Mario had achieved the American dream.

Lanza was the first descendant from either family to return to Italy in search of work. His name, once dominant on the singles charts, had been replaced by Sam Cooke, Jerry Lee Lewis, Fats Domino, Buddy Knox, Little Richard, and Elvis Presley. The tenor, who had emerged the victor in competition with Frank Sinatra, Rosemary Clooney, Johnny Ray, Nat King Cole, Frankie Laine, Guy Mitchell, Jo Stafford, and others, was now being outsold by Perry Como and Dean Martin. Not knowing how or when his audience had left him, and even less how to reclaim them, he was as much a victim of changing times as his own failings.

On 28 May, the liner passed through the Strait of Gibraltar and into the deep blue Mediterranean, past the craggy islands of Capri and Ischia, with Vesuvius and Naples in sight but yet distant. The approach to Naples, by sea, is among the most beautiful in the world. The bay slowly recedes into a safe harbor. Vesuvius, dormant but still emitting a vapor trail, is on the right and the city directly ahead, built on slopes that grow from a blur on the horizon to a conglomeration of dusty, faded grandeur, wealth, and, in the shadows and alleys, absolute hell-holes. As the *Giulio Cesare* approached the harbor, small boats sailed out to meet the liner with all hands gaily waving, shouting, and welcoming the man many viewed as the finest interpreter of their passionate music.

Thousands of cheering, banner-waving Neapolitans lined the pier. A paunchy Lanza, dressed in a dark suit and characteristically crooked tie, was visibly tired and overwhelmed as he disembarked. Once again his inclination was to avoid the press, but the throng was such that the police could only guide him to an open limousine and on to a reception. He became an honorary citizen of Naples and made a brief visit to the mausoleum of Enrico Caruso. He later said, "From the moment I got off the boat in Naples, I felt like a new man. I began to live."[2]

The singer and his family arrived in Rome the following day. They stayed briefly at the posh Bernini Bristol, where two flower-filled suites awaited them. The instant advantage of the move to Italy was that his slate was truly clean. The Europeans had read of his difficulties in Hollywood, but all that was distant and the amiable, charismatic, golden-voiced man of film and records was more real than thirdhand gossip. Ultimately, they thought of him as a charming rogue who lived by his own rule, a man of admirable spirit. Mario had not known such a time since his phenomenal 1951 concert tour. Feeling cherished and appreciated, at least for the moment, he was certain he belonged in Rome and believed he would find happiness there.

Mario Lanza's first rule of high finance was simple: if you spent a lot, it meant that you were earning a lot. His second rule was equally simple: if you spent more than you earned, it meant that you were being underpaid or cheated. Given those options, the family settled into a luxurious suite at the fabled Hotel Excelsior on the Via Veneto, where the costs of lodging and room service would exceed his Italian film earnings.

The Titanus project was a film called *The Seven Hills of Rome*. It was a low-budget project in comparison with his Hollywood work, which reflected the uncertainty of completion rather than the diminution of his box-office appeal. The tenor greatly resented that he had been forced to guarantee his own salary through St. Cloud Productions, though he claimed to understand the basis for their trepidation when he signed the contract with Titanus. He waited until the eve of production to voice his complaints.

The cast included Renato Rascel, a comedian-singer who was quite popular in Italy; Peggie Castle, a sultry blonde who played in B films during the 1950s, the last of which was *The Seven Hills of Rome*; and Marisa Allasio, known as the Brigitte Bardot of Italy. The tenor was under the impression that Bardot herself had signed to appear in the film, and he was not happy when he learned he was to play opposite Allasio. Allasio treated him with immense respect and regarded him as a great star, but his reponse to her was often contempt and rudeness. The extras were a versatile bunch who doubled as carpenters, cooks, barbers, electricians, and all-around gofers.

Production commenced with a script that was rewritten daily, outdated equipment, incomplete sets, inexperienced crews, and stars who could not speak English. The singer took the situation as a personal affront, giving rise to an excuse to eat, drink, and be anything but merry. The situation was exacerbated by Mario's insistence on bringing his family to the set. The children were usually well behaved, but the four youngsters were an inevitable distraction. Worse, Betty seemed to feel that she was on the roles as an assistant director. Her suggestions struck the crew as meddlesome and often caused her husband to explode in rage, which provided another source of delay. Titanus, headed by Geofreddo Lombardo and de Simoni, claimed that Lanza was too drunk to work. Mario countered that Titanus was not ready. As always, idle time, alcohol, studio executives, and Mario Lanza were a bad mix. By 7 June, de Simoni and Lombardo had canceled production.

They advised Greg Bautzer that they were considering a lawsuit. Bautzer discussed the situation with Al Teitelbaum, who then flew to Rome. When he arrived, Teitelbaum found Lanza in poor emotional and physical condition. The emotional problems were nothing new: Lanza felt betrayed and worried that the picture would be poor because Titanus did not appear to know much about film production. Teitelbaum and Maurice Silverstein, head of international production for MGM, reassured the tenor.

Teitelbaum regarded the physical problems too as easy enough to solve: if the tenor kept drinking, he was going back to his fur shop in California. Amazingly, Lanza agreed to stop and, for a time, actually kept his promise. Production resumed. Teitelbaum accompanied his charge to and from the site of shooting each day to ensure that he stayed away from alcohol. The tenor was cooperative and worked hard, in his own fashion, to make the film—although he continued to be as amazed by the archaic equipment and methods as de Simoni was astonished by his star's truculence.

In July 1957, another crisis hit the production. Titanus insisted that Lanza attend what was represented as a charity ball in Naples. He and Teitelbaum took the train from Rome and, upon arriving in Naples, received another banner welcome and ride through the city. He was again made an honorary citizen of Naples and was presented with something called the Enrico Caruso Award, a one-time contrivance to lure the tenor to what was actually a political rally. Among the organizers was mobster Lucky Luciano, a pathetic, puffy relic in 1957, far removed from any significant influence on major mob activities. He had been deported from the United States after being released from prison in 1947 and was now a familiar sight in Naples, walking the length of the Via Partenope along the beautiful bay, his newspaper tucked under his arm. Skimming from the proceeds of so-called charity concerts was a frequent scam for Luciano and others. Luciano tried to ingratiate himself with Lanza; the singer was uncomfortable with Luciano's interest.

Lanza and Teitelbaum returned to Rome. Mario was drunk the next day, causing a two-day delay on the set. He returned to the studio and, while in make-up, sent his chauffeur for a bottle of Chivas Regal. He began to drink with no purpose beyond getting drunk, despite his manager's warnings. When Teitelbaum escorted a very drunken Lanza home, Betty launched into Teitelbaum for allowing her husband to drink. Teitelbaum, like so many before him, was fed up. He concluded that Mario would never change and left the next day. The two men spoke via telephone from time to time, but Teitelbaum's duties as personal manager had terminated—which the furrier made official in a letter dated 21 July 1957.

Prerecordings for *The Seven Hills of Rome*, with the exception of the imitation sequence, were done in the Vatican Auditorium, which was a great source of pride for the singer: even the great Arturo Toscanini had been denied permission to record there with the NBC Orchestra. Lanza boasted that his were the first commercial recordings made in the pope's theater. Unfortunately, his marginal-to-good singing did not match the splendid surroundings. His voice was troublesome, and he had difficulties with the score. The theme song, Victor Young's "The Seven Hills of Rome," was a modest composition, indifferently performed. "There's Gonna Be a Party Tonight" was a lively but inappropriate yelling session. He did a poor job on the portion of "All the Things You Are," a demanding composition, that was included in the film. He sang "Lolita" reasonably well, broke down on "Questa o quella" (necessitating the use of a 1951 recording on the RCA soundtrack), and provided a passable performance on "Come Dance with Me."

The imitation sequence, which featured Lanza doing amateurish take-offs of Perry Como, Frankie Laine, Dean Martin, and Louis Armstrong, was touted as a human touch by a great singer—fine, if some great singing had occurred. The scene plays as an eerie documentary of dissipation.

The most memorable song from the film is "Arrivederci, Roma," which brought Mario back to the singles charts for the first time in years. The story behind the recording was vintage Lanza. Upon arriving in Rome, he and Betty were serenaded by a street singer, Luisa Di Mio, who operated in the best tradition of the Italian street urchin with her older brother-cum-agent nearby. Mario and Betty overtipped Luisa, and naturally, they saw much more of her and her brother. When the recording was scheduled, the tenor insisted it be done as a duet with Luisa in the Piazza Navona, with Bernini's fountains as background. The director, Roy Rowland, a competent but not distinguished craftsman best known for coddling difficult stars, went along with him. How difficult could it be to locate a beggar with a regular route? For a while, it seemed impossible as she was nowhere to be found. Alternates—pretty girls with sweet voices—were auditioned. None suited Lanza. "If you think they're all the same, then you sing with them," he challenged.[3]

The Roman police finally located her. Everyone but Mario judged her as filthy, unattractive, and without talent. Music director George Stoll, who had worked with the tenor on several MGM projects, advised him that Luisa's voice was too thin and limited. Mario remained adamant: he would cue her in and out and sing in her key, if necessary.

The brother, aware that a big American movie star was fighting to get his sister into the picture, overplayed his hand as much as Titanus underplayed theirs. He demanded $160; the offer was $100. Mario was livid, complaining that it was peanuts to pay for capturing a real slice of Rome. The Italians, for whom aggressive bargaining was a way of life, considered it moronic to pay a street singer more than she could earn in a month for a single song. The brother upped his demand to $5000, causing de Simoni and Lombardo to turn ashen and struggle against fainting. Luisa's brother finally concluded that nothing more than $160 was forthcoming, and the deal was struck. The scene was one of the most touching in the film, with Mario complementing Luisa's thin voice by singing softly and guiding her through a memorable sequence.

During the filming of *The Seven Hills of Rome*, his fans gathered, cheered him on, and were treated to spontaneous concerts from a man who had become a national hero. But Lanza did not sing a single challenging note in *The Seven Hills of Rome*. The producers explained that they wanted him to be accepted in a more casual role. Mario later called his performance terrible and the film lousy.

Gene Ruggerio, a veteran MGM film editor, worked miracles in splicing scenes of background and rare appearances by Lanza in order to make the storyline flow. But the film remained uneven. *The Seven Hills of Rome* opened to mostly generous reviews, though it was decidedly a film for Lanza fans only. It may have been mawkish and silly, but Mario was back to the light comedy he did best. It featured a wobbly tale about an erratic American tenor, Marc Revere (in honor of the Lanzas' youngest son, Marc) who goes to Rome to find his former fiancee (Castle), moves in with his cousin (Rascel), tries to find work, and falls in love with Raffaella (Allasio; the name was in honor of Raphaela Fasano, the young girl who had died from leukemia).

Critic A. H. Weiler (*The New York Times*, 28 January 1958) wrote: "As a Cook's Tour of the Eternal City, *The Seven Hills of Rome* proves once more that the Italian capital is 'unconsciously the most beautiful city of the Continent' and that Mr. Lanza can, at least, sing up a storm." Others called it great fun and noted that Lanza's comebacks were never ending. Many found the imitation sequence enjoyable, though it seemed like a strange choice for a singer who claimed that he left Hollywood rather than debase his voice in sappy B films.

For *The Seven Hills of Rome*, Mario was supposed to receive $150,000 plus 50 percent of the profits, boasting to reporters that stars like Jimmy Stewart, Cary Grant, and Alan Ladd did not receive as much. Nor did Mario. Titanus Films filed suit, demanding $69,710.25

for delays and cost overruns caused by Lanza's behavior on the set. The picture—despite its low budget, $2,345,686 initial run at the box office, good rental rates after Lanza's death, and current video release—never showed a "profit" that translated into payments to its star or his heirs.

The Lanzas quit the Excelsior and leased the first floor of the five-story Villa Badoglio, Mussolini's gift to Marshal Badoglio in appreciation of his conquest of Abyssinia. The massive white marble Villa, at 56 Bruxelles in the exclusive Savoia district of Rome, was a city-block long, with immense grounds and a grand facade. At $1000 per month, the rent was considerably less than the family had paid in Hollywood. Betty quickly assembled a staff of ten for the fifteen-room apartment, and the family commenced a lifestyle that exceeded their Hollywood excesses. Life at Villa Badoglio was frenzied, with frequent visitors, many of whom lodged there. The great room, larger than a jai alai fronton, and dining room with a marble table that seated twenty, became a regular stop for the interesting, the soon-to-be not-very-interesting, the hopeful-of-someday-being-interesting, and the simply uninteresting.

Mario, like his parents before him, saw no reason to complicate the personalities of his four children with discipline. Visitors recalled the youngsters signaling servants to retrieve their napkins from the floor or demanding, by phone, that a comic book be fetched from the other end of the Villa. Betty was initially invigorated by the change of scenery, and the marriage took on the glow of a second honeymoon. Clear-eyed and vivacious during those first months in Italy, she reduced her drug and alcohol intake and actually seemed to enjoy life.

That season the tenor footed the bill for mountainous spreads of Italian specialties and bottomless bottles of fine wines and champagnes, explaining that his fans expected him to live like a movie star. Then just as suddenly, the parties ceased and Mario refused to see anyone who called at the Villa. He began to boast of million-dollar offers and hinted at savings and investments sufficient to carry him through the rest of his life in grand style, while associates whispered that they were advancing hundreds of thousands of dollars to support him.

The tenor's weight was down to 194 pounds when the production of *The Seven Hills of Rome* ended, and in the months that followed, he continued to lose weight. Mario worked himself into the best condition he had known since his training for Las Vegas and spoke enthusiastically about more recordings, films, and a return to concerts. He even boasted that London's prestigious Covent Garden was courting him. When a reporter with the *New Musical Express* (23 October 1957) inquired about the status of negotiations, a spokesman there noted that none were ongoing, adding, "which is not to say that we wouldn't welcome some." Live opera, with its requirement of knowing a role from top to bottom, a demanding audience, and the tension of having to cue himself in and out of complex arrangements with conductors invariably less patient than Costa, would have been difficult to impossible for Lanza in 1957.

In October 1957, Ed Sullivan, a great admirer of Lanza's talent, visited with him in Rome. Films of Sullivan's interview show a nervous but trim and absolutely endearing Mario laughing and exclaiming that he was homesick. Sullivan ran the interview after the singer's death, earnestly pronouncing Lanza a magnificent talent and a wonderful man.

On 31 October, Mario and Betty filmed a segment for *The Christopher Program*, a Catholic charity format featuring entertainment and an inspirational message. The host, Father Keller, led them in a discussion of their lives and Mario's singing, from a perspective of the voice as a gift from God and the responsibilities of caring for and presenting a thing that brought beauty and happiness to many people. Mario was animated; he laughed and talked at a rapid clip, his eyes and hands in constant motion. He looked great and the effect—in spite of some far-fetched ideas about how, as a child, he saw his whole career in the flickering light above the altar at St. Mary Magdalene di Pazzi in Philadelphia—was as endearing as the Sullivan interview.

The tenor sang "Santa Lucia," "Because You're Mine," and Schubert's Ave Maria with Paul Baron accompanying on the piano. It was simple singing, without strings or complex arrangements. It was also beautiful singing. Betty, tastefully groomed and dressed, seemed sweet and unaffected. When she offered that her role, in support of her husband's gift, was to provide moral support and laugh when those things were needed, Mario added, while nervously toying with a pack of cigarettes, that those things were required very often.

They laughed and hugged, two attractive and vibrant people who seemed lucky enough, after thirteen years of marriage, to be very much in love.

CHAPTER 28

Command Performance

> I never knew that human lungs could produce such volume. . . .
> Your hands were very expressive, . . . I enjoyed your singing
> tremendously.
>
> Queen Elizabeth II, 1957[1]

Constantine Callinicos was under contract to conduct, part-time, with
the highly respected New York City Opera when Mario phoned him in
September 1957. Bursting with ideas and excitement about live performances and great recordings, Mario sought the man with whom he
had done his best work in both mediums. "Costa, you must come here,"
he exclaimed, "I'm singing like ten tigers. . . . We're going to sing a command performance before the queen of England."[2] The Royal Command or Royal Variety Performance is the equivalent of being invited
to the White House to perform for the First Family and their guests.
Callinicos, ever eager to share the limelight with Lanza, sought a release from his contract and joined the tenor.

When Constantine arrived in Rome, he was amazed to see Mario
so trim, so eager to work, so enthusiastic about his art. Costa hoped,
once again, that Mario at last would achieve his full potential. Lanza
swore, again, that he had stopped drinking: "I don't want to look at that
stuff! I'm off it forever!" At just under 180 pounds, he also professed to
be on the right path with regard to his diet: "No more abusing myself
with all those rich foods. Just good simple food for me."[3] As usual, his
elevated mood, which always marked the productive phases of his
career, was accompanied by rigorous attention to what he ate and
drank.

Mario and Costa prepared for his performances at the London Palladium. It was an exciting time for Mario. His movies and films had
done well in England, and he was looking forward to singing before

such loyal fans. He and Betty were optimistic, content, and excited
about one another and their future. They and Costa traveled from
Rome to Paris by train, crossed the English Channel, and pulled into
Victoria Station on Thursday, 14 November, aboard the Golden Arrow.
The tenor braced himself with two glasses of wine before confronting
the enthusiastic crowd, mostly women, that surged forward, chanting
for their hero and knocking him to the ground. He got up, still smiling,
and delivered an impromptu song. The excitement was every bit that
later created by Elvis Presley or the Beatles.

Shortly after he settled into the Oliver Messel Suite at the Dorchester, the tenor met with representatives from the London press. He
started by reflecting that his career had been a composite of many great
moments and a few failures, but that the Royal Command Performance would provide the biggest thrill of his life. But as the press
crowded around him and with his first performance before a live audience in over six years less than four days away, his insecurities turned to
hostility. He complained to the still friendly corps about how everyone
seemed to believe everything that had ever been written about him.
He carped that they were more interested in his weight than the fact
that he was the biggest-selling recording artist in the world. Downing
champagne, he chided the writers—he had come to England to sing,
not fight for the heavyweight championship of the world.

In fact, no one had mentioned his weight in a less than compli-
mentary manner, noting that he looked fit. The one-sided swaggering
continued, with Mario sneering at years-old suggestions that his career
and voice were finished, asking what career would be finished with a
voice like his, and snapping that he was not temperamental—he merely
said no more than most. He ripped into the writers for all the wrongs,
real and imagined, that had been attributed to him by others in the
past. Finally Lanza offered a champagne toast, announcing his intention to drink through the evening and to dedicate himself to singing
come morning. Many observers doubted he would appear on Monday
evening.

The binge continued through Friday. The tenor's treatment of
what had been a mostly sympathetic press produced predictable results. The good feelings ended the next day when the tabloids hit the
stands, describing him as overweight, petty, volatile, and crude. Under
attack, he drank more champagne and seemed destined to repeat the

disaster of Las Vegas. With a concert tour and more film offers hanging in the balance, it was not an error his career could withstand.

The magnums arrived regularly on Saturday. Lanza overtipped waiters so much that they fought over the privilege of attending to his needs. The singer continued to drink, until Sunday evening, at which time he grew quiet, began to weep, rose from the sofa, and sought refuge in his room.

Callinicos' phone rang early Monday morning. It was Mario, spiritedly telling him not to be concerned; they would do a wonderful show that evening. Later that day, he appeared at the rehearsal. He was nervous and tense as Costa fed him the words in the ritual they always followed. Onlookers were amazed by what they were seeing: the great Mario Lanza was unable to sing a note without being guided by his conductor. They were more amazed by what they heard: the voice was more beautiful than they had imagined. Even after the rehearsal, Callinicos wondered, with all that had occurred since the triumphant 1951 tour, if Mario would ever be able to sing before a live audience again.

Costa headed for the Palladium that evening, still uncertain about what might occur. The huge stage, marble pillars, and twenty-five hundred crimson seats had provided a setting for the greatest entertainers in the world. Whether or not Mario Lanza would add his name to the list remained to be seen.

The tuxedo-clad tenor arrived at the Palladium and joked with Callinicos. As always, he grew tense as the moment for his introduction neared. The Royal Variety Performance of 18 November 1957, like most, featured songs, dance, British vaudeville routines, and comedy. Mario paced and grimaced as each performer, from British stalwart Gracie Fields to Judy Garland, finished their segments. When his name was announced, he reminded Constantine to throw him the words to each song. He was terrified of his upper register failing him.

The tenor centered himself on the stage, extremely nervous and perspiring heavily. Callinicos was hurt by seeing the singer in such distress and paused momentarily. He then tapped his baton, and the orchestra began the introduction to "Because You're Mine." *Melody Maker* (23 November 1957) described it well: "A brief nod to the Royal Box, a wave to the audience, and he was off into 'Because You're Mine.' No tricks, no striving after effect, standing well back from the mike with the riser only half way up he proved his contention—that he is in better voice than ever." One critic noted "an uncertain air about him as he made his entry."[4] Still nervous, he muffed the introduction to his second number, "The Loveliest Night of the Year." Callinicos was pleased nonetheless: "The tones—orotund and bold—filled the Palladium. It was not Mario at his best, but I was willing to settle for it."[5]

Lanza acknowledged the applause and quickly moved into "E luce-van le stelle." He nervously shifted his weight from one leg to the other and was self-conscious about his gestures. When he finished, the applause was thunderous. Most of the critics judged his voice nothing short of superb. *Sporting Review and Show Business* (22 November 1957) concluded:

> Mario is good and he knows it—his robust top notes almost tore the roof off. I doubt if the Palladium has ever heard a tenor of such lung power before. . . . Lanza loosened his collar and tie and shows he can belt out those top notes without benefit of commercial amplification.

He took numerous bows, acknowledged Callinicos in the conductor's pit, and walked off with the crowd still applauding.

It was nothing more than three songs, well sung, by a great natural tenor, but it was more than that, a personal victory to Mario. He had run a dead heat with his fears and insecurities, accomplishing something he had not been able to do since Fresno, California, more than six years before. That he could muster the internal strength to go through with the engagement was perhaps the most amazing thing he ever did.

When the traditional greeting line for the queen was announced, the tenor refused to take his place. It was too much like the military and the ranks he so detested. At the last minute, he achieved a second victory for the evening and lined up with the other performers. Queen Elizabeth shook his hand and expressed her appreciation. Afterward, over dinner in an obscure restaurant, Mario was exuberant, willingly signing autographs and welcoming his fans.

The tenor repeated the three songs in a televised special, *Sunday Night at the Palladium*, on 24 November. The fiascoes of the past—the lip-synching on *The Chrysler Shower of Stars*, the unspeakable embarrassment of Vegas, and the years of emotional paralysis—were forgotten. He jubilantly predicted that he would perform in concerts all over the world.

Lanza's fans would line up to hear him virtually anywhere in the world. The uncertainty was this: who would awaken the morning of the concert? Mario Lanza, or Alfred Arnold Cocozza, a frightened, insecure, and tormented man?

CHAPTER 29

Grand Tour

So you are Mario Lanza. To think that this is the great Mario
Lanza. I am sorry for you.

Hamburg prostitute, 1958[1]

Interest in a concert tour of Europe began before the tenor walked
down the gangplank in Naples. He was quite popular in nearly every
country there, regarded simply as a great singer as opposed to the
blurred pop-opera image he had been saddled with by his own country.
William Judd, vice-president of Columbia Artists, Inc., with whom
Mario had been under contract since his 1942 success at Tanglewood,
knew that the tenor was obliged to tour Europe in order to settle the
lawsuit his company had filed. Judd contacted John Coast, his European concert manager in London, and mentioned that they had an
opportunity to present Mario Lanza if Coast were up to the challenge.
Judd cautioned that luring the tenor to the stage would require unprecedented fees.

Coast, who was unaware of the pressure under which the singer
would undertake the tour, responded immediately and asked about the
condition of Lanza's voice, his likes, dislikes, and needs. John Coast was
enthusiastic about the prospects and worked mightily on Mario's behalf, before and during the concert tour he planned. He never gained
adequate payment for his efforts and never lost faith in the tenor's talent or loyalty to the man .

Negotiations continued through the fall of 1957. Things remained
vague; Mario avoided communication and refused to commit to proposals, and matters were further complicated by his old habit of telling
parts of the story to different people and signing multiple contracts,
with everyone believing they had the exclusive right.

Coast's first lesson in how difficult life would become occurred when he learned, from a story in London's *Daily Mirror*, that Mario Lanza was scheduled for a Royal Variety Performance and a television special in November. He feared the exposure would reduce the tenor's box-office appeal in London but, having spent his working life with entertainers, moved ahead. The immediate effect was that prospective dates in Genoa, Turin, Milan, Rome, Paris (at the Palais de Chaillot), and Belgrade had to be turned down. The lasting impact was that all concerts in England had to be booked and promoted through Leslie Grade, Lanza's new agent in the United Kingdom courtesy of yet another contract with General Artists, which meant that Coast's commissions—a stiff 20 percent—had to be shared. Bill Judd, fully aware of Lanza's unpredictability, made the crossing from New York to Portsmouth aboard the *Queen Mary*. He installed Peter Pritchard at Villa Badoglio, as tour manager, valet, errand boy, and figurative punching bag. When he sailed back, a January 1958 start was in place.

The initial rush of excitement that had come with the new beginning in Italy was over for Betty. Her husband was back to his old business with women of varying ages and stations in life; he stood a greater risk of being harmed by an irate husband, brother, or father than from being ambushed by a Mafioso. The last gasp of the second honeymoon came when she saw her husband successfully conquer his fears and lauded by his London fans. She resented that he received all the attention and, in a country where she spoke few words of the native language, made up for lost time with her elixir of drugs and alcohol. To provide padding against her frequent falls, Mario placed carpets on the Villa's marble floors. In early December 1957 Betty was hospitalized briefly for phantom pains and malnutrition, sending her husband on a binge at a time when he should have been engaged in serious preparation for the upcoming tour.

John Coast described the tour as the finest ever planned for any tenor, with Lanza receiving vastly more than Gigli was paid for his European appearances. He also predicted that the tour would convince every major opera company that Mario Lanza was a legitimate artist. By 20 December 1957, the tour was sold out and setting records in the process. In Germany, the promoters were desperate to add dates and regretted, in hindsight, that ticket prices had not been set higher at the outset. Though a frantic Lanza worried about filling the house, all eight thousand tickets to a concert at Royal Albert Hall were sold within four hours, comprising the biggest stampede for tickets in the eighty-six-year history of the hall. A second date was added and sold out within days. A third date, expected to sell slowly, also sold out within days.

Maurice Silverstein and Charles Goldsmith, chief of operations for MGM in England, were concerned about the tenor's decision to perform at Royal Albert Hall without a microphone, as a failure might damage the prospects for future film releases. They urged that he instead appear at the Royal Festival Hall, which was somewhat smaller but far superior acoustically. William Judd assured them that Lanza's voice had always been adequate to fill the venues in which Columbia Artists, Inc., had booked him. He was confident that Mario would adapt and prove equal to his surroundings.

Sailing was not smooth at Villa Badoglio. Mario demanded piano accompaniment instead of an orchestra and insisted on working with Constantine Callinicos. As the program developed, Costa's long piano solos became an issue. Coast felt that it would be difficult and embarrassing for Callinicos to attempt to hold an audience who wanted more of Lanza. Constantine held his ground: "As far as difficulties regarding my being able to hold the audience, suffice it to say that I did it in the past while Mario was at the peak of his career and I can do it again now." He also demanded billing on the front page of the program—"Assisted by Constantine Callinicos, Pianist"—and was adamant that the word "accompanist" not appear anywhere.[2] It was a heady demand for a musician whose greatest achievement was an association with the man he was assisting and whose name, on the marquee, would not attract a single attendee.

Another problem was the program. Though it sounded formidable, with selections from Scarlatti, Verdi, and Tosti, it made few demands on Lanza's range. Coast cautiously suggested that the German promoters would insist on an additional operatic aria and correctly observed that the line-up was somewhat light.

Callinicos, writing from the Pensione Elisabetta at 146 Via Veneto, summed up the difficulties he was experiencing with a singer who was under pressure but reluctant to embark on a tour:

> I really don't know what to say regarding the extra aria for Germany. You must know that it has been a day to day and hand to hand struggle to get Mario to prepare for this program. I have gone to the house many a day at ten a.m. and waited until seven or eight

p.m. before I could bring him to a piano to go through the program, and most of the time it has been working with a man who
had been drinking beer all day or all night the night before. I have
used every ounce of my patience and of my perseverance, and
thank God I have a lot of both, and at this moment I am relieved
and confident that he will do a good job with the program.[3]

The first concert was less than two weeks away, and no aria was
added. With the exception of two movie themes ("Because You're Mine"
and "The Seven Hills of Rome") the program was comprised of material he had sung during the 1940s and early 1950s. Critic and admirer
alike would have to accept that Lanza had no interest in developing his
repertoire. The tenor enthusiastically predicted that this would be
greater than the tour of 1951. Costa merely hoped for the best.

Christmas 1957 at the Villa was festive, with an enormous, beautifully decorated tree and the best of everything to eat, as per the singer's
rigorous standards. He also enjoyed the Italian New Year's Eve custom of "out with the old, in with the new," and aggressively littered the
street in front of the Villa with odds and ends, glass, and junk.

The tour began in Sheffield, England, four days later. The first performance, before an eager crowd that had bought all three thousand
tickets in a record two hours, was a success. Lanza received tremendous
ovations after "E lucevan le stelle" and "La donna è mobile," and the
local reviews were excellent. His next appearance was at St. Andrew's
Hall in Glasgow, where he visited with relatives from the Cocozza side
of the family and angered the press by refusing to be interviewed. The
Scottish critics complained that the ninety-minute program, with long
periods featuring Callinicos at the piano, was light and far less than they
expected from Mario Lanza. Concerts in Newcastle and Leicester
followed.

The singer arrived in London on 14 January to meet Betty at
Heathrow Airport and prepare for his concert at Royal Albert Hall two
evenings later. That night, he and Betty attended Richard Tucker's
Covent Garden debut, in a production of *Tosca*. They sat with Sara
Tucker in a private box. Mario sat at the rear of the box out of consid-
eration for Richard, not wishing to attract attention to himself.

Richard and Sara joined the Lanzas for a late-night dinner in their
suite at the Dorchester. Mario ordered a sumptuous spread and made
certain that everything, including the bourbon Tucker preferred, was

the finest available. The men talked at length. Mario attentively asked
Richard about his methods and time spent training. They parted and
promised to meet again, though it too quickly became impossible. Sara
Tucker later wrote, "It was as if Mario wanted to figure out why Richard's life had gone one direction, and his own life another. . . . Richard
and I both got the impression that for all his wealth and great success,
Mario wasn't really happy. Something important, something very basic
seemed missing from his life."[4]

On the evening of 16 January, the singer walked into Royal Albert
Hall for the first time in his life. The size of the auditorium, covered by
a glass dome 155 feet high and 273 feet long, hit him hard. "It's too big,
Costa," he gasped.[5]

Callinicos reassured him and again hoped for the best. The audience of more than eight thousand wildly applauded as Lanza took the
stage. The performance began slowly, with little banter and only polite
applause after the Lamento di Federico, "Lasciatemi morire," "Già il
sole del Gange," and "Pietà, Signore." He adjusted to the hall and produced impressive volume, but he was pushing and seemed sluggish.

He seemed tired in the middle of the program, producing a ponderous version of "The House on the Hill," an uneven rendition of "E
lucevan le stelle," and a "Mamma mia, che vo' sapè" that paled in comparison with his successes of six to seven years earlier. Some noticed
that he seemed to shift his weight from leg to leg. The reason would
soon become clear; undoubtedly his trouble affected his stamina during the concert.

Later his nervousness seemed to ebb, and he engaged the audience in casual banter, slowly but surely setting the house afire with the
crescendo building through "'A Vucchella," "Marechiare," and two
popular songs. When he finished "Because You're Mine," the bond
between audience and performer was electric. Requests were called
out from all corners of the massive hall. Many requested "Be My Love,"
but the tenor would not vary from the program. His last number, "La
donna è mobile," was at times casually sung, clearly delighting the audience, with a voluminous but marginal high-B finish that caused the
crowd to cheer wildly, stomp their feet and nearly tear the benches
from their moorings. It was a triumph comprised of more parts
charisma than artistry.

The performance was recorded, and Lanza, upon hearing the playbacks, was aghast. He correctly assessed the material as being less than his best and was firm in his conviction that it should not be released. As things turned out, it was the only commercial recording ever made of Mario Lanza in concert, and RCA decided that that circumstance warranted its release. A slipshod album (called *An Evening with Mario Lanza* or *A Mario Lanza Program*) was initially made available. The recent CD, *Live from London*, features a remastered product that captures the excitement of the concert. Reviews noted the enthusiastic audience, the substantial voice, and the light program.

Katherine Field, who performed in three productions with Plácido Domingo (Messiah, *Hippolyte et Aricie*, and *La Bohème*), attended the concert and remembers it well: "[Lanza] was past his peak, but it was really something to hear a voice that was big enough to fill that hall. . . . He was uncomfortable and awkward on the stage—until he opened his mouth. Once he started to sing, he was different. In person, onstage, he was so powerful."[6]

John Coast was concerned about Costa's fee of $750 per performance plus expenses and a weekly salary of $250, which was frankly out of line for a pianist or in keeping with the revenue the tour would generate. Coast encouraged Lanza to terminate Costa and hire Geoffrey Parsons, whom he felt was among the best accompanists for concerts and recitals. When he learned that Parsons' fee would be $150 per concert, Lanza seethed with rage. Suddenly he regarded Callinicos as one of those in the legion that was out to get him. Bill Judd spoke with the singer on 17 January and, concerned about his emotional state, cautioned Coast to go easily and watch things closely.

When the tenor took the stage at Royal Albert Hall for a second concert on 19 January, he was still angry. He turned to Callinicos, stared, and hissed about being robbed.

His condition that evening remains controversial. Callinicos says he was drunk, and some who were in attendance agree. Others, perhaps sympathetic to their idol, claim that he was merely more subdued than he had been at Royal Albert Hall on 16 January. In any case, it is certain that he was in no condition to sing. He tried to placate the crowd, explaining, "I am very sorry tonight, but while househunting in your beloved London, I slipped and injured my ribs. Will you please forgive me?"[7]

Many did not. The second concert at Royal Albert Hall was an artistic disgrace. The performance was somewhere between marginal and terrible. When it ended, some were merciless. Fortunately, better evenings were ahead.

The tour resumed in Germany with concerts in Munich on 24 January and Stuttgart three days later. John Coast, who scheduled concert tours for the greatest names in opera, felt that Lanza's performance in Stuttgart was the finest he had ever heard—and he had seen Gigli in concert, and Richard Tucker at Covent Garden two weeks before. He judged the voice dark and powerful in every register and went so far as to pronounce Lanza in a class above di Stefano, Björling, and del Monaco. The audiences rushed the stage in both cities, crowding, shoving, and making it impossible for the tenor to exit. Lanza had once thrived on such adulation, but now it terrified him.

Lanza's right leg was swollen and causing him constant pain. A doctor was summoned the next day. Lanza looked fine, though some thirty pounds heavier than the 178 he weighed two months before. The physician, Dr. Fruhwein, told the singer he had high blood pressure and phlebitis; clots had formed in the deep tibial vein of his right calf, causing edema and the painful inflammation. At a minimum, phlebitis makes prolonged standing or walking painful. At its worst, Dr. Fruhwein told his patient, it can cause death if a clot of sufficient size breaks away and blocks the pulmonary artery. The cause of Lanza's phlebitis is impossible to determine. He may have injured the leg or simply have been predisposed to the condition (Mary Cocozza experienced difficulties with clotting in the same leg). His bouts with obesity, probable diabetes, and general lifestyle were certainly contributing factors.

All engagements through 1 March 1958 were canceled.[8] The tenor refused to consider hospitalization in Germany and, despite the dangers associated with his condition, returned to Rome, where he was hospitalized for thirteen days. Treatment consisted of blood thinners, antibiotics, a support stocking, and immobilization until the crisis ebbed. The cancellations were valid, but because of his reputation they were met with disbelief. Rumors circulated about temperamental outbursts and nightclub hopping in Rome. Few knew how close to death he had come.

A movie, *Largely a Question of Love*, scheduled to begin on 7 March in England, was scrapped. John Coast, more of an optimist than Callinicos had ever been, scheduled dates for March and April. He pleaded with the tenor to consider his obligation to the voice, to straighten himself out.

The singer continued to recuperate at Villa Badoglio, eager for a film or an infusion of cash to support his lifestyle. He requested payment of all funds owed him for the January concerts, which left with him approximately $16,000 from a $38,000 gross to clear up two months rent on the Villa, medical bills exceeding $2000, and Costa's fee of $2462. After commissions and an advance of $10,000 were deducted, he was short of the amount needed to meet his immediate obligations.

Lanza was reasonably well mended and anxious to resume the tour. Betty decided to join him. She and Mario made a devastating team, according to Coast. Together they had a pronounced ability to cause divisions among the managers, whose best interests were served by remaining united. Betty complained that Coast did not spend enough time with her and Mario, and that everyone was cheating them. She hated Peter Pritchard and demanded that he be fired, that a new car and driver be hired, and that all hotels be first class. In particular, she found the renowned Dorchester unacceptable. By himself, the tenor was merely impossible. With Betty in tow, they became the clients from hell.

Mario returned to London on 2 March, looking surprisingly fit, dapper, and handsome, though he used a cane. Björling's British agent Victor Hochhauser, who had promoted the January concerts in England, refused to work with Lanza any longer, which caused problems with rescheduling dates at Royal Albert Hall.

Mario appeared, as scheduled, in Bristol, Manchester, Newcastle, and Brighton. The critic for the *Manchester Guardian* (7 March 1958) found a Lanza concert to be an unusual experience:

> A concert by Mario Lanza, if what we got at the Belle Vue last night was typical, is very much like an after-dinner jollification at a club (a very large club, 6,000 strong) at which one of the members by annual tradition gets up and sings a few songs. . . .When the singer strolled to the platform ten minutes late, the audience gave a loud cheer. . . . He kicked around quietly now and again, waving breezily to different sections of the audience, talking to his accompanist, and shrugging various limbs like an athlete or a matador carelessly waiting till all was prepared for him. . . . The singing . . . was a surprise. Though untouched by artistic fastidi-

ousness, Lanza has a musical sensibility, and he sang . . . with a sense of style that although not very developed, and in some matters brutalised by bad examples among the great singers, was fundamentally and naturally musical, and instinctively observant of different musical expressions.

On 15 March, he returned to Rome for the confirmations of Colleen and Ellisa. Once back at Villa Badoglio, he argued with Betty and began to drink—which forced cancellations in Bradford, Croyden, and Birmingham. Betty often baited her husband into vicious, pointless arguments that triggered drinking episodes. Once she succeeded in provoking irresponsible behavior, she berated him for failing to appear in concert. As Costa observed, the more Mario needed her support, the less Betty had to do with him.

When he resumed the tour, Mario's discipline continued to wane. He ate, drank, cursed incessantly, sought women, and fired David Tennant, Peter Pritchard's replacement, installing in his stead Alex Revides, a frustrated Shakespearean actor who caused almost as many problems as Betty during what was left of the tour. Revides' aggressive rantings about how great and mistreated Mario was—and how conniving and unscrupulous everyone connected with the tour had been— were enough to send the tenor further down the wrong alley. That Lanza would become more and more difficult, believing Revides' nonsense, was inevitable. Desperately short of operating capital, he jumped to accept career guidance from a man who had been unsuccessful in his own endeavors. Revides introduced the tenor to producer Al Panone, who promised to arrange German financing for a film.

Lanza appeared as scheduled in Dundee, Scotland; in Belfast, before an enthusiastic crowd of more than ten thousand; and in Leicester. He was next scheduled to sing a mini-concert at the Olympia in Paris on 2 April. He checked into the Hotel George Cinq and spent three days drinking, gorging, and making lengthy phone calls to Betty, his mother, Teitelbaum, and others. The Parisians expected a great deal from him and were nonplussed with his sluggish, five-song performance for a $2800 fee. When presented with a bill for more than $1000 at the George Cinq, he created a regrettable scene.

By the spring of 1958, Lanza's Hollywood debts had been eliminated by Business Administration. The tenor now weighed 225 pounds; Coast and the others avoided him at meal times as he insisted on order-

ing enormous feasts from room service, demanding the best of everything in the manner of a potentate with endless funds. Coast complained that it was necessary to play cards with him until dawn in order
to get him tired and that he was up again shortly after sunrise, insisting
that his card-playing companions arise when he did. His fees averaged
more than $4000 per concert—enormous by European standards. Still,
he was hacking away at what came in, leaving little after expenses and
commissions were deducted.

The tour moved along to Ostend, Belgium, where he sang well. A
disappointment in Rotterdam followed, with an audience so small that
his earnings were limited to the $1000 guarantee; Costa wisely waived
his fee, now $525 per performance. The critic for the *Hannoverische
Algemeine* (12 April 1958) had mixed impressions of the next concert,
in Hanover, Germany:

> His appearance was pure American slovenliness—a lounge suit
> and a crooked tie; later, he drank water in full view of his public.
> . . . [But] there is no equal to this naturally beautiful tenor in the
> world today. The free-flowing "Bel-Canto" is an irresistible attrac-
> tion, the unsurpassing strength flowing from the heights of falsetto
> to a deep coaxing urgency. . . . Indeed, the enthusiastic reception
> knew no bounds.

Two days later, Lanza sang in the enormous outdoor stadium at
Kiel, Germany. His spirits were low, his stamina poor, and only his
drinking and weight up to the standards of his youth, but somehow he
gathered his forces. Callinicos couldn't believe what he was hearing:
"This was the man I had thought was through. . . . His voice, 'darker'
and richer than I had heard it in years, thrilled me. Its volume and sub-
stance rivaled any male voice I had heard in my life."[9] Kurt Klukist
(*Lübecker Nachtrichten*, 14 April 1958) was similarly impressed:

> One thing was obvious after the first few bars. . . . This man, who
> was not allowed to be other than the product of a well-regulated
> publicity machine, fell naturally and significantly into the greatest
> role he could play. . . . He really can sing. . . . This wonderfully
> melodious tenor [has] a natural gift. . . . It is difficult to know what
> to admire most: the faultless breathing technique, the elastic pre-
> cision of his wording, the light *piano*, the well-synchronized join
> between registers. Lanza sings emotionally, [with] a smoldering

fluency. His delivery is definitely not a technical exercise, but an event of blessed Southern fluency.

The great reviews from the concert in Kiel were his last for a live performance.

Now it was on to Hamburg. A doubtful Mario—torn between what Costa had said about his latest performance, the prattle from Revides, and his waning energies—was scheduled to perform before a full house. He arrived in Hamburg by car on 13 April; Coast and the German promoter followed. When they arrived at the Vier Jahreszeiten, they discovered that their charge had not yet registered. Well after midnight, the tenor phoned David Tennant, who was back aboard performing the duties Revides had promised to handle. Coast and Tennant were summoned to Lanza's suite. When they arrived, they found the tenor in the living room and a pretty girl in the bedroom.

The men conversed in the living room. Eventually, the young woman joined them. Lanza immediately became abusive, cursing at the top of his lungs and demanding that she perform certain sexual favors. He shouted that she must do as he requested because she was nothing more than a prostitute who had already been paid.

Tennant resigned on the spot and handed back a $1000 watch the tenor had given him. Lanza smashed the watch against a wall and returned to abusing the young woman. He called her a whore and knocked her down. Then he threw a hundred dollar bill at her and ordered her to leave.

She went to the bedroom and retrieved her things. Before leaving, the woman threw the money back at Lanza and sobbed through a stream of tears, "So you are Mario Lanza. To think that this is the great Mario Lanza. I am sorry for you."[10]

The Vier Jahreszeiten was Lanza's fourth hotel in Germany. He had already been advised not to return to the first three. He was heading for a perfect record.

The young woman returned with her boyfriend and demanded an apology. The singer strutted, raged, and called him a pimp. The boyfriend declared that it was now a matter for the police. Lanza made a call to Villa Badoglio and summoned Revides for support. The boyfriend returned the next morning and settled for $1000. No scandal resulted.

Revides arrived on 14 April and wreaked more destruction. That evening, he and Lanza argued—loudly and pointlessly—about *Otello*. Lanza guzzled beer and shouted the difficult arias over and over again until well past midnight. He was close to being ordered to leave the hotel.

On the morning of the concert, the tenor complained that he did not feel well. A doctor saw him in mid-afternoon, pronounced him fit, and sprayed his vocal chords. He remained agitated and demanded that another physician see him. He slept for several hours late in the after-noon and then was seen by two more doctors, to whom he complained about his blood pressure and throat. The physicians found nothing wrong with him. Still his fears and insecurities had won. He would not perform that evening.

The concert was scheduled to begin at 8:15 p.m. Twenty minutes before curtain time, Callinicos headed to the hall; Lanza, healthy but for his alleged sore throat, remained at the hotel, snuggled beneath the bedcovers like a child, unable to comprehend that thousands had looked forward to an evening hearing him in concert.

Callinicos took the stage and announced that the concert had been canceled. The crowd was outraged. Many stormed the stage and abused Costa. He was fortunate to escape with a police escort.

A crowd gathered outside of the Vier Jahreszeiten and chanted obscenities. The singer thanked Callinicos for handling what had been a dangerous situation.

He retreated to Rome, canceling an appearance on Belgian televi-sion that would have earned him $5600 and concerts in Wiesbaden, Cork, Dublin, and London. John Coast optimistically, and then stub-bornly, hoped that Mario would honor his commitments, but April passed with no word from Lanza—nothing but Revides' absurd pontifi-cations on his behalf. Lanza was exhausted, depressed, and thoroughly lost. The tour, which had started as a necessary but grand undertaking, ended as a disappointment. He was left with a net of approximately $29,000 from a gross exceeding $84,000 and several threatening law-suits stemming from the cancellations.

That he was unemployable as a concert artist was obvious. He had fewer than six hundred days to live.

CHAPTER 30

For the First Time

If he could only have crawled out of his own skin and listened to
his own voice, he might have lived his whole life differently.

George London[1]

Royalties from record sales, Mario's previous financial lifeline, were
down for a simple reason: his studio work during 1957 and 1958 had
been limited to seven recordings, none of which resulted in significant
sales. Movies and concerts had never produced enough income to support his lifestyle or hierarchical and subterranean leeches, and he was
barely able to meet his expenses in Europe. His royalties—down to
$300,000 a year during 1958 and 1959—kept him under the constant
stress of paying for yesterday's extravagances.

On 5 May 1958, Lanza entered into an agreement with Alex Gruter
of Corona Films to star in a film called *For the First Time*. The tenor
was to receive a lucrative $200,000 plus 40 percent of the profits, but as
usual, the singer received considerably less. None of that mattered to
Mario now; the present advance of $8000 monthly provided a badly
needed influx of cash.

Gruter took one look at Lanza—bloated, nervous, and withdrawn—
and realized that production would require a deft touch. He proposed
that Mario go to the Park Sanitarium in Walchensee, a Bavarian village
in the mountains near Garmisch and the majestic Zugspitze. The singer
declined, offering that he could rally himself, lose weight, and get ahead
of his creditors by performing in South Africa, where he was incredibly
popular and regarded as at least the equal of any tenor, past or present.
John Coast encouraged him; by now Coast felt that his mission was
more artistic than financial: to get Mario Lanza before the public.

Callinicos continued to work with his friend, finding conditions
similar to the bleak period that had followed the *Student Prince* blow-

up. Mario was easily agitated; the slightest provocation, most of them imagined, incapacitated him for hours. Betty was mixing Seconal and alcohol with her former *joie de vivre*, emerging from her room long enough to initiate a vicious argument—which left Mario feeling justified about another destructive binge. The offers from South Africa increased to a lofty $10,000 guarantee per appearance for six concerts (two each in Johannesburg, Cape Town, and Pretoria) with prepaid airfare and no commissions. Costa worked against his doubts as the tenor, unable to refuse such an offer, continued to insist that the tour take place.

As the date approached, the singer retreated to the Villa's basement kitchen, drinking one bottle of beer after another as he sat and stared out the window. When he could not stand another drink, he wandered to his bedroom and slept until it was time to begin the process again. His weight approached 260 pounds. Once again, he was losing the battle against a deep depression.

Callinicos, accustomed to Mario's last-minute recoveries, refused to give up. At the last moment, Lanza canceled the trip. Costa had pinned his hopes on fees from the tour. Instead, he was stuck in Rome with a once-prodigal talent whose tomorrows were growing short in the early winter of his life.

In July, the situation—if it were possible—deteriorated. The tenor regarded the basement kitchen as his fortress, a place where he could eat and drink away from observation, Betty, and recrimination. He resorted to unorthodox treatments, taking diuretics and Antabuse while continuing to drink, which caused nausea and shortness of breath. August brought no improvement. Lanza was as deeply mired in depression as he had been during his darkest years. His mood shifts were sudden and explosive. Nothing interested him: not music, not his children, not life. He drank and brooded. Callinicos challenged him and Mario, revealing a pathetic combination of sensitivity and hopelessness, replied, "I know, Costa. But I'm so terribly unhappy. When I'm happy, I don't do these things."[2]

Callinicos asked what made him unhappy. The list was long. Mario lamented the many broken promises from friends, his break with Sam Weiler, the MGM suspension, the troubles with Betty, the disappointment he experienced during his last film, the disappointment he was sure to experience with his next film, the sinister plots perpetrated against him by producers and others, and more. When Costa attempted to offer guidance, the tenor waved him off. He still believed he had done nothing wrong.

"Please, Costa. Tell me tomorrow. I won't be so low tomorrow. Then we'll really begin to do a job. It'll be all right. Just don't think I'm crazy. It's just that I have to get away from all these troubles in my head."[3]

It is one thing for a man to pursue a destructive path. It is quite another when he does it knowingly while wishing that things were otherwise. The powerlessness and lack of insight were harrowing to both participant and observer.

Gruter, alarmed over the singer's condition, pressed him, and Lanza finally agreed to go to Walchensee. There he submitted to a two-week, twilight sleep regimen, fed intravenously and drugged in order to lose weight. With Mario, the sedation provided two other advantages: it controlled a horribly uncompliant patient and staved off the tremors caused by withdrawal. Callinicos joined him at the end of the treatment. Lanza was lonely; even the fabulous view and crisp air meant nothing to him. The evening meal, which often consisted of canned peaches and cottage cheese, seemed like something thrown at a prisoner of war in the meanest camp to a man accustomed to too much of the best of everything.

He cheated on the drinking restrictions by sneaking into the village or cajoling the staff for an occasional beer. But he lost weight and asked Costa to rent a piano; the two old friends rehearsed daily. Mario asked Betty and the children to join him. They arrived in the family's 1958 chauffeur-driven Deluxe Micro Volkswagen bus. Lanza's preference ran to Cadillacs, but they were cumbersome in the ancient, narrow streets and too small for the entourage that accompanied Betty and the children. The tenor played and swam with the children, shopped, lifted weights, and commenced road work, which was particularly dangerous in view of his ongoing battle with phlebitis. It was like old times in Palm Springs. Mario had emerged from his depression and seemed reconciled to his surroundings, expressing his oft-told resolutions to eat simple foods, exercise, and stay away from alcohol. He viewed the heavily forested mountains and inhaled the fresh air, vowing to return and spend the rest of his life in Bavaria. After seven weeks, he returned to Rome more than forty pounds lighter.

The first order of business that fall of 1958 was prerecordings at the Rome Opera House, where Lanza was scheduled to sing "Niun mi tema" from *Otello*, the Triumphal Scene from *Aida*, "Vesti la giubba," and the trio from *Così Fan Tutte*. Most of the hundred sixty members of the house orchestra and chorus regarded the singer they were commissioned to accompany as a Hollywood creation and myth. As the session progressed, a stir began among the musicians. After each performance, they expressed amazement at what they had just heard. Many told Callinicos that they were astonished; they had been unaware that the voice was so round and glorious. Even Vitale, the general director of the Rome Opera Company, approached Callinicos and expressed surprise at hearing such a magnificent voice. Costa claimed that inquiries about Lanza's availability for operatic engagements followed, and that he was scheduled to open the 1960 season at the Rome Opera House as Cavaradossi in *Tosca*.

He sang well at the Rome Opera House that day. His "Vesti la giubba" was well sung. His "Niun mi tema" was rich and dramatic; together with his duet with Licia Albanese in *Serenade*, it provides an enticing hint of what Lanza might have done as Otello. The Triumphal Scene from *Aida* was pure spectacle. The piece, as performed on an opera stage, celebrates the return of the victorious Egyptian army. At its gaudiest, live camels, horses, elephants, and livestock parade across the stage to the accompaniment of dozens of voices in chorus. An individual voice—even with stalwarts such as Leontyne Price and Franco Corelli—is difficult to single out. The recording from *For the First Time* is exciting from the beginning, with Lanza heard above soprano, chorus, and orchestra—complete with blaring horns—throughout.

When the session was finished, Callinicos left Rome briefly for the steadier work and remuneration of his association with the New York City Opera. He was emotionally exhausted, his affairs in disarray. Since joining Lanza in Europe, he had participated in twenty-one concerts, some triumphant and some awful, and sat by as even more appearances were canceled. He had been enticed by the prospect of artistic success and decent earnings, neither of which materialized. He had seen Lanza at his worst, again.

The tenor completed his prerecordings with Carlo Savina and George Stoll, who was now a regular at Villa Badoglio, with mixed results. "Come prima" ("For the First Time") was the film's marginal theme song. "O Mon Amour," a small composition, was tastefully sung, and his rendition of Schubert's Ave Maria was excellent. Unfortunately, the "'O sole mio" was dreadful, with an obviously impaired Lanza struggling throughout. "The Hofbrauhaus Song," sung with Johannes Radiske and His Band in Berlin, was uneven. The low moment of the prerecordings was a George Stoll composition, "Pineapple Pickers," which tested Mario's crossover abilities and found him wanting as a rock 'n' roller. It is easily the worst of Lanza's recordings.

The direction of *For the First Time* was assigned to Rudy Maté, a distinguished cinematographer who had earned five Academy Award nominations (*Gilda*, with Rita Hayworth, among them). His directorial efforts, considered less successful, included *D.O.A.* and *The Mississippi Gambler*. Nonetheless, he brought a high order of technical competence to the film.

The plot had a strangely familiar ring. Mario was cast as Tony Costa (in honor of the tenor's father and Callinicos), the unpredictable, temperamental, hard-drinking sensation of the opera stage. After missing a performance, the errant star hides out on the island of Capri and falls in love with Christa, a nearly cloistered deaf girl who regains her hearing and returns the tenor's love. The plot was weak, but it all meshed well enough to come in as Lanza's best work since *The Great Caruso*. His acting was understated, and his flair for light comedy was back. Playwright Clifford Odets once said that, even if Lanza could not sing, he would have been a success in Hollywood as an actor. The tenor's natural talent was as underexploited as it was undervalued.

As to casting, the male contingent, which included Kurt Kasznar and Hans Sohnker, was decent, but the leading ladies were mind-boggling. Christa was played by twenty-six-year-old Austrian actress Johanna von Koszian, whose youthful appearance—more on the order of an eighteen-year-old—made for a distracting and improbable combination with Lanza, looking all of his thirty-seven years plus a few borrowed from the next decade. Naturally, the tenor was caught in a triangle with a wealthy countess, played by Zsa Zsa Gabor, in hot pursuit. Her best line was "Dahling," which served for "Yes," "No," "Maybe," "I don't know," and a thousand other more expressive phrases.

The film was shot in Austria, Germany, and on Capri, which provided interesting background for Maté's deft camera direction. But moving heavy production equipment across the bay from Naples by ferry and up the steep hills of Capri was time-consuming and difficult, and von Koszian was under contract with a repertory company to appear in three different plays each week, which forced an on-again off-again schedule. Once again, Mario made poor use of idle time. He drank heavily thoughout filming, resulting in the usual delays and a few scenes where he was clearly on the receiving end of a large evening. Though his weight fluctuated between 190 and 210 pounds during filming, he appeared more robust than in *The Seven Hills of Rome* because of his temporary resumption of exercise. Nevertheless, he had aged; his appearance was alarming to some in Hollywood.

The film opened to mostly decent reviews. *The New York Times* (15 August 1959) described *For the First Time* as Lanza's "most disarming vehicle in years" and further noted, "[His] Ave Maria is touching indeed. . . . One male viewer counted handkerchiefs in the hands of nine female viewers." *Pictureshow* found him delightful and on his game. The *Los Angeles Examiner* wisely questioned his portrayal of a teen idol, though it praised his voice and likened him to Caruso. *Newsweek* (24 August 1959) called it "the worst of Lanza," while its cross-town rival (*Time*, 31 August 1959) issued another diatribe:

> Outsize tenor Mario ("My voice is the greatest in the world") Lanza is an unpredictable, erratic, self-centered American singer. . . . The casting is pluperfect, but most of the picture is a pretentious bore. The prerecorded songs seem unable to locate Lanza's lips and some of the arias might even have been scraped off old Lanza sound tracks. . . . He summons little of the old Mario magic and all of the old mannerisms—aggressive smile, athletic nostrils, orbiting eyeballs, and quivering poundage.

It was the penultimate mean-spirited barrage against a singer whose enduring appeal was vastly more potent than the magazine's attacks. The last salvo, sadly enough, was a cowardly obituary that belittled his millions of fans for confusing him with a legitimate vocal talent.

For the First Time was not a box-office success. Its initial run of $2 million in theater rentals was the lowest gross for any film in which the tenor starred. With the release of the film, Mario sought payment of the final $55,605 of the $200,000 guarantee owed him by Corona Films. Gruter responded by filing a suit in the German courts seeking $95,416.66 for a variety of cost overruns, citing alleged misconduct and drunkenness. Gruter knew that Lanza would be unlikely to receive a fair hearing in the German courts, where he was already under attack for his canceled concerts; when you add the extra discouragement of the heavy legal fees associated with litigating from afar, it becomes clear that Gruter never intended to pay the singer his full salary. The ploy worked. The tenor retained local counsel and filed a cross-complaint. Not surprisingly, the German courts entered a judgment against Lanza six years after his death. The matter lingered, and both parties eventually waived their claims. Gruter remitted less than the amount recited in the contract and paid no percentage of profits to the estate. As always, the attorneys representing the tenor's interests received handsome fees.

If one sees the profound in circumstance and coincidence, the final scene of *For the First Time* is haunting. Lanza, in full regalia as Radames—with a well-muscled left leg in full view and the troublesome right concealed by his robe—sings while the fanfare of the Triumphal Scene goes on around him. At the conclusion, he turns his back to the audience as the camera rolls back and the curtain closes.

There were more film offers. But it was the last scene in Mario Lanza's film career.

CHAPTER 31

Recording Artist, Take 2

It was a voice at its best—after everything and in spite of everything.

Constantine Callinicos[1]

Though he seldom experienced inner peace for more than a few days at a time, Mario's time in Rome had brought him more happiness than his last five years in Hollywood. He loved being driven past Rome's historic sights, his dark eyes focused on everything and the questions constant. He was fond of Rome's bustling piazzas and busy streets and became a favorite with greengrocers, flower peddlers, waiters, and porters always overtipping and occasionally offering a song. It was not unusual to find him singing at the top of his lungs in a cafe, clearly enjoying the *vino da tavola* with a group of admirers. Where in Hollywood he had hidden for months and even years behind gates or walls when depression overtook him, Villa Badoglio offered nearby distractions, and the spells, though just as dark and intense, were more easily broken. Within a few blocks, he encountered people whose admiration was unconditional. The Villa itself became a waystation for friends, business associates, and hangers-on, including George London, Giuseppe di Stefano, Peter Herman Adler, Art Buchwald, Lucky Luciano, and Peter Lind Hayes.

The Roman press was mostly kind. His mother was an ocean and a continent away. And no contract bound him: more than anything, Mario Lanza could not endure long-term expectations and was seldom productive when an attempt to manage him was made. The eleven months from November 1958 to September 1959 were his most productive studio period, with more than five dozen titles recorded. The results varied from terrible to extraordinary, but his trademark interpretive intensity was never less than absolute.

His first project, an album of seldom-recorded Neapolitan songs, was cut at Cinecittà in Rome during November and December 1958, with Colleen and Ellisa Lanza in the studio. Franco Ferrara conducted; the arrangements were by Ennio Morricone, who would achieve fame with his compositions for *The Good, the Bad, and the Ugly*, *Once Upon a Time in the West*, and *The Untouchables*. Mario sang magnificently at times, delivering powerful and impassioned renditions of "Tu ca nun chiagne" (lavishly praised by José Carreras), "Dicitencello vuie," "Voce 'e notte" (the tenor's favorite recording), "Canta pe' me," and "Passione." The studio musicians, impressed by his facility with various dialects, found it difficult to believe he was not a native Italian. Reviews were good.

The album, entitled *Mario!*, was unavailable for decades and is one of two (the other being *A Cavalcade of Show Tunes*) that have been overlooked and undervalued. The titles in the collection—some long neglected—began to appear on albums by Franco Corelli and are staples at any Carreras concert. RCA released a remastered CD in 1995.

In December 1958, Lanza signed a contract with Arthur Bruner of C.C.C. Films for a production called *Granada*. The singer received advances allegedly totaling $50,000, though Bruner later settled with Lanza's estate for $15,000 and several vague contingencies. The film, along with a rumored project called *The King of Naples*, never materialized.

Temporarily flush with cash and elated with the success of his first studio album in more than two years, the tenor decided on a rare venture for the Lanza family: a vacation. Mario, Betty, and the four children spent Christmas in St. Moritz, Switzerland, romping in the snow, skating, and enjoying life away from servants, reporters, leeches, and fans. It was a happy time for Betty, whose quest for peace was frequently no more successful than that of her husband.

The respite was brief. Back at the Villa, Lanza drank and raged; though mostly marble, even this rental did not escape damage. Once again Mario retreated from his hard-won slimness to the protections afforded by extra poundage. He argued with Betty, claiming that, were it not for her, he would have pursued an operatic career rather than Hollywood money.

In April 1959, Lanza, desperately tired, consented to be admitted to the hospital. His blood pressure, never under control, was dangerously elevated, and the phlebitis was chronic despite medication. The only treatment then available for phlebitis was to thin the blood to prevent the clot from enlarging and to immobilize the patient. Immobilization was crucial. If small sections of the clot break off and pass, the crisis ebbs; standing or walking can cause movement in the vein and muscle, increasing the likelihood of a larger section's breaking away and causing a fatal pulmonary blockage. Lanza left the Clinica Valle Giulia in mid-April.

Earlier in 1959, Callinicos, anticipating work on albums or a film, had returned to the Villa to find himself dislodged by Paul Baron, who would produce the singer's next three albums. Callinicos now announced that he was leaving Villa Badoglio for an engagement in Athens. Lanza asked him to stay in touch, perhaps sensing that the commitment to Baron was a mistake. Indeed, though Lanza had told reporters that his voice had never known bad production, that it only became more settled, he would become intimately familiar with bad production—courtesy of Baron—on his next two albums.

Stereophonic sound had become the rage. In the early days, people were mesmerized by novelty albums featuring gimmicks such as the sound of a train seeming to pass from the left to the right speaker, and the mere inclusion of a "stereo sound" effect was preferable to quality singing in monaural. RCA, however well intentioned, made the mistake of deciding that its best-selling Red Seal artist should rerecord the soundtrack from *The Student Prince* in stereo. The attempt to duplicate that initial success ran against heavy odds; the degree to which it failed is astonishing.

Lanza's condition that spring foreclosed any possibility of decent recording sessions, from the quality of his voice to his ability to simply cooperate. He stalked out of the studio, threw tantrums, and produced an almost unrecognizable sound; he simply could not sustain the energy required for good voice production. The recordings, produced by Paul Baron, should never have been released, but RCA favored its stereo remake for several decades. Fortunately, the remastered CD that is currently available contains the original recordings, which remain the standard for all who sing the role.

Next Lanza, still somewhat hobbled by his phlebitis and in low spirits, was back at Cinecittà with Baron to record a stereophonic version of his earlier versions of Christmas carols. The originals—masterfully

sung, passionate versions of traditional carols—had included a powerful rendition of "O Holy Night" with a memorable high-B finish. The
remake was characterized by a thin voice, marginal breath control, and
a tedious tempo. The most telling sign of his overall condition was the
fact that he made no attempt to rerecord "O Holy Night." The tenor
could not have bought, begged, or borrowed a decent high B in May
1959.

His next recording venture proved that his voice was not lost. In
June, he was back at Cinecittà for another session of Neapolitan favorites. This time the combination of Lanza and Baron worked. Lanza's
interpretations were impassioned, and the voice was good—within the
range required by the selections. He sang a beautifully restrained "Ide-
ale," a "Lolita" that is nearly indistinguishable from his 1951 version,
and a classic rendition of "Musica proibita" ("Forbidden Music") that
brought the piece back to the repertoire of many great tenors (most
recently, Carreras and Pavarotti). Many familiar with Neapolitan *can-
zone* consider his "Senza nisciuno" to be the definitive version.

The album, *Lanza Sings Caruso Favorites*, was an artistic achievement and a best seller, jockeying for position with offerings by Elvis
Presley and the Everly Brothers, for months following its release. The
double-set (Caruso's recordings of other selections were featured
on the companion record) was well received by W. A. Chislett (*The
Gramophone*, March 1960), long a Lanza critic, who wrote, "[The
selections] reveal him at his best, for he was always more effective in
such songs, even though they were sung with more vigour than finesse.
. . . Here, the very vigour coupled with the sheer quality of the voice can
be enjoyed by all."

Constantine Callinicos returned to the Villa in June and found
Mario struggling against his well-established destructive behavior, a
force the singer could neither conquer nor comprehend. Still, a part of
him strove to achieve the artistic. He was eager to continue working.

In July, Mary Cocozza, Salvatore Lanza, Mario's Aunt Hilda, and
Betty's mother, May Hicks, traveled to Italy. The tenor, whose ease in
Rome had been tinged with homesickness, was thrilled by the visit. He
insisted his relatives stay at the Villa and experience the material success it represented. During the drive into the ancient city, Mary noticed
a group of men relieving themselves against a wall, their backs turned
but otherwise in full view of passersby. She pronounced indignantly

that such crude behavior would result in an arrest in the United States. Mario meekly countered that it was a Roman custom.

RCA suggested that he record *The Vagabond King*, *The Desert Song*, *The Merry Widow*, and a rerecording of the *Caruso* album in stereo. The tenor, bursting with ideas, agreed and also suggested several operatic projects, a collection of sacred songs, and even an album with his mother.

The next recording session, again at Cinecittà, was an interpretation of Rudolf Friml's (*Rose Marie* and *The Firefly*) 1925 score of *The Vagabond King*. Lanza and Callinicos worked well together, as they always had. Betty, May Hicks, Salvatore, Hilda, Mary, and the children sat in the control booth, wildly applauding after each successful take of an eight-song, six-hour session. Lanza sang with flashes of magnificence, once again bringing new life to material that would sound like a dated operetta with most voices.

The singing was dark, solid, and impassioned on excellent versions of "Nocturne," "Only a Rose," and "Someday." If the session was too long and the tenor's stamina compromised by his smoking, it showed in a mild rasp on "Love Me Tonight" and "Tomorrow," though Lanza's unfailing commitment to the material remains compelling. His interpretations were excellent on some outtakes, others are hurt by a metallic sharpness. Overall, his breath control was the best it had been since he left America. Callinicos judged it their smoothest session ever: Freddy had to behave—no blistering the ceiling with vile tirades or heaving the music stand—with his mother watching. It was an idea that should have occurred to someone years before.

The tapes were flown to New York, where RCA dubbed in soprano Judith Raskin's voice and a chorus. The engineering was amateurish for a prestigious company like RCA, but the album sold well nonetheless and met with decent reviews. RCA issued a remastered CD in 1995.

Mary returned to the United States in late July; her sister, her father, and May Hicks remained at the Villa, their dates of return uncertain. With his mother gone, Mario made up for lost time. In early August, an initial attempt at recording Romberg's score of *The Desert Song* was scrapped because of an inferior orchestra. The second session was also unsuccessful, but deficient musicians were not to blame. Once again the tenor's drinking had left him with no voice.

Callinicos was serving two masters. He was devoted to his old friend, but he also had to show a return on RCA's investment. He decided to record the orchestra during a third session, wait for a day, and then dub in Mario's voice. It was a wise decision.

Lanza arrived at Cinecittà spiritless, hung over, and depleted, his right leg swollen and painful. Costa worked with the orchestra while the singer sat silent, hunched forward, alternately clutching his face and hair, neither watching nor listening. He got up and took a seat in the control booth. After a time, he got up, waved at Callinicos through the glass partition, and left. The voice that made him so proud, his magnificent gift, had failed him. It was a sad moment. Pictures from the session show a tragically impaired man who bore little resemblance to his screen image.

Lanza returned to Villa Badoglio, further depressed by his failure at Cinecittà—which triggered his customary reactions of rage and heavy drinking and his wife's customary insults and recriminations. Lanza sought refuge on the marble balcony off their bedroom, lost consciousness, and lay there while a cold rain fell through the night. Members of the household staff found him the next morning. He was rushed to the Clinica Valle Giulia and incorrectly diagnosed with pneumonia. In truth, part of a clot had broken loose, causing a partial blockage of the pulmonary artery; it showed up on an x-ray as a spot on the lung. Much has been made about Mario Lanza's extreme weight swings and deteriorating health, but the only potentially fatal condition—over the short term—was his phlebitis.

Callinicos visited his old friend at the hospital and was shocked at how much older than thirty-eight he appeared. Mario laughingly pronounced himself indestructible and assured him that he would begin another diet and finish *The Desert Song*. The tenor was again rallying himself. He had an indomitable will to survive that operated, in a precise cycle, with his depression and self-destructive behavior. Once again, he vowed to eat sensibly, avoid alcohol, and live a disciplined life.

It was still August when the tenor was discharged from the hospital. He launched himself into a torturous regimen of near-starvation dieting: prerecordings for his next film, *Laugh, Clown, Laugh*, with Caterina Valente and Ted Heath's Orchestra, were scheduled to begin in London in September. Villa Badoglio was not air-conditioned, and August is a time, even today, when Romans flee the blazing heat that engulfs their city. Mario limited himself to an occasional sip of mineral water as he struggled to drive his weight below 260 pounds. He suffered greatly but made little progress.

Callinicos and Mario returned to Cinecittà to complete *The Desert Song*. Betty sat in the control booth while the engineer played each selection. The tenor concentrated and went through a quasi-rehearsal, singing while Callinicos conducted. On the third replay, Mario's voice was recorded as he listened to a tape of the orchestra. Some songs were recorded in a single attempt, but none required more than a second effort. The session was completed that morning, with uneven results. The voice was dark and powerful, the commitment and interpretation intense on "The Desert Song" and "Azuri's Dance." He was in exceptional voice on "One Alone," producing a solid high-B finish that proved his voice was still capable of magnificence. It would be misleading to assert that his production, in 1959, was equal to that of 1951. The voice had a baritonal quality and the upper register, once freely squandered, showed signs of wear with an occasional rasp and, at times, a decided thinness or break. At its best, it was still a glorious and uniquely haunting voice.

Other recordings from the session (a reprise of "One Alone" and the unreleased "My Margo") show the strain of a long session. Callinicos turned the studio tapes over to RCA but made discs for himself. The straight versions from the sessions—without enhancements or remastering   reveal a voice of considerable power and range. Once again, soprano Judith Raskin and other voices were added on separate tracks in New York.

Callinicos remembered being at Cinecittà on 10 September 1959: "Mario sang 'The Lord's Prayer' very, very beautifully . . . I believe the best he ever sang it in his life. So the Malotte Lord's Prayer—and sometimes I think about it and get chills—was the last thing Mario ever put down on record."[2]

The recording never has been located in the RCA vaults. The last title in the RCA catalogue for *The Desert Song* is prophetic: "One Good Boy Gone Wrong."

CHAPTER 32

Final Rally

I have few regrets. I've made mistakes, but if I could live my life
again, I would play most of it the same way.

Mario Lanza, 1957[1]

In September 1959 the Villa bustled with the activity associated with
the start of another film. Al Panone and Irving Pisor, who planned to co-
produce *Laugh, Clown, Laugh*, huddled with their star while lyricist
Bob Russell ("Sound Off" and "Jack and the Beanstalk") and Mischa
Spolansky ("Frenesi," "Time Was," and "Don't Get Around Much Any-
more") were in London collaborating on the score. Filming was set to
begin in October, an unrealistic starting date in view of the singer's
weight and overall condition.

Lanza's sense of resolve about dieting and drink weakened, and
Callinicos, returning to the United States for a six-week engagement
with the New York City Opera, was sent off with a fine lunch and a
warm farewell. Lavish parties continued during what was a beautiful
warm September in Rome. Try as he might, Mario made slow progress
in readying for the film; with his age and lifestyle, there was less to
retrieve. As the month wore on, he complained about left-side chest
pains. They were not related to coronary disease. Rather, a clot was
forming in the deep tibial vein of the singer's right calf. Pieces were
breaking away, causing a less than total blockage of the pulmonary
artery and intermittent pain that mimicked a heart attack.

The prerecordings scheduled for 17 September in London were
canceled; Mario was not well enough to travel. His condition failed to
slow the pace at 56 Bruxelles, however. In late September he took Betty
and the children to see a performance of *Aida* at the Imperial Baths of
Caracalla, the finest place in the world to view Verdi's epic opera. The
ruined baths are mere shells of their third-century glory, but the

226

grandeur of the outdoor setting outdoes anything Hollywood could create for the final divided tableau, with the floodlit representation of the Temple of Vulcan and the tomb against the dark Roman sky. Unfortunately, the Lanzas did not make it beyond the first act. Mario was quickly recognized and, with the crowd turning from the performance to him, left during the first intermission. Onlookers remembered that he looked very tired, which is not surprising. The pain associated with acute phlebitis is intense and persistent.

The last of Lanza's great feasts at Villa Badoglio was held on 29 September. Peter Lind Hayes, the man who had discovered him in Marfa, Texas, in 1942, attended. As the evening progressed, Lanza upended and downed a magnum of champagne; he played and sang along with some of his recordings—shouting with all the volume he could muster. Hayes, judging that the tenor had slipped beyond manageability, nevertheless interviewed the jovially intoxicated singer for a radio broadcast. Lanza spoke enthusiastically about Rome, his life, and his upcoming film, which he pronounced the long overdue but worthy successor to *The Great Caruso*.

The thing that was truly bothering Lanza was his right leg, which is precisely what he told Betty and Mary when he admitted himself to the Clinica Valle Giulia on 30 September with a fever, rapid pulse, and chest pains—all symptomatic of acute phlebitis. The plan, consistent with acceptable treatment in 1959, was that the singer would remain immobile and receive antibiotics and blood thinners. If all went well, the clot would dissolve and the crisis would pass.

Mario was a model patient for several days and then became restless. The truth was that he considered the cure worse than the disease. He craved alcohol and worried about the children, who, since Betty seldom ventured from her room, were likely being cared for by household staff. On Tuesday, 6 October, he and his wife argued bitterly over the phone. He told his physicians he was going home the next day. That evening, some claim, he sang "Come prima" or excerpts from *Tosca* for the nursing staff. The next morning, he phoned Betty again. He told her he could not stand it in the hospital and that he would be home later that day.

Later that morning, he left his bed and moved about, placing pressure on his right leg. A substantial piece of the clot broke away and was carried to a place too small for it to pass: his pulmonary artery. Lanza lost consciousness. He was discovered shortly after noon, barely breathing and flushed. Physicians and nurses worked on him, but it was too late. Nothing could save him. Mario Lanza, the one-time prodigy from Philadelphia who had both thrilled and disappointed millions, was pronounced dead at the age of thirty-eight in Room 404 of the Clinica Valle Giulia in Rome, Italy. The cause of death was listed as a heart attack. Because events surrounding the death were not suspicious, there was no autopsy or investigation.

News of a celebrity's sudden death spreads in strange ways, with no orderly notification of the next of kin. Salvatore Lanza was waiting on the front steps of Villa Badoglio when the chauffeur returned and announced, in Italian, that Mario was dead. Betty learned of the tragedy when she phoned to speak with her husband. Dr. Silvestri, with no time to rehearse the difficult moment, spoke in overly formal and literal English, advising her that it would not be possible for her to speak with her spouse as he had just died. Betty needed alcohol and drugs to survive the best of days; Dr. Silvestri, regretting his clumsiness, went to 56 Bruxelles to provide her with an immediate and potent crutch.

The story hit the wire services, making front-page headlines throughout the world. Richard Tucker often bragged that he was the greatest tenor in the world—a burden many thought rested elsewhere. But not even Tucker would have argued with the contention that Mario Lanza was the most popular and beloved tenor in the world. The grief was intense and widespread.

In Hollywood, where it was dawn, Mary and Tony Cocozza were fast asleep at 622 Toyopa Drive. A telephone call brought the news to Terry Robinson, who still lived with the couple. Disbelieving, he turned a radio on. The radio was louder than Robinson realized; it awoke Mary. She was surprised to hear "Be My Love" so early in the morning, and said so. Then the announcer broke in: Mario Lanza had died from a heart attack in Rome.

Mary went blank and then into hysteria. Tony ran into the street, shouting, over and over, his son's boyhood name of Freddy. Neighbors and friends gathered to comfort the couple, stunned to find themselves, suddenly, the saddest of people: parents who outlive their only child. Mary endured the long flight to Rome in a near trance as fellow passengers approached and offered their sympathy.

Embalming was not a rigorous practice in 1959 Rome, and after three days in an undersized coffin in the massive great room of Villa

Badoglio, the deterioration was noticeable. On Saturday, 10 October, thousands lined the funeral route as the coffin was carried to the Church of the Immaculate Heart of Mary in Rome's elegant Parioli district in a glass-walled, black and gilt carriage drawn by four plumed black horses. More than three thousand mourners, including Van Johnson, Robert Alda, Rossano Brazzi, and Xavier Cugat, attended. The crowd overflowed into the street.

Betty had requested that her husband's recording of Schubert's Ave Maria be played during the funeral mass, but the pastor refused: church regulations prohibited recorded music. Instead, an Italian baritone named Forcione sang the hymn accompanied by the Roman Polyphonic Choir. In a sad reunion with the Lanza family, Father Paul Maloney, who had baptized Damon and Marc less than two years before in California, intoned the requiem mass.

The body was temporarily interred at Rome's Verrano Cemetery while Betty floundered, unable to decide where final burial should occur. A rumor that Mario had expressed a wish to be buried beside Enrico Caruso in Naples created a media stir—exciting even the custodian of the cemetery in Naples, who envisioned tips from tourists. The rumor was unconnected with Mario, and the Caruso family's disclaimer was unnecessary.[2]

Myrt Blum of Business Administration ordered the Villa closed and all remaining possessions (some looting had occurred) shipped to the United States. Betty and the children, accompanied by two dogs, a canary, and several apparently irreplaceable employees, left for Los Angeles. The situation was not without its humorous moments. Among the household items that made the long journey from Rome to Los Angeles was the family's Volkswagen bus.

The people of Philadelphia wanted to pay their respects to their native son, and Mary, though initially opposed, decided to honor their wishes. The ornately carved, wooden coffin arrived at Leonetti's Funeral Home at 2223 South Broad Street in South Philadelphia on Thursday, 15 October. The remains were badly deteriorated, and a plate-glass cover was installed on the coffin. Mario's childhood friend, Eddie Durso, was a pallbearer: "I was shocked by his physical appearance. His face and neck were distorted and swollen. A tiny bit of blood protruded from the corner of his mouth. . . . I tried to recollect the friend I had known. . . . Thirty-three years later, I still miss him"[3]

More than fifteen thousand passed the casket the next day. When the police tried to close Leonetti's at midnight, the crowd rushed forward, forcing them to stand by until the last mourner left two hours later. Leonetti stopped his head count at twenty thousand.

On 18 October, Lanza's remains were flown to Los Angeles for yet another funeral. The condition of the body had become so bad that the funeral director required positive identification. Terry Robinson, shocked, demanded that they "make Mario look like Mario," and that the wooden casket be replaced with an expensive copper model. He advanced his own funds to ensure that it occurred.[4]

Mary Cocozza, upon seeing her son in his coffin again, glowered and raged. "How could you do this to me! It wasn't supposed to end this soon! How could you! The career . . . ."[5]

On 21 October 1959, two weeks after his death, Mario Lanza received his final funeral service at the Church of the Blessed Sacrament in Hollywood. The service was attended by stars, executives, and ordinary people. Kathryn Grayson, who reportedly wept at hearing the news, did not attend, though she did much for the family during the years ahead. No executive from Mario's troubled days at MGM was present. The singer's flag-draped coffin was taken to a temporary resting place in Calvary Cemetery and eventually laid to rest in the stately mausoleum at Holy Cross Cemetery in Century City.

At the final service, Tony Cocozza, his eyes tear-filled and swollen from days of weeping, sobbed and begged that his son be spared, that God take him because he was old and had lived his life.

Mary, grief-stricken, unwittingly provided the cornerstone of Mario Lanza's torment: "My baby! My baby!"[6]

The Aftermath and the Legacy

To millions of people the world over, myself included, his magnificent voice enriched our lives and introduced us to a wide spec-
trum of classical and popular music.

José Carreras[1]

In the absence of an autopsy or official investigation into Mario Lanza's
death, rumors thrive. Some claim that an empty IV bottle was found
pumping air into the singer's body, which is impossible: gravity causes
IV fluids to flow; there is no force or pumping action. Others say that air
was injected into the tenor's veins, creating an embolism that would
have led to the same cause of death. Nonsense. As Dr. Fruhwein
warned him in 1958, Lanza stood the danger of throwing a clot, losing
consciousness, and dying. And that is what occurred.

Another rumor was—and sadly remains in the minds of too many—
that Lucky Luciano ordered the hit on the singer for his loss of face
over Lanza's failure to appear at another "charity" concert. But a hit on
Mario Lanza would have been inconsistent with Mafia tactics. They
would have roughed him up, possibly, threatened his friends, or leaned
on members of his domestic staff. They would not have killed the goose
for a single failure to lay a golden egg when more could be had. The
singer was a national hero—even Luciano liked him. Furthermore,
Lucky often failed to deliver what had been promised at such concerts:
it was part of the scam. In his last years, Luciano was desperate for
attention and hopeful that a film would be made about his miserable
life. He badgered any journalist who would listen to him about his crim-
inal activities, including his purported order of a hit on Bugsy Siegel
over the protests of Meyer Lansky—yet he never so much as hinted
about involvement in the tenor's death in the two years that he survived him.

Rumors that the singer had borrowed money from a major New York or Sicilian family and then spurned attempts at collection are similarly baseless. Lanza was at times short of cash, but he always obtained the funds he needed from legitimate sources. At his death he had more than $300,000 in royalties on account with RCA—which converts to more than $4 million in present money. Mario Lanza had too much pride—and legitimate income—to resort to mob money.

Another rumor was that the tenor died penniless, heavily indebted to friends, promoters, and taxing authorities. When his estate was filed, there was no evidence of substantial indebtedness. Income taxes were negotiated down from a vastly inflated bill of $500,000, and without Lanza's spend-as-you-go lifestyle, the estate was quickly in the black. Royalties from RCA continued to be substantial.

Betty was left wealthy in terms of money and the comforts it provides but impoverished with regard to self-worth and vision for the future. She settled in a rented home in Beverly Hills, hired a retinue of servants, mixed her deadly escape of Seconal and alcohol, and barely functioned during the next few months, crying that life without Mario was not worth living. Nothing could brighten her outlook. Betty needed support and guidance, but the Hicks family was of little value to her, and Mary Cocozza had her own problems adjusting to life without Mario. Besides, Mary's rivalry with Betty did not die with her son.

As for the Lanza children, they were understandably bewildered by the death of their father and the sudden move to a comparatively subdued place where everyone spoke English instead of Italian. In November 1959, May Hicks took them to Chicago without Betty's permission. Subsequent events hint that the motive was, not surprisingly, money; though, in defense of May Hicks, she was misled by her greedy offspring. The children were returned after the incident was reported to the police. Betty called it a mix-up, and May Hicks explained that her daughter needed a rest.

Christmas and New Year's Eve passed with a dispirited and seldom rational Betty not caring that a new decade had begun. Her life, as troubled as it may have been, could not advance beyond 7 October 1959. Terry Robinson made arrangements to admit her to the Las Encinas Sanitarium, but she feared that hospitalization would provide her family with another opportunity to seize the children. She refused to abandon, even temporarily, her routine of oblivion. "You should've become a priest. You're always telling people how to live," she slurred at Robinson.[2]

On 11 March 1960, she was found dead in her bedroom at the age of thirty-six. Circumstances, which add nothing to an understanding of the situation, suggest that it was not a suicide. The coroner's report indicated that her blood-alcohol level was a lofty .24 and that an unknown quantity of Seconal had been ingested.[3]

That afternoon, Johnny Mobley—loyal member of the Lanzas' household staff and as devastated as anyone by the tragic turn their lives had taken—brought the four frightened children to the Cocozza home in Pacific Palisades. Until that moment, Mary had been mired in her own deep and agonizing depression, not caring if it were morning or evening or if she ate or starved. When a priest visited to offer condolences and counseling, she refused to see him. She wanted nothing to do with a God who could permit her son to die. But when she opened the door and saw Johnny Mobley and the children—Colleen, eleven; Ellisa, nine; Damon, seven; and Marc, five—she realized her life had a purpose. The children were aware only that something had occurred and that everyone was upset, but they did not know that Betty was dead. Initially Mary could only bring herself to tell them that their mother was ill; later that night she told the children that their mother was gone.

Less than one month later, May Hicks filed for custody of the four suddenly orphaned children. The Cocozzas answered the petition, and the matter was fought in the courts for more than a year. Al Teitelbaum, who was no fan of Mary Cocozza, testified that he had seen enough in the Hicks family to convince him that the best interests of the children would not be served by granting the Hickses custody.[4] On 27 May 1961 the petition was denied. It would be nice to say that this was the last sighting of a Hicks at the Lanza trough, but Betty's brother Bert, feeling literary, filed a claim alleging exclusive rights to the Lanza story. The claim was dismissed, and Bert died a short time later.

Mary and Tony, now beneficiaries of a limited portion of the insurance proceeds and without a mortgage on the Toyopa house, were comfortable, but Mario's refusal to instill discipline in his children made for a difficult start. It was Terry Robinson's assistance and guidance that pulled it all together. When he was not running his health club, Robinson lectured the children, took them to church, and provided them with the only example they ever had of a man who worked a regular job. He did as much as he could. He did more than anyone else.

The administration of Mario and Betty Lanza's estates was a case of death imitating life. Royalties, for the seven years following the tenor's death, were \$1,059,941.60. Total claims against the estates were \$27,157.16.[5] Legal fees and continued payments totaled \$592,748.46.[6] After miscellaneous fees, including a \$25,000 advance to Betty's estate for the support of the children, were paid, \$313,238.87 was left. The most amazing thing about the outcome was that it required no gun or bloodshed. Mario's estate was closed and more than \$1 million in royalties was paid to estates opened first for Betty and then the children. The final payout, \$858,611 from more than \$2 million in royalties, speaks for itself. There are words to describe such a situation, but even Mario Lanza would not have used them.

If royalties are any measure of artistry through staying power, the tenor has endured. Incredibly, heirs, original parties, or assignees of Lanza's various agents and attorneys continue to receive a percentage of his royalties, which consistently topped \$100,000 per year during the 1960s, soared to as much as \$600,000 during the 1970s, stayed slightly above and below \$200,000 during the 1980s, and have approximated \$150,000 yearly during the 1990s. The 5 percent due Business Administration was paid until 30 September 1996, when David Martin, who represents their interest, agreed to terminate the right, noting that thirty-seven-plus years was enough. The varied parties who now receive the 5 percent originally payable to Bautzer & Grant and the 2.5 percent payable to J. Everett Blum have held firm against threats of legal action.

Sam Weiler returned to peddling real estate and various singers, none of whom achieved fame. Like Colonel Tom Parker, he "managed" a talent so immense that it required little of what he provided. Weiler collected the 5 percent of royalties originally due him until his death in 1995; releases signed by Mario Lanza and his heirs preserve Weiler's heirs and assigns a right to a cut until 7 October 2026.

Al Teitelbaum, now in his eighties and living in grand style in Ashland, Oregon, receives 10 percent of the Lanza largesse; in 1997 he graciously entered into an agreement favorable to the Lanza heirs. His greatest regret about Mario and Betty Lanza was that he was unable to restore order to their lives: "To this day, I feel guilty about leaving them in Italy. If I had stayed and worked with them, perhaps they would both be alive today."[7]

Constantine Callinicos continued to pursue a varied career in New York, never mining the same hole long enough to become established. He conducted, part-time, for the New York City Opera through the 1960s, promoted Greek music, and was the house-conductor for Kapp Records. In 1983 he participated in the PBS documentary *Mario Lanza: The American Caruso*. Callinicos' recorded recollections were musically correct, but he was monotony personified; he was bitterly disappointed when the documentary ended without mention of him. Callinicos died in 1986. According to one friend, he became misty-eyed—to the end—when he heard certain Lanza recordings.[8]

Mary Cocozza contributed to the rearing of her grandchildren. She received surprisingly modest amounts from the estate for their support and feared calling for even small amounts, to be spent for the benefit of the children, as the attorneys representing the estate generally denied the requests and then assessed handsome fees for phone calls or letters. She worked hard to ensure that her beloved son would not be forgotten and even mused about a film based on Mario's life, naively insisting it would be family fare, "like *The Sound of Music*."[9] She died, following a stroke, on 7 July 1970, at the age of sixty-five. Just over a month later, Terry Robinson was appointed guardian for Ellisa, Damon, and Marc.

Tony Cocozza, who could not bear listening to his son's recordings after 1959, retreated more and more into a private world that consisted of his wonderful vegetable garden and his dog. He died on 22 May 1975, at the age of eighty-one.

Colleen Lanza, encouraged by Joe Pasternak, had a short-lived singing career, working with Lee Hazlewood, Nancy Sinatra's protégé. Her voice was pleasant but undistinguished. She married Alberto Caldera, Jr., the nephew of the president of Venezuela, on 23 July 1971. Terry Robinson gave away the bride, and Bobby Vinton sang "Because" on the brightest day of a marriage that quickly failed. Her second marriage, to Patrick Davis, lasted for more than twenty years. Colleen admitted, without regrets, to an up-and-down life. She did much to ensure that her father's legacy endured. Sadly she was struck by a car while crossing a street near her home in California on 19 July 1997; she died on 4 August 1997. Colleen was forty-eight.

Damon and Ellisa live in California. Damon is an affable man who has been badly victimized by lawyers and others purporting to represent his interests. He shared the house at 622 Toyopa Drive with brother Marc for many years. They lost the property, which had appreciated to well over $1 million, after mortgaging it to acquire venture capital for a misguided investment in a failed pizzeria/sportsbar. Marc, a pleasant and exuberant youth, turned troubled and reclusive as he grew older; his lifestyle contributed to his early death in 1991. The house on Toyopa was later demolished so that a new home could be built on the lot.

Terry Robinson, now in his eighties, is proud of his sixty years as a physical therapist and educator. In 1993 he was made an honoree of the International Fraternity of Oldetime Barbell and Strongmen of the World at the New York Downtown Athletic Club. Robinson still runs a health club, lectures, paints, and writes. He lives in West Los Angeles with his lovely and vivacious wife, Sylvia.

Honors and tributes have been commonplace, and associations devoted to preserving Mario Lanza's memory are active in most major countries, none more dedicated than the British and Philadelphia contingents. In February 1996, two trees were planted outside of Royal Albert Hall in commemoration of the tenor's 1958 concerts there; he is the only performer to be so honored. Nick Petrella, a mainstay in his record shop on Snyder Avenue in Philadelphia, promoted and planned the annual Mario Lanza Ball for more than three decades. Others have taken up where Nick left off; the event usually sells out well in advance and features performances by and scholarship awards to promising young singers. The Mario Lanza Institute maintains the Mario Lanza Museum, located in the Settlement Music School, 416 Queen Street, Philadelphia, PA 19147.

The tenor's birthplace at 636 Christian Street is still occupied by descendants of Salvatore Lanza. The Italian-American import store ceased operation decades ago; the display window is now bricked over. A plaque commemorating its historical significance hangs in front. Villa Badoglio is now the embassy for the People's Republic of China.

Lanza was a prodigy. Rosati, Koussevitzky, Adler, Schipa, Björling, Tucker, London, Merrill, Kirsten, Albanese, and others of his time admired his artistry and voice for its glorious tone, range, and size. No tenor since can ignore Lanza, nor are his achievements lost on Pavarotti, Domingo, or Carreras, all of whom lavishly praise his influence on their careers. The repertoire of the Three Tenors is laced with Lanza staples; they even do a medley in his honor. As José Carreras put it, Lanza's "glorious, ringing tenor, that freshness and vitality of performance . . . was his and his alone."[10]

When Lanza emerged from concert to film, most opera houses in the United States played to limited audiences and required subsidies to remain afloat. The masses discovered opera through Lanza's first three films and his passionate, visceral singing. No one had realized that opera could sound the way he sang it: his seductive (as Met soprano Anna Moffo categorized it) voice may be his most enduring operatic legacy. Audiences for live opera increased, and the impact has continued through four decades. The children and grandchildren of those who discovered opera through his films are now in attendance.

Lanza's name still comes up whenever voice is discussed, though the misinformation about forcing, a lack of live performances, and an electronically amplified voice survives despite the praise of those who sang with him or heard him in his more than two hundred concerts. His was a glorious and natural voice, with one of the broadest and most powerful ranges ever recorded. The worlds of music and film had not seen his like before. If he ultimately failed or disappointed, it was only when measured against his own dazzling potential.

Always, he remains the tenor in exile.

A Retrospective Diagnosis

I was there. I saw it all, and I've thought about it and thought
about it—and I still don't know why Mario did the things he did.
Terry Robinson, 1995[1]

For years before he saw Dr. Augustus Rose, Lanza's moods swung between relative stability and severe depression, interspersed with spells
of hypomania and hypermania. Such a pattern is consistent with a bipolar disorder, more commonly known as manic depression. In its simplest terms, bipolar illness is an orientation between two poles, mania
and depression. The shifts become troublesome, a disorder, when they
are sudden and explosive. Such mood swings are confounding to those
who must deal with the person.

The characteristics of a depressed state include a marked loss of
interest or pleasure in all or most activities, significant weight loss or
gain, insomnia or excessive sleep, and a diminished ability to concentrate. In Lanza's case, a period of severe depression would be interrupted by a surge of energy and ideas, such as a desire to sing in the
early morning. Those around him would believe that the worst had
passed. Just as quickly, his mood would darken. Terry Robinson remembers the tenor spending days in his robe, unresponsive and staring
downward.

Unfortunately, the manic state often becomes elevated, as it did
with Lanza. Elevated moods are typified by emotional instability, inappropriate assertiveness, excessive demands, flights of euphoria, intol-
erance of criticism, extreme affability, creativity, gregariousness, grandiose pronouncements, unpredictable hostility, feelings of persecution,
astonishing indiscretions of speech and manner, and sexual preoccu-
pations, ranging from indecent proposals to outright obscenity. Worse,
the mood can be accompanied by poor judgment and a conviction that

the person is functioning at a higher level than those around him. If the mood continues to elevate, damage to property and person may occur. If the mood is mixed *and* elevated, as it sometimes was with Mario, feelings of persecution can alternate with tearfulness or elation. Alcohol—the self-administered medication of Ernest Hemingway and Mario Lanza—feeds such states.

When Lanza's mood was stable, he was charming and generous— the host who worried that a guest might find something less than magnificent; the concerned friend who brought Raphaela Fasano to Hollywood; the doting father his daughters remember as loving and so full of humor. When he entered a mixed or depressed state, he was impossible. Critics often described him as overly bright-eyed, which was noticeable when his mood was dramatically elevated. Promiscuity is another sign of an extremely elevated mood, and the singer's tendencies were worsened by his relationship with his mother. Exhibitionism is a common compulsive, unconscious defense of a son who has begun to identify with and develop sexual feelings for a dominant mother who attempts to live through her offspring; aggression toward women is often a later, destructive acting-out against the mother. Mario Lanza's childhood set the stage for these unfortunate developments.

During production of *That Midnight Kiss*, Joe Pasternak witnessed in Lanza "a disturbing quality . . . that you couldn't quite pin down." He was thoroughly confused by Mario's behavior: "One day he was at my feet, the next day at my throat." The tenor announced that he was greater than Caruso, railed about Ethel Barrymore's plot to outshine him, and demanded top billing.[2] While filming *The Toast of New Orleans*, the tenor astonished cast and crew with crude antics, the same behavior that had marked his teen years in South Philadelphia and the Bel Canto tour. He barely staggered through *Because You're Mine*, and his depression and mixed moods sabotaged *The Student Prince*. He was taut—alternating between tearful reactions to the slightest criticism, rage, and boastfulness—when Dr. Rose made his diagnosis of megalomania in 1952.

In Dr. Rose's defense, his lack of knowledge was consistent with his time. The true diagnosis—bipolar disorder—was seldom made during the 1950s, despite its having been identified as a distinct illness in 1896. Even if Dr. Rose had made the right call, no effective treatment was available at the time. Experiments with lithium, the drug of choice for bipolar disorders, did not begin until the 1960s, in England. The drug was not approved for use in the United States until 1972; other compounds have emerged as alternatives since.

Mario drifted between deep depression and hypomania from 1952 to 1955. When the tenor was out of control he raged against his homes and was rough in his relationships, sexual and otherwise. During what should have been the prime of his career, he was inactive. Though he achieved some glorious moments in recording studios from 1956 to 1959, at the Royal Variety Performance during 1957, and on his 1958 concert tour, his overall direction was ever erratic, spiraling downward.

Hollywood did not cause Mario Lanza's troubles, though the requirements and stresses of films, concerts, recording schedules, and stardom acted as accelerants. Hollywood only succeeded in replicating his childhood, surrounding him with people who condoned his behavior, however outrageous. If he had remained in South Philadelphia and worked at any one of a thousand mainstream jobs—with a sympathetic employer who could withstand his argumentative moods, unpredictability, and long periods of absence—his life might have been less troubled. It was impossible for Mario to meet the timetables required for films and concerts—that he consistently be ready to work on a particular day at a set time in a certain place. Similarly, a career in grand opera might have produced some spectacular early results, but the adulation of opera lovers combined with his refusal to accept criticism or direction would have been more disastrous, finally, than Hollywood had been for him. He had, to that extent, the best career he could have had.

Mario Lanza was, like many, an essentially decent but imperfect man. His worst behavior was not the result of malevolence. Often he could no more be blamed for his actions than a lame man can be blamed for his limp. His mighty desire to produce and survive allowed him to achieve immense acclaim and a magnificent legacy. Few, nevertheless, would wish his lot on their own sons.

The tenor's devastating struggles are long over. As José Carreras and so many of his fans have urged, he deserves to be remembered with love and affection.

Notes

CHAPTER 1

1. Mike Tomkies, "The Mario Lanza Story," *Motion Picture*, December 1971.

2. According to a near-deathbed promise made to Lanza's paternal grandmother, a baby girl would have been named Verdun, in honor of the French city where hundreds of thousands died during World War I.

3. Records, Department of Veterans Affairs. Tony Cocozza's disability pension would exceed $700 per month at 1997 rates. It would not be taxed.

4. Russ Columbo worked successfully in film, stage, and radio venues during the 1920s and 1930s. He was particularly popular in Italian-American communities. He was killed at the age of twenty-six, when an antique pistol a friend was handling accidentally discharged.

5. Eddie Durso, as told to John Durso and Steve Vertlieb, *My Memories of Mario Lanza* (Philadelphia 1992), 7.

6. Ibid.

7. "Million Dollar Voice," *Time*, 6 August 1951.

CHAPTER 2

1. Boris Goldovsky, as told to Curtis Cate, *My Road to Opera* (Boston: Houghton Mifflin Company, 1979), 315–316.

2. So related Arthur Cosenza, in an interview with the author, 7 October 1997. Cosenza attended South Philadelphia High School for Boys three years behind Lanza and later sang with him; he served as the general director of the New Orleans Opera Association from 1970 to 1996.

3. "Million Dollar Voice," *Time*, 6 August 1951.

4. Ibid.
5. Goldovsky, 317.
6. Ibid., 316.
7. Ibid.
8. Ibid., 317.
9. So related Terry Robinson, in an interview with the author, 9 November 1995.
10. Raymond Strait and Terry Robinson, *Lanza: His Tragic Life* (Englewood Cliffs, New Jersey: Prentice-Hall, Inc., 1980), 10.

CHAPTER 3

1. Constantine Callinicos, with Ray Robinson, *The Mario Lanza Story* (New York: Coward-McCann, Inc., 1960), 50.
2. "Million Dollar Voice," *Time*, 6 August 1951.
3. This tale, like that of the piano hauler's introduction to Koussevitzky, made its way into the Lanza biographies by Constantine Callinicos and Terry Robinson.
4. Letter from Jerry Adler to Steven Pattison, 17 May 1956.
5. Matt Bernard, *Mario Lanza* (New York: McFadden-Bartell, 1971), 14.
6. According to MGM press releases, Lanza was five feet, eleven inches tall, but photos of the tenor standing next to Howard Keel, who is six-foot-three, and Kathryn Grayson, who is five-foot-six, suggest otherwise.
7. Terry Robinson, interview, 9 November 1995. Hicks' daughter, Dolores Hart, from whose movie sets he was barred because of his behavior, stunned Hollywood in 1963 when she left a successful film career (including an infamous "kiss" with Elvis Presley) for the austere life of a Benedictine nun. Robinson remembered that Hart attended a retreat at her alma mater, Marymount, and never returned to her life as a film star. He and Mary Cocozza once visited Sister Dolores, as she was now known, at a convent in Connecticut; he remembered she was quite happy and "looked like an angel." Now a ranking member of the order, she has recently broken her vow of silence to promote an album featuring religious chants performed by nuns.
8. Callinicos, 50.
9. Sanford Dody, *Robert Merrill: Once More from the Beginning* (New York: The Macmillan Company, 1965), 192.
10. Harold Diner, interview, 7 April 1995.
11. Columbia Concerts press release, 1946.
12. Ibid.

13. Callinicos, 56.
14. Jack Warner, "A Hollywood Tycoon Remembers Why He Refused to 'Discover' Mario Lanza," *Weekend*, 21 January–2 February 1965.
15. Award of Disability Compensation issued 1 December 1945 by the Veterans Administration; records, Department of Veterans Affairs.

CHAPTER 4

1. This and all subsequent quotes in this chapter are from Ida Zeitlin, "The Mario Lanza Story," *Photoplay*, September 1951.

CHAPTER 5

1. Zeitlin, "The Mario Lanza Story." Lanza was referring to *The Celanese Hour*.
2. So related Charles Handelman, in an interview with the author, 6 August 1994. Handelman, a noted and highly opinionated opera afficionado, had spoken two years earlier with the son of the great baritone. According to Handelman, "[Lanza] really was capable of wonderful things."

CHAPTER 6

1. Presumably, Toscanini meant the natural gift, the pure voice, not the production known as singing. Although this controversial remark is often quoted, direct attribution to Toscanini is sketchy. It was widely circulated only after Lanza died—two years after Toscanini's death. Constantine Callinicos claimed the remark was made in 1949, when Toscanini heard Lanza's first four recordings with RCA ("Celeste Aida," "Mamma mia, che vo' sapè," "Core 'ngrato," and "Che gelida manina"). Callinicos said that Toscanini was particularly impressed with Lanza's rendition of "Che gelida manina."
2. Arthur L. Charles, "Return Engagement," *Modern Screen*, March 1953.
3. Callinicos, 61.
4. Lanza and Weiler amended the contract on 4 August 1947, giving Weiler 10 percent of gross earnings, and again on 12 January 1951, giving Weiler 20 percent of gross earnings as well as a perpetual right to income from Lanza's royalties.
5. During the 1970s, Weiler released recordings from copies of Coke Show tapes. He was sued by the Lanza family.
6. This and all subsequent quotes in this chapter are from Callinicos, 61–65.

CHAPTER 7

1. John Rockwell, "Mario Lanza," *The New York Times*, 21 March 1982.
2. This and all subsequent quotes in this chapter are from Callinicos, 25–28.

CHAPTER 8

1. Henry Toby, "Lanza Speaks," part 2, *Picturegoer*, 14 September 1957.
2. So related Lee Berthelson, in an interview with the author, 16 April 1997. Berthelson had spoken with the conductor of the Milwaukee concert and various other eyewitnesses.
3. Callinicos, 70.
4. Ibid., 75.
5. Zeitlin, "The Mario Lanza Story."
6. Joe Pasternak, with David Chandler, *Easy the Hard Way* (New York: G. P. Putnam's Sons, 1956), 277. Pasternak, a Transylvanian-born Hungarian, was credited with saving Universal Studios from bankruptcy and salvaging the career of Marlene Dietrich.
7. Ibid.
8. Ibid., 278, 289.
9. Leonard Wallace, "Mario Lanza: The Golden Voice," *Picturegoer*, 9 June 1957.
10. Pasternak, 279.

CHAPTER 9

1. Lanza's stock reply to the frequent question.
2. Frances Yeend, interview, 17 August 1995.
3. *Mario Lanza: The American Caruso* (1983 PBS documentary).
4. Letter from Frances Yeend to the author, 11 August 1995.
5. Alan Burns, "The Lady Behind Pinkerton," *U.S. Mario Lanza Appreciation Society Newsletter* 2, no. 1 (15 December 1996).
6. So related Alan Burns, in an interview with the author, 12 January 1997.
7. Arthur Cosenza, interview, 7 October 1997.
8. Zeitlin, "The Mario Lanza Story."
9. Letter from Albert Robinson to the author, 10 November 1993.
10. Ibid.
11. Frances Yeend, interview, 17 August 1995.
12. Pasternak, 284.
13. Albert Teitelbaum, interview, 5 May 1997.

CHAPTER 10

1. Callinicos, 84.
2. Pasternak, 284.
3. Callinicos, 84.
4. Mario and Betty had officially changed their names by order of the Los Angeles Superior Court on 7 October 1948—giving the singer eleven years, to the day, as Mario Lanza.
5. Diana Altman, *Hollywood East* (New York: Carol Publishing Group, 1992), 239.
6. Callinicos, 84.
7. Ibid., 84–85.

CHAPTER 11

1. Callinicos, 191.
2. Lanza eventually refused to learn new material. During his 1958 European tour, he omitted the challenging Agnus Dei, "My Lady Walks in Loveliness," "Celeste Aida," and "Thine Alone" and added five songs he had sung before 1949 and two movie themes.
3. Callinicos, 90–91.
4. Liner notes to *The Mario Lanza Collection*, RCA Victor 09026-60889-2, 1991.
5. Callinicos, 104.
6. So related Alan Burns, in an interview with the author, 6 June 1996.
7. So related Terry Robinson, in an interview with the author, 7 December 1996.
8. Durso, 55.
9. Undated clippings.
10. Dick Tatham, "My Tribute to Mario Lanza," *New Musical Express*, 23 October 1959. Sadler's Wells became the English National Opera in 1974.
11. The owners of the duplex on Spalding sued them for $1038 in unpaid rent and damage to furniture and carpeting; the matter was later settled.
12. Terry Robinson, interview, 9 November 1995.
13. Albert Teitelbaum, interview, 5 May 1997.

CHAPTER 12

1. "Million Dollar Voice," *Time*, 6 August 1951. For the record, by age twenty-nine Caruso had appeared at Covent Garden and La Scala, had sung in the world premieres of five operas, and had made his first twenty recordings.

2. Sammy Cahn, *I Should Care: The Sammy Cahn Story* (New York: W. H. Allen, 1975).

3. Mario had been tapped to perform in *Andrea Chénier* in San Francisco with Tebaldi, but the partnership never advanced beyond negotiations.

4. Terry Robinson, interview, 9 November 1995.

5. Callinicos, 106.

6. Pasternak, 285.

7. "Faces and Places," *Parade*, 5 December 1975.

8. In his biography, Niven wrote that Humphrey Bogart told him to leave Hollywood for a while after a "stinker" like that: "You should have held out, kid. This is crap." David Niven, *The Moon's a Balloon* (New York: G. P. Putnam's Sons, 1972).

9. Letter from Burt Solomon to the author, 27 December 1993.

10. "Faces and Places," *Parade*, 5 December 1975.

11. Terry Robinson, interview, 9 November 1995.

CHAPTER 13

1. Bernard, 21.

2. Altman, 244.

3. Bernard, 21.

4. Altman, 241.

5. Ibid.

CHAPTER 14

1. Mike Tomkies, "Meet the Stars," *Weekend*, April 1958.

2. Enrico Caruso, Jr., and Andrew Farkas, *Enrico Caruso: My Father and My Family*, (Portland, Oregon: Amadeus Press, 1990), 546.

3. Albert Teitelbaum, interview, 3 September 1997.

4. Caruso, Jr., and Farkas, 546.

CHAPTER 15

1. Caruso, Jr., and Farkas, 546.

2. Jesse Lasky, with Don Weldon, *I Blow My Own Horn* (New York: Doubleday and Company, 1957), 257.

3. Virginia McPherson, "Caruso's Real Voice to Be Used in Film Bio," *The Hollywood Citizen News*, 1 February 1946.

4. *Variety*, 15 December 1949.

5. James R. Parish and Michael R. Pitts, *Hollywood Songsters* (New York: Garland Publishing, 1991), 406.

6. MGM recorded soundtracks for *That Midnight Kiss*, *The Toast of New Orleans*, *The Great Caruso*, and *Because You're Mine* but did not permit their release by RCA, which recorded highlights from each film separately. MGM and RCA cooperated on soundtracks from *The Student Prince*, *The Seven Hills of Rome*, and *For the First Time*.

7. The version recorded by MGM is more than four minutes long; approximately eight seconds were included in *The Great Caruso*.

8. Lasky, 267.

9. Callinicos, 115.

10. So related Alan Burns, in an interview with the author, 6 June 1996.

11. Dorothy Kirsten, *A Time to Sing* (New York: Doubleday and Company, 1982), 129.

12. Caruso, Jr., and Farkas, 546.

13. Domingo spoke of his debt to Lanza in *Mario Lanza: The American Caruso* (1983 PBS documentary).

14. Derek Mannering, *Mario Lanza: A Biography* (Calgary, Canada: Calgary University Press, 1993), 11.

CHAPTER 16

1. Toby, "Lanza Speaks," part 2.

2. Callinicos, 133.

3. Ibid., 137.

4. Ibid., 141.

5. Terry Robinson, interview, 9 November 1995.

6. Callinicos, 123.

7. Bernard, 191.

8. The property at 355 St. Cloud in Bel Air, California, was acquired on a land contract between the Lipperts and Albert Teitelbaum. Mario Lanza's name does not appear on any deed or document in the chain of title associated with the property.

9. Letter from Rita Barrett to the author, 27 November 1994.

10. This and all subsequent recollections in this chapter by Harold Diner are from an interview with the author, 7 April 1995.

11. Terry Robinson, interview, 7 December 1996.

12. Babs Diner, interview, 7 April 1995.

13. These and all subsequent recollections in this chapter by Gerald Vinci are from an interview with the author, 7 April 1995.

CHAPTER 17

1. Robin May, *Stage and Screen Audio*, November 1974.

2. Mannering, 11.

3. Dorothy Caruso, *Enrico Caruso: His Life and Death* (New York: Simon and Schuster, Inc., 1945), 147.

4. This and all subsequent recollections by Julius Rudel in this chapter are from an interview with the author, 9 March 1996. Rudel was musical director for the New York City Opera from 1957 to 1979 and musical director for the Kennedy Center from 1971 to 1976; he has conducted at the Met since 1978.

5. Charles Osborne, "The Art and Voice of Mario Lanza," *Hi-Fi News and Record Review*, October 1973.

6. Arthur Cosenza, interview, 7 October 1997.

7. Callinicos, 195.

8. "Million Dollar Voice," *Time*, 6 August 1951.

CHAPTER 18

1. Albert Teitelbaum, interview, 3 September 1997.

2. Albert Teitelbaum, interview, 7 May 1997.

3. Pasternak, 287.

4. Bernard, 41.

5. Terry Robinson, interview, 9 November 1995.

6. Hedda Hopper, "Lanza Talks," *Photoplay*, November 1953.

7. Contract between Mario Lanza and MGM.

CHAPTER 19

1. Strait and Robinson, 107.

2. Albert Teitelbaum, interview, 7 May 1997.

3. Pasternak, 288.

4. So related Albert Teitelbaum, in an interview with the author, 7 May 1997.

5. Terry Robinson, interview, 9 November 1995.

6. Ibid.

7. Contract between Mario Lanza and MGM.

8. Injunctive relief requires "irreparable harm." MGM's request for monetary damages eliminated the notion that it would suffer irreparable harm if the tenor pursued other forms of employment. The tenor would be responsible for any losses incurred by the studio. California law provided a distinct exception to the standards enforced in the rest of the United States.

9. Letter from Mario Lanza to Loew's, Inc., 21 September 1952.

CHAPTER 20

1. Attorney Gerald Lipsky, who represented Lanza from 1954 until his

death and then handled his and Betty's estates, made this remark during a meeting with the author and Frances Breidenbach, Esq., 7 December 1996.

2. According to several friends, associates, and relatives—notably Mary Cocozza—Lanza's career earnings ranged from $10 to $15 million; in fact, he made approximately $6 million during his twelve-year concert and film career. His film earnings, which totalled $637,395, were as follows: $26,500 for *That Midnight Kiss*; $51,500 for *The Toast of New Orleans*; $55,000 for *The Great Caruso*; $40,000 for *Because You're Mine*; $30,000 for *The Student Prince*; $150,000 for *Serenade*; $140,000 for *The Seven Hills of Rome*; and $144,395 for *For the First Time*.

3. Charles, "Return Engagement."
4. Dody, 192.
5. Pasternak, 289.
6. Ben Maddox, "My Personal Plans," *Movieland*, May 1953.

CHAPTER 21

1. Maddox, "My Personal Plans."
2. Albert Teitelbaum, interview, 7 May 1997.
3. Terry Robinson, interview, 9 November 1995.
4. So related David B. Heyler, Jr., during a meeting with Cyrus B. Godfrey, Esq., Phyllis Torres Bessette, M.D., and the author, 4 December 1996.
5. Callinicos, 169.
6. Terry Robinson, interview, 9 November 1995.

CHAPTER 22

1. Maddox, "My Personal Plans."
2. Colleen Lanza, interview, 16 February 1997.
3. Bernard, 92.

CHAPTER 23

1. Lanza's expressed preference, rather than misusing his voice in gambling casinos or grade-B potboilers for the grasping of "the easy buck." Jim Newton, "He Knows What He Wants," *Modern Screen*, June 1953.
2. Albert Teitelbaum, interview, 4 September 1997. Teitelbaum recalled his discussion with Sammy Lewis, manager of Las Vegas' New Frontier Hotel, in detail. Lewis asked, "What would it take to get Lanza in Vegas?" Teitelbaum, caught off guard, responded with another ques-

tion: "What is the most anyone has ever gotten?" "Twenty-five thousand a week." "Fifty thousand," Teitelbaum countered. Lewis looked away, considering for no more than a few seconds. Then—"You got it." Teitelbaum now says he should have asked for $100,000: "They would have gone for it."

3. Ibid.
4. Ibid.
5. Bernard, 138.
6. Albert Teitelbaum, interview, 20 June 1997.
7. Ibid.

CHAPTER 24

1. Helen Gould, "Is Lanza a Changed Man?" *Movieland*, April 1956.
2. Albert Teitelbaum, interview, 20 June 1997.
3. Terry Robinson, interview, 30 May 1997.
4. Harold Diner, interview, 7 April 1995.
5. Callinicos, 191.
6. Robin May, "The Art and Voice of Mario Lanza," *Audio*, March 1974.
7. Osborne, "The Art and Voice of Mario Lanza."
8. Callinicos, 193.
9. Lloyd Shearer, "The Mario Lanzas: A Tragedy of Success," *Parade*, 1 May 1960.

CHAPTER 25

1. "Golden-Voiced Lanza Is Dead," *Daily Mirror*, 8 October 1959.
2. *The People of the State of California v Albert Teitelbaum, et al.*, 163 Cal.App.2d 184.
3. Vault tapes, BMG/RCA.
4. Albert Teitelbaum, interview, 4 September 1997.
5. So related his daughter, Bobbi Hill, in an interview with the author, 11 March 1996.
6. Plans were underway in 1998 to release a remastered CD.

CHAPTER 26

1. Terry Robinson, Albert Teitelbaum, and many others recalled this as Lanza's favorite toast.
2. Terry Robinson, interview, 9 November 1995.
3. Ibid.
4. Lee Berthelson, interview, 16 April 1997.

CHAPTER 27

1. Toby, "Lanza Speaks," part 1, *Picturegoer*, 7 September 1957.
2. Ralph Cooper, *Empire News*, November 1957.
3. Albert Teitelbaum, interview, 3 September 1997.

CHAPTER 28

1. *Daily Express*, 29 November 1957.
2. Callinicos, 12, 201–202.
3. Ibid., 203.
4. Isadore Green, "The Nervous Mario Lanza," *Record Mirror*, 28 December 1957.
5. Callinicos, 22.

CHAPTER 29

1. Letter from John Coast to Ercola Grazienei, 17 April 1958, recalling events that took place at the Vier Jahreszeiten, Hamburg, Germany, in the wee hours of 14 April 1958.
2. Letter from Constantine Callinicos to John Coast, 10 December 1957.
3. Letter from Constantine Callinicos to John Coast, 23 December 1957.
4. James A. Drake, *Richard Tucker* (New York: E. P. Dutton, Inc., 1984), p. 169.
5. Callinicos, 208.
6. Katherine Field, interview, 30 August 1995.
7. Callinicos, 213.
8. Concerts had been scheduled as follows: 30 January (Wiesbaden, Germany); 2 February (Hamburg, Germany); 4 February (Kiel, Germany); 6 February (Hanover, Germany); 9 February (Nuremberg, Germany); 12 February (Paris); 16 February (London, Royal Albert Hall); 18 February (Leicester, England); 20 February (Birmingham, England); 23 February (Croyden, England); 25 February (Manchester, England); 1 March (Belfast, Northern Ireland).
9. Callinicos, 214.
10. Letter from John Coast to Ercola Grazienei, 17 April 1958, recalling events that took place at the Vier Jahreszeiten, Hamburg, Germany, in the wee hours of 14 April 1958.

CHAPTER 30

1. Callinicos, 73. George London died in 1985.
2. Ibid., 226.
3. Ibid.

CHAPTER 31

1. Callinicos, 247.
2. *Mario Lanza: The American Caruso* (1983 PBS documentary).

CHAPTER 32

1. Toby, "Lanza Speaks," part 2.
2. "We had nothing against Lanza, living or dead, but his screen imper-
   sonation of Caruso gave him no more claim to a burial place in the
   family chapel than playing Lincoln gave Raymond Massey claim to
   burial in Arlington Cemetery." Caruso, Jr., and Farkas, 550.
3. Durso, 70, 73.
4. Strait and Robinson, 170.
5. Terry Robinson, interview, 9 November 1995.
6. Ibid.

CHAPTER 33

1. Mannering, 12.
2. Terry Robinson, interview, 30 May 1997.
3. Union Central Life Insurance Company declined to pay on a $200,000
   life insurance policy, claiming that Betty had concealed her addiction
   to barbiturates. The attorneys representing her estate accepted
   $35,000 three years later.
4. Albert Teitelbaum, interview, 16 June 1997.
5. Total claims against the estate of Mario Lanza were as follows:
   Transworld Airlines $267.58; Kathryn Reitzle $1700 (clerical services);
   Giacomo Spadoni $3400 (vocal coaching); Imperial Glass $18.33
   (plate glass on coffin); Terry Robinson $822.56 (funeral expenses),
   $2336.81 (salary); Bell & Croyden $59.26 (steam equipment for European tour); Società Telefonica Tirrena di Roma $1451.43 (last phone
   bill at Villa Badoglio); Inland Revenue $2101.19 (British income tax);
   and Arthur Bruner/C.C.C. Films $15,000 (advance). A second claim
   by Transworld Airlines of approximately $4000 (for transport of
   Lanza's body and the Lanza family from Rome to Los Angeles) was
   submitted too late to be handled by the probate court, and Lipsky and
   TWA wrangled over the issue. By assessing handsome legal fees
   against the estate, which diminished any savings, Lipsky effectively
   shirked the most moral of debts.
6. Payments made from royalties during the seven years following
   Lanza's death were as follows: Albert Teitelbaum $102,752.87; Baut-
   zer & Grant $79,765.46; Business Administration $79,765.46; J. Ever-

ett Blum $98,889.75; Samuel E. Weiler $129,765.46; O'Melveny & Meyers $6609.46; and Gerald Lipsky $95,200.00.

7. Albert Teitelbaum, interview, 7 May 1997.
8. Clyde Smith, interview, 15 February 1993.
9. Joseph Curreri, "Mario Lanza Never Should Have Died!" *Motion Picture*, April 1967.
10. Mannering, 11.

AFTERWORD

1. Terry Robinson, interview, 9 November 1995.
2. Callinicos, 84.

Selected Bibliography

Bernard, Matt. 1971. *Mario Lanza*. New York: McFadden-Bartell.

Burns, Alan. 1996. "The Lady Behind Pinkerton." *U.S. Mario Lanza Appreciation Society Newsletter* 2, no. 1 (15 December).

Burrows, Michael. 1971. *Mario Lanza and Max Steiner*. Cornwall, United Kingdom: St. Austell.

Callinicos, Constantine, with Ray Robinson. 1960. *The Mario Lanza Story*. New York: Coward-McCann, Inc.

Carreras, José. 1994. Introduction, liner notes to *A Tribute to Mario Lanza*. Teldec 4509-92369-2.

Charles, Arthur L. 1953. "Return Engagement." *Modern Screen*, March.

Cocozza, Mary. 1962. "Mario Lanza Lives!" *Photoplay*, December.

———. 1963. "Bringing Up Mario Lanza's Children." *Photoplay*, March.

Crumpacker, C. E. 1991. Liner notes to *The Mario Lanza Collection*. RCA Victor 09026-60889-2.

Curreri, Joseph. 1962. "The Great Mario." *Opera News*, 21 April.

———. 1967. "Mario Lanza Never Should Have Died." *Motion Picture*, April.

Durso, Eddie, as told to John Durso and Steve Vertleib. 1992. *My Memories of Mario Lanza*. Philadelphia.

Finch, Hilary. 1994. "The Calm Before the Storm." *BBC Magazine*, October.

Gould, Helen. 1956. "Is Lanza a Changed Man?" *Movieland*, April.

Green, Isadore. 1957. "The Nervous Mario Lanza." *Record Mirror*, 28 December.

Hirst, David. 1990. "The Great Tenors: Lanza the Inspiration." *Opera Now*. December.

Hopper, Hedda. 1953. "Lanza Talks." *Photoplay*, November.

Maddox, Ben. 1953. "My Personal Plans." *Movieland*, May.

Mannering, Derek. 1993. *Mario Lanza: A Biography*. Calgary, Canada: Calgary University Press.

May, Robin. 1974. "The Art and Voice of Mario Lanza." *Audio*, March.

———. 1974. *Stage and Screen Audio*, November.

"Million Dollar Voice." 1951. *Time*, 6 August.

Newton, Jim. 1953. "He Knows What He Wants." *Modern Screen*, June.

Ornadel, Cyril. 1974. "The Mario Lanza Story." *BBC Radio*, March.

Osborne, Charles. 1973. "The Art and Voice of Mario Lanza." *Hi-Fi News and Record Review*, October.

Robinson, Terry, and Raymond Strait. 1980. *Lanza: His Tragic Life*. Englewood Cliffs, N.J.: Prentice-Hall.

Rockwell, John. 1982. "Mario Lanza." *The New York Times*, 21 March.

Schlierf, Werner. 1993. *Mario Lanza: Schicksel einer Stimme*. Munich: Baumgartner.

Shearer, Lloyd. 1960. "The Mario Lanzas: A Tragedy of Success." *Parade*, 1 May.

Tatham, Dick. 1959. "My Tribute to Mario Lanza." *New Musical Express*, 23 October.

Toby, Henry. 1957. "Lanza Speaks." Parts 1–3. *Picturegoer*, 7 September; 14 September; 21 September.

Tomkies, Mike. 1958. "Meet The Stars." *Weekend*, April.

———. 1971. "The Mario Lanza Story." *Motion Picture*, December.

Wallace, Leonard. 1957. "Mario Lanza: The Golden Voice." *Picturegoer*, 9 June.

Warner, Jack. 1965. "A Hollywood Tycoon Remembers Why He Refused to 'Discover' Mario Lanza." *Weekend*, 21 January–2 February.

Zeitlin, Ida. 19518. "The Mario Lanza Story." *Photoplay*.

Compact Disc Discography

BMG/RCA

Love Songs by Mario Lanza (BMG/Ranwood 8268-2)

Christmas with Mario Lanza (64274-RG)

Don't Forget Me (09026-61420-2)

Lanza: Greatest Hits (09026-68134-2)

The Magic of Mario Lanza (DVK-20808)

Mario! Lanza at His Best (09026-68130-2)

Mario Lanza: Be My Love (60720-2-RG)

Mario Lanza: Christmas Hymns and Carols (CAD1-777)

The Mario Lanza Collection [3 CD set] (09026-60889-2)

Mario Lanza: Double Feature—For the First Time and That Midnight Kiss (60516-2-RG)

Mario Lanza: The Great Caruso and Other Caruso Favorites (60049-2-RG)

Mario Lanza: The Legendary Tenor (62182-RC)

Mario Lanza: Live from London (09026-61884-2)

Mario Lanza: The Student Prince and The Desert Song (60048-2-RG)

Mario Lanza: You Do Something to Me (CAD1-450)

Mario Lanza: You'll Never Walk Alone (09026-68073-2)

RHINO

Be My Love: Mario Lanza's Greatest Performances at MGM (R2 72958)

MELODRAM

Mario Lanza/Frances Yeend: Hollywood Bowl [recorded live 27 August 1947] (MEL 16512)

GALA

Mario Lanza: Live at the Hollywood Bowl (GL311)

Filmography

That Midnight Kiss (MGM) (Sept. 1949) (96 min.) (Technicolor)
Producer, Joe Pasternak; director, Norman Taurog; screenplay, Bruce Manning and Tamara Hovey. Cast: Kathryn Grayson, José Iturbi, Ethel Barrymore, Mario Lanza, Keenan Wynn, Jules Munshin, J. Carrol Naish, Thomas Gomez, Arthur Treacher, Marjorie Reynolds, Amparo Iturbi.

The Toast of New Orleans (MGM) (Sept. 1950) (97 min.)
(Technicolor)
Producer, Joe Pasternak; director, Norman Taurog; screenplay, Sy Gomberg and George Wells. Cast: Kathryn Grayson, Mario Lanza, David Niven, Rita Moreno, Richard Hageman, J. Carrol Naish, James Mitchell, Clinton Sundberg, Sig Arno.

The Great Caruso (MGM) (Apr. 1951) (109 min.) (Technicolor)
Producer, Joe Pasternak; director, Richard Thorpe; screenplay, Sonia Levien and William Ludwig. Cast: Mario Lanza, Ann Blyth, Dorothy Kirsten, Jarmila Novotná, Richard Hageman, Gilbert Russell, Carl Benton Reid, Eduard Franz, Ludwig Donath, Alan Napier, Paul Javor, Carl Milletaire, Shepard Menken, Vincent Renno, Nestor Paiva, Peter Edward Price, Mario Siletti, Angela Clarke, Ian Wolfe, Yvette Duguay, Argentina Brunetti, Maurice Samuels, Blanche Thebom, Lucine Amara, Teresa Celli, Nicola Moscona, Marina Koshetz, Giuseppe Valdengo.

Because You're Mine (MGM) (Oct. 1952) (103 min.) (Technicolor)
Producer, Joe Pasternak; director, Alexander Hall; screenplay, Karl Tunberg and Leonard Spigelgass. Cast: Mario Lanza, Doretta Morrow, James Whitmore, Dean Miller, Paula Corday, Jeff Donnell, Spring Byington, Don Porter, Eduard Franz, Bobby Van.

The Student Prince (MGM) (June 1954) (107 min.) (Anscocolor) (CinemaScope)
Producer, Joe Pasternak; director, Richard Thorpe; screenplay, Sonia Levien and William Ludwig. Cast: Ann Blyth, Edmund Purdom (sung by Mario Lanza), John Ericson, Louis Calhern, Edmund Gwenn, S. Z. Sakall, Betta St. John, John Williams, Richard Anderson, Evelyn Varden, John Hoyt, Steve Rowland, John Qualen.

Serenade (Warner Bros.) (Apr. 1956) (121 min.) (WarnerColor)
Producer, Henry Blanke; director, Anthony Mann; screenplay, Ivan Goff, Ben Roberts, and John Twist, from the novel by James M. Cain. Cast: Mario Lanza, Joan Fontaine, Sarita Montiel, Vincent Price, Harry Bellaver, Joseph Calleia, Vince Edwards, Licia Albanese, Jean Fenn.

The Seven Hills of Rome (MGM) (Jan. 1958) (104 min.) (Technirama)
Producer, Lester Welch; director, Roy Rowland; screenplay, Art Cohn and Giorgio Prosperi. Cast: Mario Lanza, Peggie Castle, Marisa Allasio, Renato Rascel, Rosella Como.

For the First Time (MGM) (Aug. 1959) (97 min.) (Technirama)
Producer, Alexander Gruter; director, Rudy Maté; screenplay, Andrew Solt. Cast: Mario Lanza, Johanna von Koszian, Zsa Zsa Gabor, Kurt Kasznar, Hans Sohnker.

Index